Day by Day

IN THE GOSPEL OF MATTHEW

Day by Day in the Gospel of Matthew

Chuck Gianotti

Day by Day in the Gospel of Matthew
Chuck Gianotti

Published by:
ECS Ministries
PO Box 1028
Dubuque, IA 52004-1028
phone: (563) 585-2070
email: ecsorders@ecsministries.org
website: www.ecsministries.org

First Edition 2013

ISBN 978-1-59387-204-5

Code: B-DBD

For additional information, contact:
Chuck Gianotti
27 Watchman Court
Rochester, NY 14624 USA
chuckgianotti@hotmail.com
www.bible-equip.org
www.BiblicalEldership.com

Other books by Chuck Gianotti:
Cosmic Drama: Men, Women & the Church
The Formation of the New Testament

Printed in the United States of America

To my wife and life partner, Mary.
Thank you for your model of devotion
to our Lord and Savior.

Introduction

These expositional meditations follow the Gospel According to Matthew verse by verse. The Bible text is accompanied by short textual commentaries and devotional thoughts for each day spanning an entire year. The Bible version used is the New American Standard Version (NASB).

The reader will notice that the devotionals are divided up to suit a typical five-day work week. We have included suggested readings for the weekends from the books of Psalms, Proverbs, and Job.

Space has been left at the end of each week of readings for your own personal notes on either Matthew or the Old Testament portions. One time-honored way to stimulate one's thinking about the Bible text itself is to answer the following questions:

- What have I discovered here about God?
- What have I discovered here about man (people in general)?
- What have I discovered here about the relationship between God and man?

We suggest you spend a few minutes in prayer, using the prayer at the end of each day's meditation and adding your own thoughts.

For your reference, a general outline of the book is provided on page xi.

May God use these brief daily thoughts to spur you on to greater discipleship of our Lord and King, Jesus Christ, and to enjoy ever deepening contemplations about His person and work.

Acknowledgments

As with any writing, many have contributed to bringing it to completion. Ruth Rodger and Sue Tyler have been faithful and excellent editors. Bill Mantel, Cathy Gretzinger, and the many who have received these devotionals in blog form and responded with comments, corrections, and general feedback—thanks to all. Greatly appreciated is Rob Tyler, Executive Director of ECS Ministries, for believing in this project to the point of publishing it. Of course, any errors that remain go back to the one who originally made them, which would be the author. I take full responsibility.

Finally, nothing I do in ministry lacks the encouragement of my wife and life partner, Mary. She remains the primary instrument God uses to spur me on.

To God be all the glory,
Chuck Gianotti, 2013

General Outline

Christ the *King* Introduced

Descent of the Messiah–part 1

Matthew 1:1-4

[1] The record of the genealogy of Jesus the Messiah, the son of David, the son of Abraham: [2] Abraham was the father of Isaac, Isaac the father of Jacob, and Jacob the father of Judah and his brothers. [3] Judah was the father of Perez and Zerah by Tamar, Perez was the father of Hezron, and Hezron the father of Ram. [4] Ram was the father of Amminadab, Amminadab the father of Nahshon, and Nahshon the father of Salmon.

The Gospel According to Matthew is the first of four biographies of Jesus Christ in the New Testament (NT). Portraying Jesus as the promised King, the Messiah of the Jewish people, and Savior of the world, this book is rich in prophetic fulfillment. Being Jewish in flavor, it begins with Jesus Christ's all-important genealogy. (Note, the term *Messiah* is a Hebrew word, the translation of which is *Christos* in the Greek language, transliterated "Christ" in English. Both words mean "anointed one." English translations vary over which term is used.)

For the Jews, genealogy was a source of authentication, establishing one's tribal connection and any ancestral link to a great historical personage that might be claimed. In the first four verses, Jesus is linked to two of the three greatest names in Jewish history, namely Abraham and David (Moses being the third). The first, the father of the Jewish nation, demonstrated the epitome of faith. The second, the greatest king of the monarchy, was the supreme model of godly loyalty.

Also included are those of less admirable character, like Tamar, a direct ancestor of our Lord. She was the widowed daughter-in-law of Judah (one of the twelve sons of Jacob and thus the patriarch of the tribe named after him). After her husband died, leaving her childless, she posed as a prostitute to trick her father-in-law into impregnating her. Judah, unaware of her identity, fell for the ruse. The result was two children, one of whom was this Perez through whom God ultimately brought Jesus into the world! This is one of a number of "blemishes" in the ancestral line from Abraham down to Jesus Christ. Most people would avoid such associations in their backgrounds, but He was not ashamed of being connected with "sinners." In fact, Jesus was characteristically called "a friend of sinners" (11:19), and He is recorded by the writer of Hebrews as not being ashamed to call anyone "brother" whom God has set apart and made "one" with Him (Heb. 2:11).

Thank you, Lord, that even though I am a sinner, You are not ashamed to associate with me and call me friend (John 15:14) and brother.

Week 1
Day 2

Descent of the Messiah–part 2

Matthew 1:5-8

[5] *Salmon was the father of Boaz by Rahab, Boaz was the father of Obed by Ruth, and Obed the father of Jesse.* [6] *Jesse was the father of David the king. David was the father of Solomon by Bathsheba who had been the wife of Uriah.* [7] *Solomon was the father of Rehoboam, Rehoboam the father of Abijah, and Abijah the father of Asa.* [8] *Asa was the father of Jehoshaphat, Jehoshaphat the father of Joram, and Joram the father of Uzziah.*

The ancestors of Jesus numbered many less-than-admirable characters. Matthew (the author) himself had a background of blatant dishonesty and self-indulgence. Formerly a turncoat, Matthew used his service of Roman tax collecting to extort his countrymen. His inclusion of those like Tamar and now Rahab reflects his great appreciation for the mercy and grace of God.

Rahab was a well-known prostitute of Jericho who showed faith in God by rescuing the two spies who had been sent by Joshua to scout the land, especially Jericho, prior to invading it (Joshua chapters 2 & 6). Directly related to Rahab was Boaz, a godly man, and his wife, Ruth (see the book of Ruth for details). While Boaz was clearly a devout Israelite in his background and upbringing, Ruth was a Moabitess, and, as such, had been raised as an idol worshiper. Yet, like Rahab, she recognized the God of Israel as the one true God and is included as one of four women specially mentioned in Jesus' genealogy.

Boaz and Ruth's great-grandson David is well known, both for being the greatest of all the Israelite kings and for his extramarital affair with the wife of Uriah (some translations supply her name, *Bathsheba*)! She is the third woman mentioned. That this relationship is even included bodes significance not only for Jesus' rightful claim to the Davidic throne, but also to God's grace evident in Jesus' heritage. No sin is too great to completely block God's blessing.

David's son Solomon, considered the wisest man ever, ended his life in foolishness, falling into idolatry. His book of Ecclesiastes has warned people, ever since he wrote it, of the vanity of a life lived apart from God.

Following Solomon was his unwise son Rehoboam, under whose incompetent leadership Israel divided into two nations. The northern kingdom, known as Israel (or Ephraim), fell headlong into idolatry. The dynasty of King David continued in the southern kingdom, called Judah, though with checkered devotion to God. Conflict between the two nations reigned from that point on.

Lord, thank you for the heritage of godly people and redeemed people who have gone before us. We stand in Your grace and mercy. Amen.

Descent of the Messiah–part 3

Matthew 1:9-12

[9] Uzziah was the father of Jotham, Jotham the father of Ahaz, and Ahaz the father of Hezekiah. [10] Hezekiah was the father of Manasseh, Manasseh the father of Amon, and Amon the father of Josiah. [11] Josiah became the father of Jeconiah and his brothers, at the time of the deportation to Babylon. [12] After the deportation to Babylon: Jeconiah became the father of Shealtiel, and Shealtiel the father of Zerubbabel.

The march of interesting characters in Jesus' ancestral line continues. Uzziah was a great king until he presumed upon God's holiness, entering the sanctuary where only the priests were allowed (2 Chron. 26). He was known thereafter by this epithet: "He was a leper." In the very year he died, Isaiah saw the Lord "lofty and exalted" and the angels crying, "Holy, Holy, Holy, is the Lord of hosts" (Isa. 6:3).

Others followed Uzziah, including Hezekiah, who brought reform and restoration to the worship of Yahweh (God's personal name). Manasseh was so wicked that during his reign God stopped warning of judgment, but then confirmed that it would indeed happen. Even the godliness of his grandson Josiah could not avert this!

Then Jeconiah (also called Coniah) extended God's censure to the Davidic dynasty: "No man of his descendants will prosper sitting on the throne of David" (Jer. 22:30). Thus the direct blood descendants, the rightful heirs to David's throne, were now barred from fulfilling that destiny. But would that not mean the end of the line for God's promise to David? "For thus says the Lord, 'David shall never lack a man to sit on the throne of the house of Israel'" (Jer. 33:17). How then could Jesus qualify to be the King of Israel?

The answer is really quite simple. One thing we can be sure of is that God always keeps His promises (Heb. 6:17-18). Jesus was *not*, in fact, a direct blood descendant of Jeconiah. He was adopted into the kingly line by Joseph (1:16). By virtue of His adoption, He obtained legal right to the throne. Yet He was still a blood descendant of David, as made clear in the complementary genealogy provided by Luke in his gospel. In that genealogy, Jesus' blood line is traced back to David through his biological mother, Mary, but through a different family line which bypasses Jeconiah. In other words, the virgin birth allows the fulfillment of *both* promises!

Lord, thank you that Your ways are above our ways, and Your thoughts above ours. We can trust You for what at first sight seems conflicting.

Descent of the Messiah–part 4

Matthew 1:13-17

[13] Zerubbabel was the father of Abihud, Abihud the father of Eliakim, and Eliakim the father of Azor. [14] Azor was the father of Zadok, Zadok the father of Achim, and Achim the father of Eliud. [15] Eliud was the father of Eleazar, Eleazar the father of Matthan, and Matthan the father of Jacob. [16] Jacob was the father of Joseph the husband of Mary, by whom Jesus was born, who is called the Messiah. [17] So all the generations from Abraham to David are fourteen generations; from David to the deportation to Babylon, fourteen generations; and from the deportation to Babylon to the Messiah, fourteen generations.

The genealogy of Christ contains a variety of individuals—some highly revered, some shady characters, and many nondescript people. In fact, some in His background are mentioned only in this list. While Zerubbabel was in the line of David and a significant governor of Israel after the Babylonian captivity, his immediate descendants, Achim, Eliud, Eleazar, and Matthan, were somewhat obscure in Jewish history, except for their mention in the heritage of Jesus. Indeed, the line of David fell into relative obscurity after the Babylonian captivity.

Is this just an unimportant, extraneous, and unnecessary detail in a boring section of Scripture? There is great importance in the inclusion of these names. First, they establish the direct tie between Jesus and the dynasty of David to His right to inherit David's throne. Second, they demonstrate God's faithfulness to fulfill His promise to David that his throne would last forever. In Jesus, this would be the case. Third, and on a more personal note, the mere mention of a man's name in Scripture was a high honor for that man. It reminds us that it is extremely significant that the name of every single believer is written down in the Lamb's book of life (Rev. 13:8; 21:27)!

The blood line in Matthew's list ends with Joseph, the husband of Mary, who was the earthly mother of Jesus. The original Greek clearly establishes Jesus' biological relationship to Mary but not to Joseph—the adoptive father. Joseph was married to Mary, through whom deity infiltrated humanity. Jesus had no biological father, the Holy Spirit having impregnated Mary (Luke 1:35). Mary, the fourth woman mentioned, was herself a woman of scandal, supposed by some Jews of that day to have borne an illegitimate child. Yet her role provided the fulfillment of God's promise to provide a Messiah for Israel in the line of David. God always keeps His promises!

Father, thank you that in Your grand plan for saving the world through the Davidic descendant, Jesus, You have recorded my name in the Lamb's book of life because I have believed He died for me.

Birth of the Messiah

Matthew 1:18-21

[18] Now the birth of Jesus Christ was as follows: when His mother Mary had been betrothed to Joseph, before they came together she was found to be with child by the Holy Spirit. [19] And Joseph her husband, being a righteous man and not wanting to disgrace her, planned to send her away secretly. [20] But when he had considered this, behold, an angel of the Lord appeared to him in a dream, saying, "Joseph, son of David, do not be afraid to take Mary as your wife; for the Child who has been conceived in her is of the Holy Spirit. [21] She will bear a Son; and you shall call His name Jesus, for He will save His people from their sins."

The heritage of Jesus Christ having been established, the story of His birth begins. The facts are well known: a young couple engaged, who had been saving themselves sexually for marriage, the girl (probably a young teen, as was customary for marriage in that culture) became pregnant, but not by Joseph. This proved to be a crisis of monstrous proportions for Joseph. According to Luke's account, Mary's pregnancy became known to him *after* she had returned from her visit with Cousin Elizabeth from the hill country of Judah (where there were many military outposts). Try as he might, it would have been impossible for him to believe Mary's story that she had not been unfaithful while away.

Joseph, being of gracious and merciful character, wanted to protect Mary's reputation. His tenderhearted care for her was obvious, despite her seemingly obvious infidelity. It was not a matter of forgiveness, for Mary could not confess to any wrongdoing without perjuring herself. The only righteous course of action was divorce, albeit a quiet one. Engagement in that day and culture was considered as binding as marriage, though the sexual consummation took place after a waiting period.

Nothing but a supernatural announcement could convince Joseph of this. The truth of the matter was simply that she was to be the entry point of God's Messiah into the world. On the one hand, it was preposterously mythical to unbelievers. But on the other hand, it was overwhelmingly fantastic for this godly young couple! In a matter beyond scientific observation or explanation, the Holy Spirit impregnated Mary. This unique event changed the course of human history.

Joseph was told, "Do not be afraid," and no wonder. The idea is mind-numbing. Deity was about to invade the natural world. The God of the universe, the long-awaited Messiah, the One who would "save His people from their sins"—Jesus—was about to be born to a young woman named Mary.

Lord, You are immense as the Creator God of the universe, yet You have come into my small life and saved me from my sin. Thank you.

Weekend Reading

Saturday – Proverbs 1
Sunday – Psalms 1–5

Personal Reflections

Miraculous Birth

Matthew 1:22-25

[22] Now all this took place to fulfill what was spoken by the Lord through the prophet: [23] "BEHOLD, THE VIRGIN SHALL BE WITH CHILD AND SHALL BEAR A SON, AND THEY SHALL CALL HIS NAME IMMANUEL," which translated means, "GOD WITH US." [24] And Joseph awoke from his sleep and did as the angel of the Lord commanded him, and took Mary as his wife, [25] but kept her a virgin until she gave birth to a Son; and he called His name Jesus.

Our section includes the first of numerous references to Old Testament (OT) prophecies in Matthew's gospel. Matthew was intent on demonstrating that Jesus, besides having a Davidic pedigree, also had the messianic pedigree. Isaiah 7:14 foretold a miraculous event: a child born of a virgin, given the name *Immanuel*, which literally means, "God with us." In Scripture, names often were descriptions. Jesus had many of them, the most commonly used one, *Jesus,* means "savior." *Immanuel* conveys the idea that God was present in this Child and would take up residence among His people. Nothing more significant could be contemplated than this marvelous truth—to have the God of the universe, the Creator of the cosmos, the Almighty and Eternal and Unique Deity (in theological terms, He who is transcendent) now among us in the person of Jesus (again, in theological terms, now *immanent*). John's gospel says He "dwelt among us" (John 1:14). He came down to our level!

How is it possible for God to limit Himself to a mere human body? This comprises one of the great mysteries of the Christian faith. It required an event of unparalleled proportions, namely a virgin birth. Critics are quick to point out that in Isaiah the word translated *virgin* can be rendered "young marriageable woman." However, the translators of the Greek Septuagint version of the OT, working about two hundred years before Christ, translated the Hebrew with the Greek word *parthenos*, clearly carrying our contemporary connotation of "virgin"—not having had sexual intercourse. Matthew makes clear, under the inspiration of the Holy Spirit, that Mary remained a virgin until Jesus was born. That she did not remain a virgin after that is plain from the fact that Jesus had brothers (see Matthew 12:47 and Mark 6:3). Truly, He was not the biological son of Joseph. He was the Son of God.

It is one thing to believe that God is with *us*, but can I really believe that He is with *me?* More than just a correct theological belief, this truth is personal—to be experienced individually. Though Jesus is no longer here physically, He promised, "I am with you always, even to the end of the age" (28:20).

Lord, infinite Creator of the universe, help me to sense Your personal presence in my life so that I will never stray from You.

Week 2
Day 2

Wisdom Seekers

Matthew 2:1-4

[1] Now after Jesus was born in Bethlehem of Judea in the days of Herod the king, magi from the east arrived in Jerusalem, saying, [2] "Where is He who has been born King of the Jews? For we saw His star in the east and have come to worship Him." [3] When Herod the king heard this, he was troubled, and all Jerusalem with him. [4] Gathering together all the chief priests and scribes of the people, he inquired of them where the Messiah was to be born.

Following the birth of Christ, the familiar story of the magi becomes prominent in Matthew's rendition of the birth narrative. The author emphasizes Christ as the promised King and Messiah. The contrast with King Herod, the magi looking for the King of the Jews, and the star in the east, all stress the monarchial nature of the birth.

The magi, coming from the east, traveled a great distance and at great sacrifice to find the One signaled by the miraculous star. They had a sincere desire to find the Child and "worship Him." They were from a class of men known for their wisdom and their study of the stars. So their extraordinary insight concerning the event in Bethlehem of Israel was nothing short of inspired. The concept of worshiping a human being (and a child, no less). was no ordinary thing.

King Herod, being controlled by the insecurity of his tentative standing with Rome, certainly took seriously the threatening news of a king being born. This Roman puppet consulted the Jewish chief priests and scribes for details about where the Messiah/Christ would be born, and the intrigue began to unfold. Clearly, Herod knew enough of popular Jewish prophecy to put the pieces together. The Jewish people had long anticipated a deliverer to free them from Roman domination. Certainly, the general populace was "troubled" by the prospect of political instability from a competitor to the throne who was not part of the Herodian dynasty. In time (about thirty years), many of them would rally around the grown-up Jesus and excitedly welcome Him into Jerusalem that fateful Sunday before He was executed on a Roman cross.

Lord, You have come to take up residence on the throne of my life. I commit today to worship You as King and Sovereign of my life. Amen.

The First Conflict

Matthew 2:5-8

[5] They said to him, "In Bethlehem of Judea; for this is what has been written by the prophet: [6] 'And you, Bethlehem, land of Judah, Are by no means least among the leaders of Judah; For out of you shall come forth a Ruler Who will shepherd My people Israel.'" [7] Then Herod secretly called the magi and determined from them the exact time the star appeared. [8] And he sent them to Bethlehem and said, "Go and search carefully for the Child; and when you have found Him, report to me, so that I too may come and worship Him."

Herod's ruse, though quite clear to us as readers, must have been transparent to the religious leaders in the "nudge, nudge, wink, wink" sort of way: "I want to worship the child-king also." Always currying concessions from the obstinate Jewish leaders, this insecure Roman puppet was laying a trap.

The chief priests and scribes, themselves anxious in the face of the threat to *their* positions of prominence, saw an opportunity to take advantage of Herod's obsessive insecurity. They readily tell him of Micah's prophecy of the importance of Bethlehem of Judea as the birthplace of the God-promised leader of His people. Their ambivalence is borne out, though, by the most notable observation: there is no record in all of history, biblical or otherwise, that these religious leaders lifted even a foot to walk the five miles or so to Bethlehem to check out the rumor. Let Herod take care of the situation! This is truly amazing, if not pathetic. They preached and taught the Scripture but did not submit to Scripture.

Herod, guided by jealousy, consulted with the magi—the foreign scholars, as it were—to figure out the exact timetable they were following. "Go find him and let me know where he is so I can worship him as well." This response seemed to indicate that he was joining in the anticipation of participating in the event as a worshiper. This subterfuge, though obvious to us readers, perhaps seemed benign to the magi, or at least did not arouse their suspicions. They seemed too preoccupied with their own excitement to recognize duplicity in others.

Oh, that it were true that every person, upon hearing the Good News of Christ, had as sincere a heart as the magi and genuinely desired to worship Christ as they did.

Father, forgive me for my pride, insecurity, and fear. Help me worship the Lord Jesus Christ in humility, confidence, and love.

Week 2

Day 4

The Wise Bow Before Him

Matthew 2:9-12

[9] After hearing the king, they went their way; and the star, which they had seen in the east, went on before them until it came and stood over the place where the Child was. [10] When they saw the star, they rejoiced exceedingly with great joy. [11] After coming into the house they saw the Child with Mary His mother; and they fell to the ground and worshiped Him. Then, opening their treasures, they presented to Him gifts of gold, frankincense, and myrrh. [12] And having been warned by God in a dream not to return to Herod, the magi left for their own country by another way.

The magi had followed the star as far as Jerusalem, probably having circled north of the Moab mountains, come down through Galilee, and finally reached Judea. Apparently the star was not visible for at least a while, hence their stopping for directions. Once they set on their way to Bethlehem, in response to the prophetic directions received, the star appeared once again. It has been in vogue for some time for astronomers to search for a naturalistic cause for the phenomenon the magi observed. Some have suggested it was either a confluence of planets lining up or a comet. What *is* clear is that the stellar manifestation proved an infallible guide for finding the newborn King. In fact, the reemergence of the star was cause for rejoicing. Note the abundance of superlatives, *exceedingly* and *great*. Imagine the exhilaration, the adrenaline! They had spent a fortune in travel costs and gifts, and now they were almost there!

After they found the Child, their audience with Him had an immediate effect. They fell to their knees. They worshiped. Literally, from its Greek roots, the word *worship* means "to kiss towards." Their affection was singular, and all else lost focus as He came into view. Their worship was also tangible, however, as they laid before Him the three gifts included in many Sunday schools and in song: gold, frankincense, and myrrh. (The popular notion that there were "three kings" comes not from Scripture but from the Christmas carol, possibly reflecting the number of gifts presented.)

As God guided the magi by means of pagan astrological studies, celestial signs, prophetic interpretations, and a Roman governor's jealousy, He also guided them through direct intervention in a dream. He warned them to ignore Herod's request to report back to him. God's heart always turns specially toward those who worship and honor His Son.

Father, may our worship of Your Son not just be in word or outward religious form, but involve our whole selves, including our possessions!

Joseph to the Rescue

Matthew 2:13-15

[13] Now when they had gone, behold, an angel of the Lord appeared to Joseph in a dream and said, "Get up! Take the Child and His mother and flee to Egypt, and remain there until I tell you; for Herod is going to search for the Child to destroy Him." [14] So Joseph got up and took the Child and His mother while it was still night, and left for Egypt. [15] He remained there until the death of Herod. This was to fulfill what had been spoken by the Lord through the prophet: "OUT OF EGYPT I CALLED MY SON."

The visit of the magi must have bewildered Joseph, the newly adoptive father of Jesus. We know little of his background other than that he was a skilled tradesman (3:55). The enormity of the events likely left him with a lack of perspective, an inherent insecurity, and indecision about the next course of action. Fortunately, God provided angelic guidance, warning him to get out of town, as it were, because Herod had set his sights on murdering the Child. Note how early Jesus encounters conflict!

Not only did Joseph and Mary have to deal with the nasty rumors of having an illegitimate child, but now the child's life was in danger. The only remedy? Flee the country. It's not hard to imagine the difficulties of establishing a marriage and family under such conditions, apart from the support of extended family and friends. This poor young couple, blessed and unfortunate at the same time, had been dealt a difficult hand in life.

Interestingly, God speaks directly to Joseph (the non-birth parent) rather than Mary (the biological/birth parent) about what to do next, which justifies our assumption that Joseph was considered the adoptive parent with all its responsibilities, legal and otherwise. He was not just a parent, but a father. Indeed, God gives the father greater responsibility in guiding and protecting the family (see Genesis 2, Ephesians 5:22ff).

Few things stir masculinity in a man like a threat to his children. So Joseph immediately ("while it was still night") responds to the divine warning to protect his family and flees with them to Egypt.

Matthew, inspired by the Holy Spirit, adds that this action, in addition to the safety factor, sets the stage for the fulfillment of prophecy (Hos. 11:1). Thus Matthew continues his book-long effort to show Jesus as the fulfillment of OT prophecies for Israel.

Lord, help me accept both the blessings in my life as well as the hardships You allow, for both give opportunity for Your glory.

Weekend Reading

Saturday – Proverbs 2
Sunday – Psalms 6–10

Personal Reflections

Tragedy in the Nursery

Matthew 2:16-20

[16] Then when Herod saw that he had been tricked by the magi, he became very enraged, and sent and slew all the male children who were in Bethlehem and all its vicinity, from two years old and under, according to the time which he had determined from the magi. [17] Then what had been spoken through Jeremiah the prophet was fulfilled: [18] "A voice was heard in Ramah, Weeping and great mourning, Rachel weeping for her children; And she refused to be comforted, Because they were no more." [19] But when Herod died, behold, an angel of the Lord appeared in a dream to Joseph in Egypt, and said, [20] "Get up, take the Child and His mother, and go into the land of Israel; for those who sought the Child's life are dead."

Killing babies represents the extreme depravity to which an insecure mind can sink. Herod had been duped by the magi, so he sent his soldiers on a rampage with the intention of destroying all possibility of the Child growing up. (Targeting all boys up to two years old suggests the amount of time that may have passed since the birth of Christ.) Psalm 2:2 foretold, "The kings of the earth take their stand and the rulers take counsel together against the LORD and against His Anointed." Herod was the first of such kings! The psalm goes on, "Now therefore, O kings, show discernment; take warning, O judges of the earth. Worship the LORD with reverence and rejoice with trembling" (vv. 10-11). Herod's lip service and failure to do as warned is pure irony, especially in contrast to the wise men who traveled a great distance to do the very thing Herod should have done.

The priests and religious leaders were of the same sentiment, though their opposition was postponed for about thirty years. When Jesus was born, they would not even bother to walk the five or so miles to Bethlehem and at least check out the report. Obviously, if this were truly the Messiah, they would be exposed as holding only to a form of religion and not really being loyal to God. Better, they thought, to ignore what was happening. Maybe it would go away—or, at least, let Herod do the dirty work. However, one ignores God at one's own peril!

Only after Herod died did Joseph, Mary, and Jesus make their way back to Israel—again at the direction of an angel. By now Joseph, being convinced of the danger, needed a divine push to return.

A sobering side thought: We live in a fallen world among fallen people who do terrible things, so sometimes people suffer because of the sins of others.

Lord, I confess the hollowness of my spiritual life when I am more concerned about how I appear rather than truly walking faithfully with You. Help me not to let my self-centeredness cause damage to others.

A Circuitous Return

Matthew 2:21-23

[21] *So Joseph got up, took the Child and His mother, and came into the land of Israel.* [22] *But when he heard that Archelaus was reigning over Judea in place of his father Herod, he was afraid to go there. Then after being warned by God in a dream, he left for the regions of Galilee,* [23] *and came and lived in a city called Nazareth. This was to fulfill what was spoken through the prophets: "He shall be called a Nazarene."*

Following God's leading is sometimes messy. Things don't always work out the way some popular preachers proclaim. The sequence in God's guidance of Joseph included the following: a God-ordained "unwanted" pregnancy, a nocturnal warning of the threat upon the Child's life, divine instructions to flee to safeguard himself and his family, the uncomfortable culture shock of living in Egypt, and a second God-inspired dream directing him to return to Israel. The latter seemed like good news: the one who had threatened the Child's life was now dead!

Indeed, relief from the intense longing for their home country *had* finally come, so Joseph, Mary, and the Child began their return. Quite a bit had happened in about two years, give or take. (Consider these facts: Herod ordered the killing of all children up to two years of age. Christ's birth took place roughly between 7 and 5 BC. And Herod died between March 12 and April 11, in the year 4 BC.)

At this juncture, a great story of God's faithfulness and protection took another ominous turn. On the trip home, they heard rumors that Archelaus, son and successor of Herod, was now in power. Until otherwise demonstrated, we might default to the conclusion "like father, like son." This would justifiably frighten any family man. It is one thing to risk one's own life in a defiant show of bravery, but quite another when such actions endanger loved ones.

Despite God's revelation in Egypt, God then gave Joseph further clarification during his return to the homeland. In a third supernatural communiqué, God directed Joseph to adjust his itinerary with a new destination in view. Rather than return to Judea (where they last resided, in Bethlehem), they made their way to Galilee, to Mary's (and presumably Joseph's) hometown.

Lord, help me follow You faithfully even when Your guidance seems confusing. Direct each step of the way, even when I don't always perceive the final picture. "Your word is a lamp to my feet and a light to my path" (Ps. 119:105).

Preparing for Messiah

Matthew 3:1-5

[1] Now in those days John the Baptist came, preaching in the wilderness of Judea, saying, [2] "Repent, for the kingdom of heaven is at hand." [3] For this is the one referred to by Isaiah the prophet when he said, "The voice of one crying in the wilderness, 'Make ready the way of the Lord, Make His paths straight!'" [4] Now John himself had a garment of camel's hair and a leather belt around his waist; and his food was locusts and wild honey. [5] Then Jerusalem was going out to him, and all Judea and all the district around the Jordan.

Fascination with the childhood of Jesus became rampant in the early centuries of the church. Much was written on the subject, most of which lacks authenticity. We find only a brief mention in the inspired record of Scripture: Luke 2:41-52. Matthew's record omits any mention of Jesus' childhood and simply fast-forwards to some three decades later, to the ministry of John the Baptist (whose birth is only recorded in Luke). John the Baptist introduces Jesus Christ to the Jewish world.

John's message was a foretaste of Jesus' message. In fact, it was identical: "Repent, for the kingdom of heaven is at hand" (4:17). It was simple in its challenge, and clear in its goal. Something good was being offered, but something bad must be taken care of first. The promised kingdom would soon be established, but the people were not yet ready for it. The remedy, the only one needed, was repentance. The rest was up to God.

Repentance meant a complete turning away from the direction in which they were walking. (They were out of step with God and His laws despite a superficial show of conformity). And repentance meant turning back to walking with God. It was an admission of guilt over sins committed under the first covenant (Heb. 9:15) and turning to the genuine expectation of the new way, the kingdom of heaven.

John's role was that of an advance man, so to speak. It was a prophet's task foretold by a prophet, Isaiah. John's lifestyle and dress certainly evoked the image of an OT prophet (see 2 Kings 1:8), all of which helped him gain the public relations coup that drew huge, curious crowds to the relatively remote area of the Jordan River.

With a momentary advance on the story, we see that in the end (at least from the Jewish point of view), the people rejected the message of the forerunner because they rejected the One of whom John *was* the forerunner—namely, Jesus. As Herod did, the nation (despite the initial showing at the Jordan) ultimately rejected her King.

Lord, as You point out sin in my life when I am out of step with Your ways,
I confess and repent of it, turning again to walk obediently in Your ways.

Day 4

Repentance Must Be Genuine

Matthew 3:6-9

...[6] and they were being baptized by him in the Jordan River, as they confessed their sins. [7] But when he saw many of the Pharisees and Sadducees coming for baptism, he said to them, "You brood of vipers, who warned you to flee from the wrath to come? [8] Therefore bear fruit in keeping with repentance; [9] and do not suppose that you can say to yourselves, 'We have Abraham for our father'; for I say to you that from these stones God is able to raise up children to Abraham."

The mass of Jews went out to see John the Baptist and, in turn, to be baptized by him. For many this was a genuine experience of repentance and confession of sins, to be sure. But mixed in with the wheat were the tares (to borrow against a parable Jesus later told)—the religious leaders who came as well. These Pharisees and Sadducees, religious/political parties—often were at odds with each other, but they rallied together at times against a common enemy, namely Jesus. John, seeing through their duplicity at once, thundered at them with the strongest possible denunciation. That's hardly what we would expect from the forerunner of Him who referred to Himself as "gentle and humble of heart" (11:28)!

One of the greatest misrepresentations of Christianity today is a gospel message that excludes the judgment of God. This may result from an over-reaction to past "hell-fire and damnation" methods of scaring people into the kingdom. Such pendulum swings are seldom good, and certainly not balanced. John's message, preparing for Christ, wasn't calling for a religious observance that would count for spiritual brownie points with God (or with people). No, God demanded a genuine response of repentance!

John called the religious leaders a "brood of vipers" which poison with their bite and strike terror in the heart. John further intimated that the only reason they conformed to his message of baptism was their fear of God's anger. This was not an adequate motivation for repentance. Indeed, man-made religion often centers on the people's terror of deity, and the leaders use fear to manipulate them. On the contrary, Paul tells us in Romans 2:4 that what genuinely leads to repentance is the kindness of God.

John therefore challenged those leaders to give proof of repentance. Words and religious observances are cheap. Being Jewish, or being related to people of faith, carried only secondary benefit. What matters when approaching God is being completely honest and open before Him about the state of one's heart (see Psalm 51:6). It's foundational to relating to God.

Lord, show me when I'm "going through the motions" of religious activity and not walking by humble faith. I confess my superficiality to You.

A Tirade Laced with Grace

Matthew 3:10-12

[10] *"The axe is already laid at the root of the trees; therefore every tree that does not bear good fruit is cut down and thrown into the fire.* [11] *As for me, I baptize you with water for repentance, but He who is coming after me is mightier than I, and I am not fit to remove His sandals; He will baptize you with the Holy Spirit and fire.*
[12] *His winnowing fork is in His hand, and He will thoroughly clear His threshing floor; and He will gather His wheat into the barn, but He will burn up the chaff with unquenchable fire."*

The tenor of John the Baptist's thundering tirade does not make for good Sunday school reading. To be sure, modern (or should I say, postmodern?) sentiments recoil at such a negative message. Is not the good news supposed to be about love and kindness, grace and meekness? Yes, but virtues like grace, love, kindness, and meekness turn up shallow if hearts are not prepared. Such things become nothing more than sentimentalism and emotion, temporary, not at all life sustaining, and certainly lacking genuine power.

The extent of grace's significance is directly proportional to our ability to live fruitful lives. Unfortunately, in today's mind-set, grace is nothing more than a human characteristic, however noble, extended to objects worthy of it. But in God's estimation, and the estimation of Christians who understand the meaning of Jeremiah 17:9 ("The heart is more deceitful than all else and is desperately sick; who can understand it?"), grace is a hundred times greater.

John is of the same mind as Jeremiah. There is a serious flaw in all of us. Judgment is not based on a person's words but on his actions. But John takes it further: if there is no good fruit, the tree is to be destroyed. Therefore, since this truth seems to be universally embraced in all religions to at least some degree, humans work hard to produce good fruit through their works to secure salvation for themselves (however that may be defined in their religious system).

Does this mean some can be good enough to attain a favorable eternity? Not at all! Everyone is called to repentance and confession, for "all have sinned and come short of the glory of God" (Rom. 3:23). Christ separates those who are not sinners from those who are. Christ Himself is the lone Occupant of the one side, and all of us are on the other. There are none who can fool the One who will baptize with the "Holy Spirit and fire."

Father, I strive to be salt and light in the world in order to be fruitful. I do it not to gain Your approval, least of all to pad my qualifications for eternal security. Rather, I live so as to please You and glorify Your Son.

Weekend Reading

Saturday – Proverbs 3
Sunday – Psalms 11–15

Personal Reflections

The Father's Pleasure

Matthew 3:13-17

[13] *Then Jesus arrived from Galilee at the Jordan coming to John, to be baptized
by him.* [14] *But John tried to prevent Him, saying, "I have need to be baptized by
You, and do You come to me?"* [15] *But Jesus answering said to him, "Permit it at
this time; for in this way it is fitting for us to fulfill all righteousness." Then he
permitted Him.* [16] *After being baptized, Jesus came up immediately from the water;*
[17] *and behold, the heavens were opened, and he saw the Spirit of God descending
as a dove and lighting on Him, and behold, a voice out of the heavens said, "This
is My beloved Son, in whom I am well-pleased."*

Enter Jesus—the inauguration of the King, if you will. Somewhat inauspiciously, He slips in among the crowd without fanfare on His part. He was one among peasants, Pharisees, Sadducees, and others. The humble and the proud. Merchants and tradesmen, men and women, weak and mighty. Almost invisible, except that John couldn't help but notice Him.

John was immediately humbled in Jesus' self-effacing presence. Whereas the baptizer had been the center of attention until then, John knew his role was to point people to Christ, the promised Coming One. Even the most significant of men are overwhelmed with their own need in the presence of the all-sufficient One. So John rightly questions the propriety of baptizing a person who is obviously greater than himself.

But Jesus insisted that John baptize Him. Jesus came to fulfill the Law, and part of that fulfillment was to do as the prophet John was calling all to do: to be baptized and make ready for the kingdom. This was the righteous thing to do. Jesus showed His humility by condescending to identify with the people He came to save.

Immediately, when Jesus came out of the water, we catch a glimpse of the Trinity: Jesus the Son of God, the Holy Spirit of God (appearing as a dove to "light on Him") and the Father (booming His approval and affirming the Father/Son relationship). In it all, the Father is immensely pleased, thrilled—like a proud Father announcing His Son's coming of age, expecting everyone else to be just as excited. Until this point Jesus had done no miracles, taught no one, nor, of course, had He paid for our sins on the cross. However, the Father was overwhelmed with pleasure in His Son. What a beautiful relationship of affirmation and affection!

The apostle relishes this relationship: "See how great a love the Father has bestowed on us, that we would be called children of God ..." (1 John 3:1a).

Father, thank you for bringing me into Your Father/Son relationship with Christ. You are my Father, He is my Brother. (Heb. 2:10-11)

Week 4

Day 2

The Terms of Temptation

Matthew 4:1-4

[1] *Then Jesus was led up by the Spirit into the wilderness to be tempted by the devil.*
[2] *And after He had fasted forty days and forty nights, He then became hungry.* [3] *And the tempter came and said to Him, "If You are the Son of God, command that these stones become bread."* [4] *But He answered and said, "It is written, 'Man shall not live on bread alone, but on every word that proceeds out of the mouth of God.' "*

Jesus, who taught us to pray, "Our Father who is in heaven … lead us not into temptation" (6:9, 13) was Himself led into temptation. But was this period of testing for Christ a real temptation, or was it just all play-acting? Some suggest Jesus couldn't really have been tempted because, after all, He was God, and God cannot be tempted to sin, nor *can* God sin. Others think Christ was very much capable of sinning, otherwise it would have been no temptation. The word *tempt* used here, however, can also mean "to examine, to test, to learn the true nature or character." Jesus was subjected to microscopic scrutiny. The experience shows His true character while being subjected to Satan's best shot! Although Satan meant it for evil, the Spirit meant it for good (cf. Gen. 50:20). Jesus was *proved* incapable of sinning!

The tempter presented three challenges to Jesus. But first we note the Greek grammatical construction rendering Satan's rules of engagement: "If you are the Son of God, and we will for the sake of argument assume that to be true ..." Satan doesn't argue the nature of who Christ is; he acknowledges it. What he challenges is whether or not Jesus would use divine abilities to satisfy His human needs. If Jesus did so, He would distance Himself from human experience and disqualify Himself as an example of depending upon (and obeying) His Father. In addition, the question is, would He follow Satan's lead rather that of the Spirit, the One who had led Him into this wilderness experience? Jesus' experience provides background to Hebrews 4:15, which reads, "We do not have a high priest who cannot sympathize with our weaknesses, but One who has been tempted in all things as we are, yet without [apart from] sin." Jesus is, therefore, "able to come to the aid of those who are tempted" (Heb. 2:18).

God promises us through the apostle Paul's letter to the Corinthians (1 Cor. 10:13) that no trial we face is outside our ability to endure when we look to the Lord for supernatural help. All we need to do is ask for that help!

Father, as Your Son taught me to pray, please do not lead me into temptation as Your Spirit led Him into temptation. You know what I can handle, so help me to trust You and not my own abilities.

The Model of Resistance

Matthew 4:5-10

[5] Then the devil took Him into the holy city and had Him stand on the pinnacle of the temple, [6] and said to Him, "If You are the Son of God, throw Yourself down; for it is written, 'He will command His angels concerning You'; and 'On their hands they will bear You up, So that You will not strike Your foot against a stone.'" [7] Jesus said to him, "On the other hand, it is written, 'You shall not put the Lord your God to the test.'" [8] Again, the devil took Him to a very high mountain and showed Him all the kingdoms of the world and their glory; [9] and he said to Him, "All these things I will give You, if You fall down and worship me." [10] Then Jesus said to him, "Go, Satan! For it is written, 'You shall worship the Lord your God, and serve Him only.'"

Having lost the first volley, Satan attempts twice more to divert Jesus from following the Spirit's lead. Again the tempter predicates his challenge on the question of Jesus being the Son of God. Ironically, the Father had just affirmed that relationship at Jesus' baptism (3:17). And He would do it again later on what we call the Mount of Transfiguration (17:5). Satan accedes to it only for the sake of argument.

The first temptation, turning stone into bread, challenged Jesus' bottom line. Would He trust His Father and walk by the Spirit's guidance, or would He act independently in order to meet His own need by supernatural means?

The second temptation questions God's faithfulness. Satan suggests a simple test that Jesus could use to prove the Father would really protect Him from harm, as promised in Psalm 91:11-12. Yet Jesus did not need to prove His Father's promise. Jesus again responds with Scripture—that one ought not to test God. The real import of the "temptation" is that Satan was trying to get Jesus to tempt in the sense of "test" His Father. But our impeccable Lord was not about to show the same disrespect for His Father that Satan was showing to the Son.

The final temptation was designed to test Jesus' allegiance. The archenemy of God was putting all his cards on the table, so to speak, and in an unabashed way. He was betting all on the possibility of attaining what he has wanted from the first: "You said in your heart, 'I will ascend to heaven; I will raise my throne above the stars of God, … I will make myself like the Most High'" (Isa. 14:13–14). To this blatant rebellion, Jesus simply dismisses the would-be usurper, for only God is to be worshiped. No one can ever be greater.

O Lord, help me not be influenced to live independently of You, questioning the faithfulness of Your word or exalting things as more valuable than You.

Week 4
Day 4

Resistance Supported

Matthew 4:11-13

[11] Then the devil left Him; and behold, angels came and began to minister to Him. [12] Now when Jesus heard that John had been taken into custody, He withdrew into Galilee; [13] and leaving Nazareth, He came and settled in Capernaum, which is by the sea, in the region of Zebulun and Naphtali.

At the word of Jesus, the devil left. As in the case of Job, Satan's temptation came only at God's permission. For a brief time the tempter was allowed the illusion of power and the thought that, possibly, he might gain success. In the end, Jesus dismisses him with a mere statement. The Evil One had no other option than to obey. What promise this holds for us who are Christ-followers! God gives permission for testing—only to a certain point! He never cedes ultimate authority or control.

Yet the spiritual struggle was real enough, as evidenced by the angels coming to "minister" to Jesus. As Son of God, He needed angels only to do His bidding. But as a man, He needed their help to sustain Him. This should warn us that although we have the ability and divine help to resist temptation, it can at times be exhausting to resist. Praise God, He supplies angels to help, as is attested in many other Scripture passages.

Now that our Lord Jesus has been inaugurated and has completed His time of testing, He is ready for ministry. Not that the Son of God *needed* anything to get ready, but He was also the "Son of Man," and as such His preparation was required. He did all things to "fulfill all righteousness" (3:14), and He came "to do the will of Him who sent [Him] and to accomplish His work" (John 4:34). He did things in an orderly pattern according to the leading of the Holy Spirit.

Matthew's gospel account was not necessarily written in chronological order, and the report Jesus received of the arrest of John the Baptist actually came at a later date. However, the author includes it here as a summary statement explaining Jesus' relocation and frequent returns to Capernaum—in an area in the north called Galilee. He often went into other areas of Palestine, particularly into Judea (where Jerusalem lay, to the south). But when opposition came, He often "withdrew" to Galilee until things settled down. Strategically, He waited until the time was right to penetrate Jerusalem on the fateful day that Christians have called *the triumphal entry*. The book of Matthew builds to that time.

Father, thank you that You supply the help we need when we become exhausted in our fight with temptation. Knowing Christ went through it helps us resist.

Light Shining in Darkness

Matthew 4:14-17

14 This was to fulfill what was spoken through Isaiah the prophet: 15 "The land of Zebulun and the land of Naphtali, by the way of the sea, beyond the Jordan, Galilee of the Gentiles— 16 The people who were sitting in darkness saw a great Light, And those who were sitting in the land and shadow of death, upon them a Light dawned." 17 From that time Jesus began to preach and say, "Repent, for the kingdom of heaven is at hand."

Jesus relocated to Capernaum (4:13) on the western shore of the Sea of Galilee, a large lake about 13 miles long and 7.5 miles wide (the present-day Sea of Tiberias). Much of Jesus' pre-Jerusalem teaching took place at various locales on the shores of this lake. Capernaum was situated on a common travel route about 83 miles directly north of Jerusalem—a multiple-day journey by foot.

This area was historically occupied by two of the less significant tribes of Israel, comprised of descendants of Zebulun, the sixth son of Leah, and Naphtali, the second son of Rachel's maid. Largely overlooked in Israel's history, these tribes figured prominently in the early ministry of the Messiah.

Matthew quotes Isaiah 9:1-2, which in context leads to Isaiah 9:5, the prophecy of the "Son" who would be "given." The people of Israel, beginning with these lesser tribes, would be shown a great Light, that is, a special Son, virgin born—none other than the Lord Jesus Christ. God saw His people as living in darkness, in the shadow of death. But that darkness would not deter His love from touching them or His commitment from restoring them. His message was to reach the Jews first and then, through them, the Gentiles (Rom. 1:16).

Such a movement by God must be matched by a readiness of the people, so Jesus preached the same message John the Baptist preached: "Repent, for the kingdom of heaven is at hand." Repentance is the first action for humans in responding to God's call. It means a person changes his mind about himself and his relationship with God. For the Jews it meant acknowledging their failure to live in holiness as God's law required. Their failure resulted in "sitting in darkness" and the "shadow of death." They needed to turn from such carnal, superficial thinking and behavior and make themselves ready for God's kingdom. For non-Jews it means acknowledging we are sinners who have fallen short of God's glory, whether through our religious activities or our blatant rejection of what we know to be true. Now is the time to repent!

Father, I am a sinner, just like everyone else. Thank you for sending a great Light in the Person of the Lord Jesus Christ.

Weekend Reading

Saturday – Proverbs 4
Sunday – Psalms 16–18

Personal Reflections

Foundation for Discipleship

Matthew 4:18-22

18 Now as Jesus was walking by the Sea of Galilee, He saw two brothers, Simon who was called Peter, and Andrew his brother, casting a net into the sea; for they were fishermen. 19 And He said to them, "Follow Me, and I will make you fishers of men." 20 Immediately they left their nets and followed Him. 21 Going on from there He saw two other brothers, James the son of Zebedee, and John his brother, in the boat with Zebedee their father, mending their nets; and He called them. 22 Immediately they left the boat and their father and followed Him.

Jesus began assembling His leaders-in-training team. According to Luke's rendition of events (chapter 4), He had already spent some time teaching in and around Capernaum, and these men had accompanied Him in His travels (see John chapters 1–4), so the invitation to these first four did not come, as it were, from a stranger.

Matthew records simply that Jesus called to them with two statements. First, He invited them to become His followers, a career and life change. Up to this point, they had followed their respective fathers into the family fishing businesses, learning the trade as apprentices, watching, working alongside, and imitating their fathers. The second (and surprising) statement Jesus made was that He would form them into a new kind of fisherman. They were invited to apprentice with a new Teacher, a new Master, for a new "business." Instead of catching fish, they would "catch" men. The disciples were to be trained to reach others for God with the message of Jesus, namely, "Repent, for the kingdom of heaven is at hand."

Observe that the only qualification Jesus required was to follow Him. He would do the rest. He didn't ask for pledges of fidelity. He didn't require prior religious achievements. Jesus today is still looking for people who will simply commit to being His followers, people who are not doubleminded (note the four men left their nets "immediately"). It was only after His death that they doubted the whole campaign for which they had "signed up" (see Luke 24:21).

So, follow they did, and the world has not been the same since. Along with eight others they became Jesus' core group, His official representatives in spreading the Good News after His departure (Acts 1:8). Since our Lord wrote nothing down, the only way we know what He taught was through His twelve disciples, later called *apostles*. Today the only way people will learn about Christ is via others who faithfully follow Him and share His teachings (28:18-20).

Father, I want to be a faithful follower of Your Son, the Lord Jesus Christ, to witness for Him and to become a fisher of men. I set aside my fears, my comfort, and my security, and I choose to follow Christ.

Caring for Social Needs

Matthew 4:23-25

[23] Jesus was going throughout all Galilee, teaching in their synagogues and proclaiming the gospel of the kingdom, and healing every kind of disease and every kind of sickness among the people. [24] The news about Him spread throughout all Syria; and they brought to Him all who were ill, those suffering with various diseases and pains, demoniacs, epileptics, paralytics; and He healed them. [25] Large crowds followed Him from Galilee and the Decapolis and Jerusalem and Judea and from beyond the Jordan.

Jesus didn't just teach and preach, He healed many people. Every time I visit someone in the hospital my heart longs for physical healing like that today. Certainly, we believe God *can* and sometimes still *does* heal people; that is why we pray when people are sick. Some have tried to imitate Jesus' ministry today with healing and miracle services. Others promote a so-called "power evangelism," which promotes the use of miraculous signs as a means to win people to Christ. Missionary reports abound of God doing miraculous works in third-world countries, even with testimonies of people being raised from the dead. Are all these things really happening? If we in our country don't see many of these things, is it because we lack faith?

Paul, who was used of God to heal others, and who himself experienced the miraculous, also knew limitations to supernatural healings (see 2 Timothy 4:20, where he left Trophimus sick, and 1 Timothy 5:23, where he recommends Timothy take "wine for the stomach's sake"). Even the most adamant promoters of miracles today are subject to physical weaknesses and die from diseases! Throughout the NT we are told to pray for endurance in suffering even when no healing comes. Yet James 5:14-18 encourages us to pray for healing. So how do we reconcile that? Simply put, biblical evidence shows that following Christ does not mean all sickness goes away. Nor does the miraculous prove that a person has faith.

Jesus' miracles authenticated His messiahship and demonstrated that God cares about people. But His healings served a higher purpose than simply the removal of hardship because suffering is a constant companion to life in a fallen world. Healings were attention getters, pointing to that which is far greater than physical healings. He met peoples' "felt" needs (the ones they were most aware of) in order to speak to them about their spiritual needs. And this method worked! Large crowds heard and followed Him. Word got around. And for those who came to faith, He met their *greatest* need—forgiveness of sins!

Father, help us care for the felt needs of others, as attention-getters, pointing them to Your Son, the Lord Jesus Christ. In the face of suffering we ask for perseverance that we may faithfully serve You and others.

Character of the *Kingdom*

Blessings of the Kingdom

Matthew 5:1-4

[1] When Jesus saw the crowds, He went up on the mountain; and after He sat down, His disciples came to Him. [2] He opened His mouth and began to teach them, saying, [3] "Blessed are the poor in spirit, for theirs is the kingdom of heaven. [4] Blessed are those who mourn, for they shall be comforted."

Now begins what is probably the most well-known discourse in Christian history, the Sermon on the Mount. It is one of five lengthy messages Jesus gave, unique in its literary form, and uncompromising in its spiritual acuity. Simple words, yet riveting truth. Counterintuitive—even ironic—this "religion" of His is a "not what you would think" kind of spirituality. It strikes us this way because we humans have strayed so far from living out God's intended purpose for us on earth. Jesus' teaching is normative in the kingdom of heaven, which both Jesus and John the Baptist said was near. In the Sermon on the Mount Jesus is preparing the people for what is expected in the coming new order of things.

He speaks to His disciples, though it is not clear whether this refers to the Twelve (more strictly defined) or to the multitude (which at various times were referred to as disciples). Regardless, the message's impact remains the same. He begins with what are called *the Beatitudes*. Often printed on bookmarks and wall plaques, they are like a preamble to the constitution of the kingdom. Whereas the preamble to the constitution of the United States, for example, speaks of the *right* to happiness, this preamble—that is, the Beatitudes of the kingdom of heaven—speaks about the *means* to happiness. (The core meaning of the word *blessed* is "happiness" or "to be congratulated.")

Jesus makes eight third-person statements, referring to people in general, not only the twelve disciples. The first has to do with the "poor in spirit," best understood in contrast to being "haughty or arrogant in spirit." A person who is poor in spirit is not self-centered. He doesn't think of himself as more important than others. Followers of Christ humble themselves while keeping in view the greatness of attaining what far surpasses the things of this world. The kingdom of heaven is at their disposal, and this means something great!

The second beatitude addresses those who mourn. Expanded further elsewhere, this foundational concept promises that the hardships and losses of this earthly life are not the final word. There is comfort in kingdom living.

Lord, the basic principles of this world, though they seem sensible, nevertheless bring death. I desire to walk in Your principles, which bring life, to live humbly and to know that the joy of comfort only comes through the sorrow of grief.

Week 5

Day 4

More Blessings of the Kingdom

Matthew 5:5-8

[5] *"Blessed are the gentle, for they shall inherit the earth.* [6] *Blessed are those who hunger and thirst for righteousness, for they shall be satisfied.* [7] *Blessed are the merciful, for they shall receive mercy.* [8] *Blessed are the pure in heart, for they shall see God."*

Jesus continues giving the Beatitudes, the blessings of the kingdom. Scholars debate what is actually meant by the *kingdom of heaven*. Does it refer to the Spirit rule of God on earth now, what some might call the church age, in contrast with the earlier age of Mosaic law? Or does it refer to the future millennial kingdom depicted in Revelation 20, the thousand-year reign of Christ? What is the difference between *the kingdom of heaven* and *the kingdom of God*? Such questions involve great systems of doctrine, so-called *covenant theology* versus *dispensational theology*. Are these debates really important?

Jesus placed great importance on this teaching, so we need to understand to whom it applies. Clearly He expected His followers to emulate this teaching: "Repent, for the kingdom of heaven is at hand" (5:17). While we believe the kingdom is yet future (in line with dispensational theology, because Israel rejected their Messiah), part of the preparation for that coming kingdom is to begin behaving in the kingdom sort of way now. So for all intents and purposes it is immaterial whether the kingdom of heaven is present or future. The Beatitudes outline how we should live *now*.

The next four beatitudes address those who are gentle (*meek* NIV, NKJV), who desire righteousness, who are merciful, and who are pure in heart—all challenges to the heart for those who desire to live for God. *Meekness* can be defined as "strength under control." It involves deferring to others (and in the Bible, particularly to God) when we could be asserting ourselves. This is difficult when confronted with those whose goal in life is to gather stuff for themselves at the expense of others. The natural mind demands social justice; we should force the rich to distribute wealth to the poor. Yet God's economy, often counterintuitive, will eventually vindicate those who choose to be meek.

Righteousness will be hugely satisfying to those who yearn for it. Mercy is its own reward; we focus on giving it rather than receiving it. The pure in heart, who "see" with simple integrity, will find immense joy in seeing God in all *His* purity. That is what the preparation for the kingdom of heaven is all about. We do *now* what we will experience fully *then*.

Lord, even though You are not yet reigning on the earth, I desire to submit to Your control and to live Your way now. Help me walk by faith, because the world presses me to walk by sight.

Even More Blessings of the Kingdom

Matthew 5:9-12

9 *"Blessed are the peacemakers, for they shall be called sons of God.* 10 *Blessed*
are those who have been persecuted for the sake of righteousness, for theirs is
the kingdom of heaven. 11 *Blessed are you when people insult you and persecute*
you, and falsely say all kinds of evil against you because of Me. 12 *Rejoice and be*
glad, for your reward in heaven is great; for in the same way they persecuted the
prophets who were before you."

Peacemaking is a rare commodity. Wars abound around the world, and things are not getting better. Conflicts between individuals continue unabated in this broken, fallen world. Despite advances in the social sciences and the abundance of self-help gurus, most people, it seems, live with considerable interpersonal conflict and tension. Daily, we hear of famous couples divorcing, and perhaps society's morbid interest in these stories reflects people's desperate desire to see their own struggles as normal.

Peacemaking is the territory of kingdom living, for it is the providence of none other than God Himself—a peacemaking God. The greatest need, of course, was to restore peace between Himself and human beings, who were created in His image. Ever since the fall, His passionate desire has been to win back His image bearers. Followers of Christ who work at bringing peace demonstrate that they're related to God. Thus they are described as "sons of God" (a figure of speech used to picture a person as being like the divine).

Following Christ is not a peaceful cakewalk though. The last beatitude implies followers of Christ will be persecuted. (Incidentally, we may infer that the Sermon on the Mount is *not* just to be applied to the future millennial reign of Christ, when "the wolf will dwell with the lamb … and the calf with the young lion," Isa. 11:6). When Christians are persecuted, they can find blessedness in the midst of it. They can truly be contented even when being treated badly because of their faith. When they live that way by faith, they fully experience the kingdom of heaven. In fact, they own it. That is kingdom living at its finest!

The sentiment here is so strong here that the Lord expounds on it more directly. He changes the pronoun from *those* to *you.* When persecution comes to you as a follower of Christ, you are in good company, namely that of the prophets. You should rejoice, for your reward will be great!

Lord, I gladly accept the persecution, the insults, the evil treatment that comes my way from following You. This is only temporary; the kingdom of heaven is eternal.

Weekend Reading

Saturday – Proverbs 5
Sunday – Psalms 19–22

Personal Reflections

Salt and Light Ministry

Matthew 5:13-16

[13] "You are the salt of the earth; but if the salt has become tasteless, how can it be made salty again? It is no longer good for anything, except to be thrown out and trampled underfoot by men. [14] You are the light of the world. A city set on a hill cannot be hidden; [15] nor does anyone light a lamp and put it under a basket, but on the lampstand, and it gives light to all who are in the house. [16] Let your light shine before men in such a way that they may see your good works, and glorify your Father who is in heaven."

Our Lord continues His radical lifestyle proclamation, relying continually on simple words rather than sophisticated oration. His message now is that His followers should have an impact on the world as basic as salt and light. Salt in the ancient Near East was used for both flavoring and preserving food. Jesus uses it here primarily in the first sense. Christians are to add spice to the world, not just to intermix with it unnoticed. In the workplace, the community, the neighborhood, and family gatherings, Christians bring moral perspective, relational balance, and spiritual insight.

Salt that loses its taste is good for only one thing: being "thrown out and trampled underfoot by men." Today salt is thrown down on roads or walkways to melt ice; it is cheap and coarse, to be walked on and driven on, but it adds no "flavor"! When the Romans quelled the Jewish rebellion in AD 70 they poured massive amounts of salt on the farmland, destroying its agricultural use for centuries. God has not called Christians to be destructive, or even neutral. Rather, our presence should bring constructive fresh air and a sense of well-being to life situations—in other words, flavor.

Christ-followers are called also to be shining lights in the world. They give clarity to relationships, concerns, and discussions. They may not have the answers to all life's issues, but they can help others gain perspective. By their gracious, clearmindedness, not arrogance, Christ's followers draw attention to "[their] Father who is in heaven."

Being a follower of Christ involves more than knowing the right words, experiencing great blessings, or even enjoying eternal salvation. It also involves our behavior (see James 1:22). The Christian's good works, motivated by the desire to enhance God's reputation, should be apparent to all. Indeed, we are saved by grace through faith so that we might do the "works" God created us for in the first place (Eph. 2:8-10). This reflects His character well.

Lord, help me be a doer of Your word, not just one who hears it. I commit to being salt and light today in my work and my community, and to live in such a way that people gain a favorable impression of You.

Week 6

Day 2

The Righteousness of the Law

Matthew 5:17-20

---

[17] "Do not think that I came to abolish the Law or the Prophets; I did not come to abolish but to fulfill. [18] For truly I say to you, until heaven and earth pass away, not the smallest letter or stroke shall pass from the Law until all is accomplished. [19] Whoever then annuls one of the least of these commandments, and teaches others to do the same, shall be called least in the kingdom of heaven; but whoever keeps and teaches them, he shall be called great in the kingdom of heaven. [20] For I say to you that unless your righteousness surpasses that of the scribes and Pharisees, you will not enter the kingdom of heaven."

Jesus endorsed the law of Moses, which was summarized in the Ten Commandments and detailed in the book of Exodus and other sections of the OT. It is true no one can be saved by the Law, for "By the works of the Law no flesh will be justified in His sight; for through the Law comes the knowledge of sin…. We maintain that a man is justified by faith apart from works of the Law…. Do we then nullify the Law through faith? May it never be! On the contrary, we establish the Law" (Rom. 3:20, 28, 31).

Yet Jesus stressed the Law's absolute importance! It follows that even though salvation cannot come through keeping the Law, the Law should be important to Christ-followers nonetheless. Precisely because we follow Him, our regard for God's righteous standards should increase. The Law spells out that righteousness in specific terms so as to unmistakably show the standard of life God desires for everyone. Only one Person could and did keep the Law perfectly, and that was the Lord Jesus Christ. All others failed—including you and me. The Law establishes that beyond all doubt. The saved person, however, has been put back on track to live according to the good works God has ordained for him (Eph. 2:10). That style of holy living is well laid out in the Law, according to Jesus. It does no good to dismiss this as applying only to a future time. Jesus clearly expects His followers to live holy, righteous lives.

He makes His point in three ways: (1) The Law is more durable than the present heaven and earth (see Revelation 21:1). The reference to the smallest letter (KJV *jot*) or stroke (KJV *tittle*) implies that God's inspiration extends to the smallest detail of what is written. Jesus here speaks of the durability of God's righteousness. (2) A person's attitude toward the Law will affect a person's standing in the kingdom of heaven. (3) Entry into the kingdom of heaven requires a righteousness that exceeds that of the religious leaders, who keep the Law, presumably better than everyone else.

Lord, though I am not saved by keeping the Mosaic law,
I commit to studying Your Word on a daily basis so that I
may know more of Your holy standard for living.

Kingdom Relationships

Matthew 5:21-24

[21] "You have heard that the ancients were told, 'You shall not commit murder' and 'Whoever commits murder shall be liable to the court.' [22] But I say to you that everyone who is angry with his brother shall be guilty before the court; and whoever says to his brother, 'You good-for-nothing,' shall be guilty before the supreme court; and whoever says, 'You fool,' shall be guilty enough to go into the fiery hell. [23] Therefore if you are presenting your offering at the altar, and there remember that your brother has something against you, [24] leave your offering there before the altar and go; first be reconciled to your brother, and then come and present your offering."

Jesus has just affirmed the importance of the Mosaic law and now goes on to demonstrate how it applies to the kingdom of heaven. The sixth commandment is God's prohibition against murder. It is true that at times God instructed His people in the OT to take the lives of their enemies. Murder, however, was to do this without God's sanction, such as in vengeance or selfishness. In OT times, "cities of refuge," complete with judges, were designated to hold court for those accused of murder (see 2 Chronicles 19). These would pronounce innocence or guilt, as appropriate. At the time of Christ, the various courts including the Sanhedrin would decide cases of capital consequences.

Jesus' interpretation of the injunction against murder went below the surface. The core of the commandment deals with the heart—not just the outward act, as the "ancients" thought. In fact, being angry with a "brother" brings a person into similar liability as physical murder. If this applies to a relationship with someone who is close, like a brother, it would certainly apply to all other relationships as well. For those accustomed to keeping "the letter of the law," this would have been unsettling.

Jesus lays out a righteousness that exceeds that of the Pharisees and scribes, using three scenarios: being angry with someone, calling someone "good for nothing," and naming someone a "fool." Each violates God's righteousness. Sin is an attitude of the heart, the symptom of which is the outward action.

Jesus applies this to a practical situation: If you become aware of conflict between yourself and someone else, reconciliation takes priority over worship. It makes no sense to bring an offering to God (indicating a heart's desire for a relationship with Him) while animosity exists with a fellow image bearer of God who is following Christ.

"Search me, O God, and know my heart; try me and know my anxious thoughts; and see if there be any hurtful way in me, and lead me in the everlasting way." (Ps. 139:23-24)

Kingdom Morality

Matthew 5:25-28

[25] "Make friends quickly with your opponent at law while you are with him on the way, so that your opponent may not hand you over to the judge, and the judge to the officer, and you be thrown into prison. [26] Truly I say to you, you will not come out of there until you have paid up the last cent. [27] You have heard that it was said, 'You shall not commit adultery'; [28] but I say to you that everyone who looks at a woman with lust for her has already committed adultery with her in his heart."

Following up His commentary on the sixth commandment concerning the heart of murder, Jesus offers the alternative for dealing with relational conflict. Rather than carrying around a bad attitude toward the other person, a member of the kingdom of heaven should resolve the situation in a personal way rather than a legal way. He said earlier that one of the characteristics of kingdom living is peacemaking. He described peacemakers as "sons of God." Here Jesus adds, "Deal with it. Don't just stew about it. Go to the person!" Reminiscent of the book of Proverbs, this wise application of the beatitude is common sense. Worldly ways of doing things involve power, revenge, and gossip. Kingdom living is peace-loving, interactive, and reasonable.

Jesus' teaching here is simply foundational. In Matthew 18:15-18 He further addresses the situation in which the other person does not respond to the overture. Paul adds in 1 Corinthians 5 that believers should not take other believers to the legal courts—rather, they ought to be able to resolve conflicts among themselves in the church.

Jesus moves to the seventh commandment, regarding adultery. (The numbering of the Ten Commandments differs based upon various Christian traditions.) Adultery, like murder, is a sin of the heart. The adage, "It's OK to look; just don't touch" is patently wrong. James 1:15 says that "when lust has conceived, it gives birth to sin; and when sin is accomplished, it brings forth death." Looking can and often does lead to actuality! Job knew his own weakness and took strong measures with himself. "I have made a covenant with my eyes not to look lustfully at a girl." Many, especially in today's Internet world, have fallen prey to the "roaring lion." Proverbs 7 pictures a young man being led down the road of sexual temptation, foolishly succumbing. The Christian echoes with Paul, "Wretched man that I am! Who will set me free from the body of this death? Thanks be to God through Jesus Christ our Lord!" (Rom. 7:25).

Father, "With my whole heart I have sought You; do not let me wander from Your commandments. Your word I have treasured in my heart, that I may not sin against You." (Ps. 119:10-11)

Kingdom Self-Discipline

Matthew 5:29-30

[29]"If your right eye makes you stumble, tear it out and throw it from you; for it is better for you to lose one of the parts of your body, than for your whole body to be thrown into hell. [30] If your right hand makes you stumble, cut it off and throw it from you; for it is better for you to lose one of the parts of your body, than for your whole body to go into hell."

On first reading, this section seems bizarre. As He often does in the Sermon on the Mount, our Lord speaks in binary terms, presenting truth as either one way or the other, black and white, no shades of gray. Such hyperbole is common when laying down foundational principles of any kind. The rest of Jesus' ministry and the teaching in the remainder of the NT fill in the gray areas. His point here is that those who want to follow Him need to settle once and for all their ultimate priorities. The stakes are high: heaven or hell. Popular Christianity seems to downplay these otherworldly "intangibles" in deference to down-to-earth tangibles. The pendulum of emphasis has swung to counter years of "hellfire and damnation" preaching and its scare tactics. Pendulums, however, often swing too far. Jesus speaks of heaven and hell as both relevant *and* tangible. Their reality ought to affect our life priorities and behavior here and now.

The argument is very simple: If a physical part of your body is the instrument causing you to merit God's condemnation in hell, then get rid of that body part! When the extent of eternity is considered, the logic of this argument is irrefutable. He refers to the eye first, a natural follow-up to verse 28 about lusting. Then His illustration of a hand indicates He is not only talking about lust.

Does this mean our salvation is in question? For those who are still seeking Christ, these words should lead to repentance, which was the summary message of Jesus from the beginning of His ministry. In fact, by the terms of the whole Sermon on the Mount, no one can be justified before God. We all fall short. Those who have already become followers of Christ, who have already been justified, ought to endeavor to remove all hindrances to holy living.

Father, I consider myself "to be dead to sin, but alive to God in Christ Jesus." I present myself to You as "alive from the dead" and my "members as instruments of righteousness to God" (Rom. 6:12-13).

Weekend Reading

Saturday – Proverbs 6
Sunday – Psalms 23–27

Personal Reflections

Kingdom Commitments

Matthew 5:31-37

[31] "It was said, 'Whoever sends his wife away, let him give her a certificate of divorce'; [32] but I say to you that everyone who divorces his wife, except for the reason of unchastity, makes her commit adultery; and whoever marries a divorced woman commits adultery. [33] Again, you have heard that the ancients were told, 'You shall not make false vows, but shall fulfill your vows to the Lord.' [34] But I say to you, make no oath at all, either by heaven, for it is the throne of God, [35] or by the earth, for it is the footstool of His feet, or by Jerusalem, for it is the city of the great King. [36] Nor shall you make an oath by your head, for you cannot make one hair white or black. [37] But let your statement be, 'Yes, yes' or 'No, no'; anything beyond these is of evil."

Today it seems that about the only *permanent* decision a person makes that is binding to his future self is the choice to get a tattoo, which is essentially an oath written in ink on flesh. All other commitments seem short lived. Jesus, however, spoke of another permanent commitment that binds a person's entire future: marriage vows. Scholars of His day enjoyed debating legitimate loopholes for getting out of that commitment. Opinions varied from lenient to strict. Jesus dispelled the notion of an easy divorce, giving only one exception—unfaithfulness. Today, Christians debate this issue as well. Some hold to a no-divorce view regardless of circumstance. Others allow for dissolution of marriage for reasons such as unfaithfulness, abandonment, abuse, and an unbelieving spouse. Add to that the question of when remarriage is permissible! The issue is just as divisive today as it was in Jesus' day.

Our Lord held a high view of marriage. He comes back to this subject again in 19:6, where He affirms that, yes, at times a married person who commits adultery does, in fact, "put asunder" what "God has joined together" (KJV). His point here is that unfaithfulness in marriage is serious, having a huge potential for destroying what was designed to be a permanent arrangement.

Jesus' reason for keeping one's word in reference to marriage also applies to all of life. Christians should be known for being people of their word. I once had a friend who would try to convince people of the truth of some story he was telling by proclaiming, "I swear on a stack of Bibles!" Of course that cast doubt on the veracity of other stories he told. Behavior that reflects citizenship in Christ's kingdom calls for our words to be clear and straightforward, accurately representing reality. Jesus says, "Let your yes be yes and your no be no," whether in taking marriage vows or in any area of life.

Lord, may my life and my words faithfully reflect an integrity of character, that I might keep my commitments before You.

Week 7
Day 2

Kingdom Deference

Matthew 5:38-42

[38] "You have heard that it was said, 'An eye for an eye, and a tooth for a tooth.'
[39] But I say to you, do not resist an evil person; but whoever slaps you on your right cheek, turn the other to him also. *[40] If anyone wants to sue you and take your shirt, let him have your coat also.* *[41] Whoever forces you to go one mile, go with him two.* *[42] Give to him who asks of you, and do not turn away from him who wants to borrow from you."*

The OT legal system, given by God, dealt with many things, including how to provide redress in cases of personal injury. The punishment should fit the crime—a simple concept. It should not exceed the offense. If a person unjustly caused someone to lose his eye, then the offender's punishment was for him to lose one of his own eyes—but not to lose his life! Leviticus 24:20 says, "As he has injured the other, so he is to be injured."

This law also served as a deterrent, possibly best explained this way: "Don't do to others what you wouldn't want done to yourself," an inverse of the so-called Golden Rule (7:12). Like all laws, this one was taken out of the judicial system and applied in Jesus' day to justify personal revenge. Today is no different. We can easily react to injustices with vengeful thoughts. "You gossiped about me, so I will gossip about you. Now you can see what it feels like!" "You drove your car on my lawn; I'll drive mine on yours and leave big ruts." "You bragged about your kids; I'll brag about mine to show you they are better than yours." The logic seems justifiable to the offended person, but if he follows through, he also becomes an offender. This bears out the truth of Proverbs 4:12, "There is a way which seems right to a man, but its end is the way of death." We act like spiritually dead people when we reduce ourselves to acting out the level of injustice that we receive from others.

Jesus turns this way of thinking on its ear by rejecting retaliation altogether. When confronted with an evil person, Jesus calls for a response of nonresistance, whether the situation involves a slap to the cheek, a lawsuit, or forceful subservience. This is radical to the nth degree. Jesus lived up to His own standard: "While being reviled, He did not revile in return; while suffering, He uttered no threats, but kept entrusting Himself to Him who judges righteously" (1 Pet. 2:23).

The Lord Jesus allowed His enemies to torture Him. At others times He reacted assertively, as when He drove out the moneychangers from the temple or commanded demons. When it came to personal offenses, however, He entrusted Himself to His Father.

Lord, I trust that You will settle all accounts and will attend to all grievances and injustices against me. Until then I trust You and "turn the other cheek."

Love to the Nth Degree

Matthew 5:43-47

[43] *"You have heard that it was said, 'You shall love your neighbor and hate your enemy.' [44] But I say to you, love your enemies and pray for those who persecute you, [45] so that you may be sons of your Father who is in heaven; for He causes His sun to rise on the evil and the good, and sends rain on the righteous and the unrighteous. [46] For if you love those who love you, what reward do you have? Do not even the tax collectors do the same? [47] If you greet only your brothers, what more are you doing than others? Do not even the Gentiles do the same?"*

The concept that all religions teach the same thing concerning moral behavior, while failing miserably on the larger issues of truth, is largely accurate. Many faith systems in the world share the basic tenet of today's passage—love. God has built into all humans a sense of a higher moral standard (Rom. 2:4-16), which religions of the world recognize. The larger issues of truth have to do with whether or not humans can meet that standard. Christianity gives a unique and unequivocal answer: *No!* At least, not without the transforming work of grace in people's lives. The Scripture is clear: "All have sinned and come short of the glory of God" (Rom. 3:23). So why this teaching of Jesus?

As pointed out previously, kingdom living pictures a coming day when Christ will reign on the earth in fulfillment of OT messianic prophecies. Revelation 22 refers to this as the millennial reign of Christ. Yet we are motivated to live by that standard of behavior now. It is the life for which we were created (Eph. 2:10) and to which Christ is calling us to live.

While the law of God does say to love our neighbors as ourselves, it nowhere commands us to hate our enemies, as some in Jesus' day taught. At times, the psalmist expressed animosity toward evil people in his attempt to express loyalty to God (Ps. 139:21). Progressive revelation in Scripture, however, moves us to a better way of expressing loyalty—to love those whom God loves. This includes the whole world (John 3:16), even those we consider "enemies."

A sub-Christian level of morality is nothing to be proud of! To love your neighbor, brother, and those who love *you* takes no great depth of spirituality. Further, love goes beyond simply holding back hatred. Jesus calls us to intentionally *love* our enemies, *pray* for them, and *greet* them in public. A big order to fill, but that is the true essence of the law of God.

Lord, I confess my preferential treatment of those who treat me well over those who are against me. Help me not to respond to them as their offense against me deserves, just as You do not treat me as my sins deserve.

The Perfect Standard

Matthew 5:48

48 *"Therefore you are to be perfect, as your heavenly Father is perfect."*

How can this be possible? The modern-day quip, "No one is perfect," contradicts this terse statement from the Lord. Is this the proverbial carrot dangling in front of the donkey—always motivating, but never attained?

Peter apparently reflected on this later: "Like the Holy One who called you, be holy yourselves also in all your behavior; because it is written, 'You shall be holy, for I am holy'" (1 Pet. 1:15-16). Actually, he was quoting Leviticus 19:2 (the thrust of which is found in other OT passages as well). So this was not a new idea. Those who follow Christ are called to be like God, perfect and holy! Some sects of Christianity claim it is possible to reach a state of perfection in this life. The apostle John, however, dispels that notion: "If we say that we have no sin, we are deceiving ourselves and the truth is not in us" (1 John 1:8).

Today's verse provides a key to understanding Jesus' discourse on the mountain. He presented a standard that far exceeds normal, humanly accepted righteousness. To the Jews the standard was the outward, superficial teaching and behavior of the Pharisees and the scribes (see Matthew 5:20). Religious people today, likewise, tend to create or accept religious standards that, while seemingly difficult, are well within reach of human endeavor—things like giving to the poor, attending church, etc.

Jesus calls us to begin our return to God with repentance precisely because God's standard, as Jesus interprets it, proves we are sinners. None of us meets the perfect requirements, measured against God Himself—perfect holiness. Rather than acknowledging spiritual failure, humans tend to substitute a lower standard, a righteousness of their own more attuned to human pride than to humility.

The word *perfect* translates the Greek word *teleios,* which can also be rendered "genuine," "complete," or "mature." Jesus calls His followers to return to God's original design. He made us in His image, to walk in His ways, under His leadership. He calls us to fulfill our true humanity, to be like God—in other words, aim for perfection!

Lord, I find my true identity in the realization that I was created in Your image. My greatest desire is to return to that ancient yet future calling, namely, to walk in Your ways.

Week 7
Day 5

An Unassuming Righteousness

Matthew 6:1-6

[1] "Beware of practicing your righteousness before men to be noticed by them; otherwise you have no reward with your Father who is in heaven. [2] So when you give to the poor, do not sound a trumpet before you, as the hypocrites do in the synagogues and in the streets, so that they may be honored by men. Truly I say to you, they have their reward in full. [3] But when you give to the poor, do not let your left hand know what your right hand is doing, [4] so that your giving will be in secret; and your Father who sees what is done in secret will reward you. [5] When you pray, you are not to be like the hypocrites; for they love to stand and pray in the synagogues and on the street corners so that they may be seen by men. Truly I say to you, they have their reward in full. [6] But you, when you pray, go into your inner room, close your door and pray to your Father who is in secret, and your Father who sees what is done in secret will reward you."

Giving and praying are on everyone's list of good religious things to do. Individuals and businesses give to charity because they know it enhances their reputation in the community. Plaques abound recognizing people's philanthropic contributions. The "advanced" religious person can manufacture eloquent prayers, seeking adulation. Jesus, however, goes for the proverbial jugular. If good works are done for earthly notice, others may be impressed, but that will be the only reward! Cheap rewards reflect cheap activity. The fleeting praise of men compares poorly to the lavish praise of the Perfect One.

Earlier, Jesus told His disciples to let their good works shine before men, not to hide them "under a bushel." Is this a contradiction? No. The issue is one of motivation. God wants our efforts to bring attention to Him, not to ourselves—to build His reputation, not our own. Though the difference is outwardly subtle, Jesus uses strong words to convey huge disparity. Righteousness, in one sense, should be out there for everyone to see. We shouldn't cover up the power of God working in us and through us. But in another sense, our actions should not be ostentatious; we should guard against self-aggrandizement, which so easily betrays us. We need to consciously counter our natural tendency to draw attention to ourselves, especially in areas such as prayer and giving.

Notice Jesus' use of the word *hypocrite*. Ouch! Though He doesn't link the identification with the Pharisees and scribes until later, we can be sure they began to squirm, along with all self-exalting religious people.

By faith we believe our Father in heaven sees everything we do, and He will give appropriate rewards. Why do we need human praise?

Lord, I confess my hypocrisy in wanting praise from people, cheap reward that it is. Your commendation is better: "Well done, good and faithful servant."

Weekend Reading

Saturday – Proverbs 7
Sunday – Psalms 28–31

Personal Reflections

The Disciples' Prayer–part 1

Matthew 6:7-10

[7] "And when you are praying, do not use meaningless repetition as the Gentiles do, for they suppose that they will be heard for their many words. [8] So do not be like them; for your Father knows what you need before you ask Him. [9] Pray, then, in this way: 'Our Father who is in heaven, hallowed be Your name. [10] Your kingdom come. Your will be done, on earth as it is in heaven.'"

I was raised in a tradition that emphasized repeating memorized prayers, including what is commonly called *The Lord's Prayer.* We used beads to keep track of how many prayers we said. The more I repeated, the more God would hear me and add to my merit of righteousness—or so I was taught. During a visit to Tibet some years ago, the memory of those repetitious prayers came back when I saw "prayer wheels" conspicuous everywhere. Each wheel was a drum containing a written-out prayer, and each time the wheel spun, the people believed, the prayer ascended to the gods. Older women in particular would keep those things spinning for hours on end.

Jesus called such practices worthless. It seems a peculiar property of human nature to believe that repetition equals effectiveness. It begins early. A young child wants something, so he repeats his whiny request *ad infinitum, ad nauseam.* But prayer has nothing to do with coercing God as though He were a reluctant parent. He already knows our needs! Prayer has a different purpose.

A few simple observations are in order: (1) Jesus' model prayer is better called *The Disciples' Prayer* because the Lord had no need of saying this prayer Himself. He had no debts of His own that needed forgiveness. (2) This was not intended as a religious practice for rote repetition. He was specifically teaching against such false practices. He did not say, "Repeat after Me ..." (3) This was more of a sample prayer or an outline for prayer. He instructed, "Pray in this way..." I don't suppose it is wrong to repeat the prayer per se as a prompter for our prayer life. But because of its traditional abuse as a religious practice somehow meriting grace, we would do well to take Jesus' warning seriously.

The first movement of godly prayer concerns God Himself. We lift our thoughts from the mundane of this world to the realm of Him who is over all and sees all. What better place to focus when being pressed in with the troubles of this world. He is our Father, not a benevolent overlord. He is holy and He wants His program and desire at the forefront of our lives. So we begin our communication with God, focusing on Him and His desires.

Father, as Your Son prayed, I pray, "Let not My will be done but Yours." Today, I submit my plans to Your guidance and direction. Show me what You want me to do.

Week 8

Day 2

The Disciples' Prayer–part 2

Matthew 6:11-15

11 "'Give us this day our daily bread. 12 And forgive us our debts, as we also have forgiven our debtors. 13 And do not lead us into temptation, but deliver us from evil. [For Yours is the kingdom and the power and the glory forever. Amen.]' 14 For if you forgive others for their transgressions, your heavenly Father will also forgive you. 15 But if you do not forgive others, then your Father will not forgive your transgressions."

By starting prayer focused on God, our perceived needs align better with His purposes. We bring our concerns to Him in the right context of His glory and desires. Otherwise our requests are purely selfish, to make life more comfortable and enjoyable. Our ultimate purpose is to enhance God's reputation and to live with His purposes in mind. Therefore we are to pray for daily food rations (or any other physical need) so that we can serve the Lord better. And when we pray like that, the Lord is inclined to give us what we ask for.

Turning from material needs, we need vigilance in dealing with our offenses against others and the temptations that so easily trap us. Following Christ heightens our awareness of failings in both areas, but we realize that any measure of success with them requires nothing less than God's help. Therefore we talk to Him about them.

The last phrase of the prayer, as rendered in the translation we're using (NASB), is not in the earliest ancient manuscripts. But it is found in the majority of later ones from the ninth to eleventh centuries. This is one of a very few places in Scripture where biblical scholars debate its genuineness. The translators indicate this with the brackets. Clearly the sentiment is biblically true and is reflected elsewhere in the NT, so the issue is moot.

Jesus' concluding commentary seems to make God's forgiveness of us contingent upon our forgiveness of others (cf. 18:23-35). Strictly speaking, forgiveness for salvation depends only upon our repentance and faith, as Jesus has been preaching all along. But those who are part of the kingdom of heaven need the daily forgiveness of God for our "debts" and "sins." This doesn't affect our eternal salvation, but it does affect our fellowship with the Lord. We do not further God's purposes and glory if we accept His daily forgiveness yet do not forgive others' offenses against us. Such behavior does not follow in the steps of the Master who calls people to "repent, for the kingdom of heaven is near."

Father, open my eyes to people I need to forgive. By freeing them from their offense I want to show You I truly repent of my own sin.

The Disciples' Fast

Matthew 6:16-18

[16] "Whenever you fast, do not put on a gloomy face as the hypocrites do, for they neglect their appearance so that they will be noticed by men when they are fasting. Truly I say to you, they have their reward in full. [17] But you, when you fast, anoint your head and wash your face [18] so that your fasting will not be noticed by men, but by your Father who is in secret; and your Father who sees what is done in secret will reward you."

Certain Christian activities have worth when only the Lord knows you are engaged in them. The propensity for human nature, however, is to just want to *appear* righteous before others. We so want the praise of people. Jesus, as the God-Man, understood this perfectly well. He was tempted in every way as we are but never succumbed to sin (see Hebrews 2:15). Some hold to the view that giving in to temptation cuts short the experience of being tempted; since Jesus never gave up in His resistance to sin, He experienced to a much greater degree the temptation to live righteously simply for the praise of men. Nevertheless, He lived to please His Father and for His praise only.

Billy Graham was asked about his greatest temptation. His response? "Pride." Having preached to millions of people, being constantly in the limelight and frequently praised, he had to continually remind himself he was simply a servant of the Lord. How much more would the Lord Jesus Christ—God in human flesh, who knew the Father had given all things to Him—would He be tempted to pride, to show His glory and holiness outwardly for the praise of men.

Knowing this temptation so well, Jesus warns His followers to make a great effort to hide their acts of personal holiness, particularly in the area of fasting. This seems to be one of the most intense, personal commitments one can make—to deprive oneself of eating for a period of time for the sake of the Lord. Fasting is a way of setting spiritual priorities ahead of physical needs for a period of time. God is not asking us to be ascetics or monks. Neither does the Lord here *command* us to fast nor even give detailed teaching of it. The point is that *when* you fast, do it privately and not for show. In fact, cover it up so others will not notice. This requires faith to really believe the Lord is there. He knows. Don't ruin its value by making sure others know you are doing it.

Lord, strengthen my faith so that I see the value of doing my personal acts of righteousness before Your eyes only.

The Disciples' Wealth

Matthew 6:19-24

[19] "Do not store up for yourselves treasures on earth, where moth and rust destroy, and where thieves break in and steal. [20] But store up for yourselves treasures in heaven, where neither moth nor rust destroys, and where thieves do not break in or steal; [21] for where your treasure is, there your heart will be also. [22] The eye is the lamp of the body; so then if your eye is clear, your whole body will be full of light. [23] But if your eye is bad, your whole body will be full of darkness. If then the light that is in you is darkness, how great is the darkness! [24] No one can serve two masters; for either he will hate the one and love the other, or he will be devoted to one and despise the other. You cannot serve God and wealth."

A man's portfolio and his possessions can become demanding gods. They require much but give so little back. Yet many people spend their lives accumulating stuff that in the end will wear out, rust out, or give out. Extended credit card debt or other financial obligations incurred in order to get more stuff now can increasingly absorb larger and larger portions of one's income. Even financial investments can suffer huge losses. Recession, inflation, embezzlement, and mismanagement can wipe away value. What's more, a health catastrophe can destroy the best laid plans for financial independence.

A god in our lives is anything that commands our unbending loyalty, and/or determines our bottom line. It affects all our decisions. Money and possessions (inextricably related) take their toll: stress on marriages, need for increased income resulting in multiple jobs, parents with little time for children, obsession with possessions, lack of sharing, anxiety—the list goes on. It's a well-known fact that many marriages are marred by conflict over money. In reality it is a clashing of the gods!

Such deities as money and possessions distort a person's view of life and lead to irrational decisions and behavior. For a follower of Jesus Christ, a decision needs to be made, sometimes on a daily basis. Whom do you serve, God or money? To be sure, we need to provide for the necessities of life and plan responsibly for future needs. But the question is this: What is the ultimate goal in your life—wealth, possessions, and stockpiled finances or being a faithful follower of the Lord Jesus Christ? You cannot do both. Make your choice. Jesus, in His customary approach in this Sermon on the Mount, paints the picture in black and white. If you are devoted to wealth, in Jesus' words, you despise God. There is no in between.

Lord, I choose to put You first, before all my decisions concerning finances and purchases. Show me how I can share what You have given me with others.

The Disciples' Needs

Matthew 6:25-30

[25] "For this reason I say to you, do not be worried about your life, as to what you will eat or what you will drink; nor for your body, as to what you will put on. Is not life more than food, and the body more than clothing? [26] Look at the birds of the air, that they do not sow, nor reap nor gather into barns, and yet your heavenly Father feeds them. Are you not worth much more than they? [27] And who of you by being worried can add a single hour to his life? [28] And why are you worried about clothing? Observe how the lilies of the field grow; they do not toil nor do they spin, [29] yet I say to you that not even Solomon in all his glory clothed himself like one of these. [30] But if God so clothes the grass of the field, which is alive today and tomorrow is thrown into the furnace, will He not much more clothe you? You of little faith!

So much of life revolves around food and clothing. Think about the hours spent in grocery shopping, meal preparation, drink selections, eating out, clothes shopping, thinking about what you will wear on any given day, and how it will look. How big is your wardrobe? How many pairs of shoes do you own? Where on the anxiety meter do you fall when thinking about these things?

To be sure, we must spend some time and expense on these things. And the amount varies from culture to culture. But Jesus gently reminds us, with simple logic, to trust Him for these things. First, the law of proportion: life is far more important than food, drink, or clothing. Earlier He told us to simply place our needs before Him: "Give us this day our daily bread." That should be the end of our worry, and other things should occupy way more of our concern.

Second, the law of comparison: since God cares for lesser entities (such as birds and flowers), He will care for us who are created in His image.

Third, the law of futility: being anxious will not do us much good in terms of our life experience or length. It is true that taking no care for our physical well-being portends irresponsibility, but Jesus addresses the opposite extreme—that of worrying about those things we can do nothing about. Simply put, many factors in our life are beyond our control, so why waste energy being anxious about them?

Fourth, the law of example: for all the trouble King Solomon went to to cater to his own needs and wants, he did little for himself by comparison with the *least* God does in taking care of us!

Fifth, the law of value: look at the beauty of flowers for a sampling of His level of care. The floral world displays God's beauty briefly, then dies. But we humans live forever. How could we think God would not take care of us?

Father, forgive me for doubting Your care in my life. I have foolishly been too focused on outward things. I turn my worry and anxiety over to You.

Weekend Reading

Saturday – Proverbs 8
Sunday – Psalms 32–35

Personal Reflections

First Things First

Matthew 6:31-34

---

[31] "Do not worry then, saying, 'What will we eat?' or 'What will we drink?' or 'What will we wear for clothing?' [32] For the Gentiles eagerly seek all these things; for your heavenly Father knows that you need all these things. [33] But seek first His kingdom and His righteousness, and all these things will be added to you. [34] So do not worry about tomorrow; for tomorrow will care for itself. Each day has enough trouble of its own."

Anxiety and stress characterize our twenty-first century. Work, family, relatives, the economy, health, international conflicts—all bring various levels of fretting. We kick into self-survival mode in smaller things, too—the daily "necessities" of life, things we can't seem to live without, like our food and clothing selections. Our multitude of options can be overwhelming. We have choices between five brands of cereal, each having many varieties of flavors, textures, vitamin supplements, and calorie counts. Toilet paper comes in multiplied options, plies, textures, designs, and even scents. Clothing fashions change every year, most of the time only slightly—the oh-so-important slight widening or narrowing of the pant legs, the width of a lapel, men's shirts tucked in or left out, just the right color of shoe to go with a certain outfit, the ruffle in just the right place, plaid or polka dot or stripes, pastels or bolds, slim or full or relaxed fit, crew or turtle or v-neck—the list goes on and on with innumerable choices.

Jesus tells His disciples to get beyond the "small stuff" and focus on the big picture, the kingdom of God. Otherwise a person can be consumed with worry. God knows we need the basics of life, and Scripture tells us elsewhere that we have a responsibility to work and not be lazy, to provide for our needs (1 Tim. 5:8; 1 Thess. 4:8; 2 Thess. 3:10-12; Acts 20:34). And true, life will never be without its pressures and concerns. But the only way to keep those things at bay is to keep God's plan and purposes in the forefront of our lives. Jesus speaks of our ultimate priorities, and this is key to life in a busy, pressurized world.

From a practical perspective, too many people today worry about the "what ifs" of the future. Jesus says there is enough in each day to occupy our concerns without worrying about the next day's. He wants us to be "in the moment," to focus on what is really important—the things of the kingdom of God—and not to let the worries of life drag us down or keep us from being useful in the King's service.

Lord, thank you that You care for my smallest needs. Since I don't have to worry about those things, I am free to follow Your will in my life.

Week 9

Day 2

Unrighteous Judging

Matthew 7:1-5

[1] "Do not judge so that you will not be judged. [2] For in the way you judge, you will be judged; and by your standard of measure, it will be measured to you. [3] Why do you look at the speck that is in your brother's eye, but do not notice the log that is in your own eye? [4] Or how can you say to your brother, 'Let me take the speck out of your eye,' and behold, the log is in your own eye? [5] You hypocrite, first take the log out of your own eye, and then you will see clearly to take the speck out of your brother's eye."

One common vice is judging and being blind to one's own faults. This was as common in Jesus' day as it is today. But judging can't be all bad. Normal-thinking, moral people evaluate the behavior of others, and it is wise to learn from others' mistakes. In fact, even Jesus affirmed Peter's "judging correctly" (Luke 7:43). The church is called to maturity in judging the behavior of its members, specifically that which is clearly immoral and blatant (1 Corinthians 6). Paul implies judging is required when he challenges "those who are spiritual" to "restore" a person "caught in a trespass" (Gal. 6:1).

We all know, however, that at some point a line is crossed. It's most apparent when we are wrongly "judged" by others. Jesus lays down a pithy statement in our passage, "Do not judge so that you will not be judged," but He does not at all mean that we are not to make moral evaluation of others' behavior. In fact He lays down the criterion for judging properly: "First take the log out of your own eye, and then you will see clearly to take the speck out of your brother's eye." The problem comes in dealing with others' sin with a double standard and in a self-righteous sort of way. To the observer, the fault in another is like a log, but Jesus says that that fault is very small (a speck) in comparison with the fault in the life of the observer (a log). That should be the perspective of a follower of Christ, of one who anticipates the kingdom of God. In other words, be more concerned with your own faults than the faults of others.

Scripture affirms the principle in other places: Romans 14 warns against judging one another in the "gray" areas of life; John 7:24 cautions against judging based on external appearances; James 2:4 speaks of judging with evil motives. If I truly love my brother, I will want to live in holiness, removing the faults in my own life, so I can see clearly to help him when he falls.

Lord, Your word reveals the thoughts and intents of my heart (Heb. 4:12). Help me to see and confess my own faults, that I may follow You more closely.

Learning to Ask

Matthew 7:7-11

[7] "Ask, and it will be given to you; seek, and you will find; knock, and it will be opened to you. [8] For everyone who asks receives, and he who seeks finds, and to him who knocks it will be opened. [9] Or what man is there among you who, when his son asks for a loaf, will give him a stone? [10] Or if he asks for a fish, he will not give him a snake, will he? [11] If you then, being evil, know how to give good gifts to your children, how much more will your Father who is in heaven give what is good to those who ask Him!"

Prayer is the wonderful access we have to God, yet many Christians struggle with it. Our Lord here lays out the simple concept, foundational to everything else Scripture has to say about this subject. Such a teaching is not exhaustive, saying everything there is to say about prayer. Rather, the Lord here is setting the overall tone that undergirds all efforts in communicating with God.

First, Jesus invites us to take the initiative in approaching God. Second, in whatever way we approach God—whether having a question to ask, a favor to seek or a desire to be in His presence (i.e. politely knocking on a door so as to gain entrance)—God is open to our approach. He is leaning toward us, not away from us; open to us, not resistant or reluctant.

Third, Jesus assures us that when we approach God, He is disposed to responding favorably toward us. We will receive what we ask for, find what we seek, and be welcomed into His presence. What a great incentive to pray! Yet what a contrast to unbelief, the impression that God really doesn't want to answer our prayer, so we have to somehow twist His arm, so to speak, to convince Him to do what we ask. That gets old fast!

Jesus, being the Master Teacher, illustrates this truth by using the "lesser to greater" argument: if caring, earthly fathers give good things to their children, how much more will our heavenly Father give *His* children good things. When Jesus refers to "you then, being evil," He is using rhetorical license to accentuate the point: we humans are so far different in goodness from God's perfect and absolute goodness, that by comparison Jesus refers to us as "evil." From this extreme perspective, Jesus' makes His point more powerfully. If human fathers are responsive, how much more will our "Father who is in heaven" give us what is good when we ask? Scripture has much more to say about prayer, but the bottom line is that God has an open-door policy for the followers of Jesus Christ who are seeking first the kingdom of God.

Lord, thank you for the standing invitation to ask, seek, and knock. Please continue to teach me to pray so that my fellowship with You may increase.

Week 9
Day 4

Pearls and Gold

Matthew 7:6, 12

[6] "Do not give what is holy to dogs, and do not throw your pearls before swine, or they will trample them under their feet, and turn and tear you to pieces ... [12] In everything, therefore, treat people the same way you want them to treat you, for this is the Law and the Prophets."

Some verses stand alone in their import and pithiness. Our reading for today focuses on two of these. The first seems quite odd, though the imagery itself makes perfectly good sense. How does this apply to followers of the Lord? How does one throw his pearls before swine? Traditionally we understand this to mean we shouldn't take holy things of God and allow non-believers to trample them. In other words, don't give them any unnecessary reason to ridicule you as a Christian or to unnecessarily malign the truth, particularly with things they, as unregenerate beings, cannot understand or appreciate. Talking to unbelievers about election, predestination, or free will is an exercise in futility. (They are hard enough for believers to wrestle with!) And such topics will certainly incur scorn. Making an elaborate show of praying at lunch in a cafeteria crowded with unbelievers qualifies for this injunction as well. This is not to say one should hide one's devotion to the Lord, but is that really a witness to unbelievers, or is it "throwing pearls before swine"? Would Jesus be suggesting that discretion is in order? Why subject our personal devotion to the Lord to unnecessary ridicule?

In the other stand-alone teaching under our consideration, Jesus gives what is popularly called the Golden Rule, "Do to others what you would have them do to you." Much has been made about the fact that just about every major religion has a similar teaching, with the misguided implication that all religions really teach the same thing. However, truth is true, regardless of where it is found, and it makes sense that this basic concept of ethical behavior authored by Jesus Christ would be imitated in other religions. He taught much more than just ethical conduct between people, though. Right behavior is rooted in a right relationship with God. That's why He said earlier, "Seek first the kingdom of God ..." All else is secondary.

Having said this, Jesus' statement provides the succinct and memorable reminder of how we should treat others—namely, as we ourselves would like to be treated. Much conflict would be averted before it happened if this principle were at the forefront of all our relationships.

Lord, help me not to "merely look out for [my] own interests but also for the interests of others" (Phil. 2:4).

Only Two Options

Matthew 7:13-17

[13] "Enter through the narrow gate; for the gate is wide and the way is broad that leads to destruction, and there are many who enter through it. [14] For the gate is small and the way is narrow that leads to life, and there are few who find it. [15] Beware of the false prophets, who come to you in sheep's clothing, but inwardly are ravenous wolves.[16] You will know them by their fruits. Grapes are not gathered from thorn bushes nor figs from thistles, are they? [17] So every good tree bears good fruit, but the bad tree bears bad fruit."

Today's reading comprises Jesus' *magnum opus* on the relative balance of who and how many will ultimately be saved to eternal life. The vast majority will *not* because men love darkness rather than light (John 3:19). This sad assessment might seem like a prediction of failure for our Lord. However, we see His love and patience in the fact that He came to die for the whole world—not just for those who would eventually believe—even if believers would be few. It may be difficult for our finite minds to comprehend that most will go to hell, but that is the teaching of our Lord Jesus Christ who, as God, is infinitely knowledgeable as well as loving. His love, compassion, fairness, and justice far exceed ours, so we can trust His teachings more than we can our own thought processes.

His message here is actually good news. The knowledge that the vast majority would reject Him does not deter Him from reaching those who would respond. In His earthly ministry, relatively few remained with Him until the cross. The multitudes abandoned Him.

The truth is narrow, by definition, and the untruth (false teaching) is vast. Look at the multiplicity of religious systems and cults in the world, the abundance of false teachers, and the plethora of self-help books, all of which attempt to present answers to life. Together they pave a broad way that leads ultimately to the destruction of the soul. This destruction is inherent because they do not choose to take the true, narrow way that leads to life. Jesus would later say, "I am the way, the truth, and the life. No man comes to the Father but through Me" (John 14:6).

How do you know, then, which teachings are true and which are false? One thing to look for, says Jesus, are the fruits in the lives of those teaching. Is there good fruit or bad fruit? Good fruit comes from the teachings of Christ and bears His characteristics.

Lord, thank you for showing me the straight and narrow way that leads to life. May the fruit of my life validate the good news I share with others.

Weekend Reading

Saturday – Proverbs 9
Sunday – Psalms 36–38

Personal Reflections

Avoiding Pseudoconfessions

Matthew 7:18-23

18 "A good tree cannot produce bad fruit, nor can a bad tree produce good fruit. 19 Every tree that does not bear good fruit is cut down and thrown into the fire. 20 So then, you will know them by their fruits. 21 Not everyone who says to Me, 'Lord, Lord,' will enter the kingdom of heaven, but he who does the will of My Father who is in heaven will enter. 22 Many will say to Me on that day, 'Lord, Lord, did we not prophesy in Your name, and in Your name cast out demons, and in Your name perform many miracles?' 23 And then I will declare to them, 'I never knew you; depart from Me, you who practice lawlessness.'"

The appearance of spirituality does not equate with walking faithfully in the Lord. What counts with the Lord is obedience, which He alone can judge, for this is a heart issue. When looking at others from the outside, what counts should be their "fruit," not their words. No amount of self-proclaimed loyalty, assertions of one's own obedience, or even miraculous feats proclaimed to be done out of fidelity to Christ will cut it with God.

The propensity of the human heart is to give greater value to words over actions. Jesus used a well-understood illustration that the quality of a tree can be identified by the quality of its fruit. That which has bad fruit is worthless (see Hebrews 6:7-8). With an economy of words, He applies this to His pseudofollowers, those who give lip service to His lordship. They will not enter the kingdom of heaven just because they can "talk the talk"!

This should be a wake-up call to those who, in cavalier fashion, presume to act or speak on His behalf, yet do not live in obedience to Christ and lack the genuine fruit of righteousness and peace. Jesus doesn't take to such behavior lightly. What a startling surprise it will be when such false purveyors of Christianity hear those fateful words, "I never knew you! Depart from Me!"

If that is how Christ treats pseudofollowers, then true believers need to take warning as well. James exhorts his readers in James 3:1, "Let not many of you become teachers, my brethren, knowing that as such we will incur a stricter judgment." Condemnation to hell is not in view for the believer here. But certainly those who teach the Lord's ways need to convey only the truth and, above all else, live what they preach. If hypocrisy is not acceptable among non-believers, we certainly can't tolerate it among believers.

Lord, I believe; help my unbelief (Mark 9:24). I obey You in many areas, but I confess my "un-obedience" in many other ways. Help me keep walking faithfully, demonstrating the power of Your name through fruitfulness.

Week 10
Day 2

Life Built on His Words

Matthew 7:24-25

[24] *"Therefore everyone who hears these words of Mine and acts on them, may be compared to a wise man who built his house on the rock.* [25] *And the rain fell, and the floods came, and the winds blew and slammed against that house; and yet it did not fall, for it had been founded on the rock."*

These would comprise the most audacious words a mere human teacher could ever speak, but Jesus is no mere human. He is the God-Man, and He speaks the truth of God. Whoever builds his life squarely on the Lord's teachings will have a solid life that no tragedy or difficulty can shake. What a promise!

The disciples heard this early in Jesus' ministry and, to be sure, gave mental assent to it. But, as with all spiritual truth, there comes a time when the truth becomes internalized through a testing process. The disciples endured many storms that battered them. On more than one occasion, the literal storms of the Sea of Galilee threatened to swamp their lives into an early, watery demise. They experienced failures in ministry, such as when they could not cast out a demon. And don't forget the rebukes of the Lord, "You men of little faith." That must have plagued them with a sense of spiritual inadequacy. All these things together don't seem like an unshakable house built on a rock, do they?

The Lord, on more than one occasion, rebuked Peter and once even identified him with Satan in his intentions (16:22-23)! What about when he denied the Lord three times? He, in particular of all the disciples, miserably failed to build upon the solid foundation of the Lord's teaching.

Then finally the disciples abandoned all hope when their Messiah was crucified as a common criminal and died. They had left all, and had at least attempted to build their lives on the solid foundation of His teachings. But now, this seemed not much of a rock to build the house of their lives on (Luke 24:21)!

In the end, though, the Rock held up against the worst storm that could buffet it. Death could not hold Jesus! He arose, proving He was who He said He was, the Son of God (Rom. 1:4). Everything He taught was true: forgiveness of sin, spiritual rebirth, and citizenship in the kingdom. When Jesus arose from the dead, He restored hope.

The teachings of Jesus Christ are not just wise counsel (though they are that). They form the very core, the base of truth on which our life must be built. He is truly *the* solid, substantial, indestructible foundation for all of life.

Lord, Your word is the foundation on which I stand. Everything else is flimsy and fleeting. Help me not to just stand but to build the life You want for me.

Life Apart from His Words

Matthew 7:26-29

[26] *"Everyone who hears these words of Mine and does not act on them, will be like a foolish man who built his house on the sand.* [27] *The rain fell, and the floods came, and the winds blew and slammed against that house; and it fell—and great was its fall."* [28] *When Jesus had finished these words, the crowds were amazed at His teaching;* [29] *for He was teaching them as one having authority, and not as their scribes.*

These verses are the complementary opposite of the previous two verses. Jesus' teachings are not just one system of philosophy to choose from among many (and in the world there are certainly many competing worldviews, religious perspectives, and ethical schemes). On the contrary, to ignore, neglect, or minimize *His* teachings is tantamount to building a house on a sand foundation. Apart from Christ we will not stand up to the rigors of life.

Now some may argue that many people who have never heard His teachings make it through life without Christ. What's the big deal? But Jesus is not talking about just making it to retirement and weathering the storms of financial struggles, health issues, and other earthly things. The focus of His coming to earth was to restore people who are lost and put them on a firm foundation to live out God's purposes in creating them.

All of what Jesus taught up to this point in the Sermon on the Mount recasts life in a truer light. We are not to focus on things such as what we eat or drink or wear. Many people do that and get those things in abundance. Rather, we are to seek the kingdom of God above all else. He will take care of the temporal things. "Kingdom living," built on the foundation of Jesus' teaching, raises life to a much higher plane than mundane living with a modicum of enjoyment and comfort. God created us to live life to the max and now Jesus calls us *back* to live life to the max! This kind of life will bring an inner equilibrium that nothing else can supply.

Jesus concluded His sermon, and the people were dumbfounded. His whole message was unique and riveting. It carried an inherent authority, and it should have done so, for the One who spoke these words about kingdom living was none other than the King Himself! Ought we not commit to daily meditating on God's written Word, studying it, memorizing it, internalizing it, and living it so that we stand fast and build our lives well on the solid Rock?

Lord, in my quest for learning and understanding, help me filter everything through the knowledge of Your Word so that I might not be led astray by any false perspective on life.

Week 10
Day 4

No Need Too Small

Matthew 8:1-4

[1] When Jesus came down from the mountain, large crowds followed Him. [2] And a leper came to Him and bowed down before Him, and said, "Lord, if You are willing, You can make me clean." [3] Jesus stretched out His hand and touched him, saying, "I am willing; be cleansed." And immediately his leprosy was cleansed. [4] And Jesus said to him, "See that you tell no one; but go, show yourself to the priest and present the offering that Moses commanded, as a testimony to them."

Leprosy, as referred to in the Bible and in biblical times, covered a variety of skin conditions and was often incurable. It brought social isolation, like HIV/AIDS do today. A person with leprosy, when approached in public, was required to call out, "Unclean, unclean" (Lev. 13:45-46). Such a person lived in poverty, being supported by relatives if they were fortunate. It was a life of misery and extreme boredom.

After Jesus' great sermon, huge crowds continued to follow Him, yet He never lost sight of individuals in the midst of the masses. A man sick with leprosy broke with the requirement of warning others of his presence and bowed down before Christ with a request. For him, the question was not about the Lord's ability but His willingness. This illustrates Jesus' teaching, "Ask, and it will be given to you" (7:7-8).

Jesus took the risk of contaminating Himself (or so it would seem) by touching the man. As Haggai the prophet pointed out, when a "clean" thing came into contact with a thing that was "unclean," the clean thing became unclean (see Haggai 2:11-15). In this incident, though, it was the "unclean" man that became "clean," that is, healed of leprosy. (Note: the concept of clean and unclean had to do with the ceremonial condition of individuals. It represented either fitness or unfitness for serving the Lord.) This demonstrates the larger truth that God "made Him who knew no sin to be sin on our behalf, so that we might become the righteousness of God in Him" (2 Cor. 5:21). Jesus was not afraid to be "contaminated" with our sin!

He gave the healed leper two instructions: (1) Don't tell anyone. Often commanding people this after healing, Jesus focused on faith, not on wowing people through the miraculous—something present-day "faith-healers" need to understand. (2) Tell the priests only. The leper, as instructed in the OT, was to show himself to the priests so they could provide objective verification of healing.

Lord, out of the billions on earth, thank you that You hear me and are aware of my needs. "Surely, our griefs He Himself bore, and our sorrows He carried" (Isa. 53:4).

No Need Too Unworthy

Matthew 8:5-8

[5] *And when Jesus entered Capernaum, a centurion came to Him, imploring Him,*
[6] *and saying, "Lord, my servant is lying paralyzed at home, fearfully tormented."*
[7] *Jesus said to him, "I will come and heal him."* [8] *But the centurion said, "Lord,*
I am not worthy for You to come under my roof, but just say the word, and my servant will be healed."

A centurion was a Roman soldier of fairly high rank, typically commanding a troop of up to 1000 men. They were often educated men, of substantial means (not always legitimate), and had all the authority of Rome behind them, which they wielded mercilessly if needed. One simply did not mess with men like that!

Centurions in the NT offer an "outsider's" perspective of Jesus Christ at times. The centurion at the cross was so struck by what he witnessed there that he openly declared he believed Jesus was divine (Mark 15:39). It was a God-fearing, Jewish-respecting centurion named Cornelius who desired to hear the gospel Peter preached. As a result, he and his household believed it and received the Holy Spirit (Acts 10). In fact, this event became the turning point in the expansion of the gospel beyond the Jews.

Here in our passage, back in Jesus' home base, we see an unnamed centurion coming to Jesus with a compassionate concern for his personal servant, who was paralyzed. The Greek term *pais* refers to a young child-slave. While we may hold such practices in contempt today, the centurion obviously treated this child quite well in the context of first-century culture and practice.

Rather than debating the morality of slavery, Jesus simply responded to the centurion's genuine request. He was no respecter of persons; social status did not affect Jesus. He was fully at ease embracing a leper, fellowshipping with despised tax collectors, dining with the religious elite, and speaking with prostitutes. He was even comfortable going to the home of a military proponent of the oppressive Roman regime. Jesus' goal was not to bring a new social, economic, or political agenda but a new spiritual order (Heb. 9:10).

Notice that this Gentile commander, despised in general by Jews, considered himself unworthy of the humble Jewish teacher. What a remarkable exhibit of modesty, of self-effacing faith before the One who would one day be exalted above the heavens. While Jesus was not beneath going to the man's home, the man considered *him*self beneath such an honor of having Jesus as his guest!

Lord, I too am not worthy that You should come into my life. You are the infinite God of the universe, holy and perfect. Thank you for Your grace and mercy.

Weekend Reading

Saturday – Proverbs 10
Sunday – Psalms 39–43

Personal Reflections

Authority and Faith

Matthew 8:9-13

9 *"For I also am a man under authority, with soldiers under me; and I say to this one, 'Go!' and he goes, and to another, 'Come!' and he comes, and to my slave, 'Do this!' and he does it."*
10 *Now when Jesus heard this, He marveled and said to those who were following, "Truly I say to you, I have not found such great faith with anyone in Israel.*
11 *I say to you that many will come from east and west, and recline at the table with Abraham, Isaac and Jacob in the kingdom of heaven;*
12 *but the sons of the kingdom will be cast out into the outer darkness; in that place there will be weeping and gnashing of teeth."*
13 *And Jesus said to the centurion, "Go; it shall be done for you as you have believed." And the servant was healed that very moment.*

Here is a man who is an illustration of what Jesus called "poor in spirit" in the Beatitudes. He was humble, sensing his unworthiness before One of great authority—greater than his own, a kind of authority that overrides the sin curse of death in our fallen world. Being a man with insight into the real nature of Christ's position over life itself, he dared to approach, seeking healing for his beloved servant.

Few things impressed Jesus, but this was one of them: the centurion's faith hit the mark! (Another time Jesus was "impressed," though in a negative way, was at the unbelief of the Jews, God's own chosen ones, in Mark 6:6.) It wasn't just that the centurion believed Jesus could heal his servant. His response proved unique (in Jesus' own words) when compared to the *lack* of faith of God's own chosen people. As one author puts it, "This Gentile penetrated more deeply into the nature of Jesus' person and authority than any Jew of His time" (*Expositor's Bible Commentary*).

This story anticipates the expansion of the gospel to the Gentile world that began with the conversion of another Gentile centurion, Cornelius (Acts 10–11). The messianic banquet referred to in today's passage is pictured in a number of places in the OT (e.g., Isa. 25:6-9), normally with little or no thought of Gentile attendance. But the Lord Jesus clearly reverses things. What bitter irony coming from Jesus' lips—that the very people through whom He came to reach the world of fallen humanity would themselves be rejected because of their lack of faith. The consequences are terrible: a hell described as outer darkness, weeping, and wailing. But this Gentile centurion's faith resulted in the merciful healing of his servant.

Lord, like the centurion, I deserve nothing, but I ask that in Your mercy and with Your authority, You counteract the death curse of sin on my life.

Week 11
Day 2

The Healer Heals

Matthew 8:14-17

[14] When Jesus came into Peter's home, He saw his mother-in-law lying sick in bed with a fever. [15] He touched her hand, and the fever left her; and she got up and waited on Him. [16] When evening came, they brought to Him many who were demon-possessed; and He cast out the spirits with a word, and healed all who were ill. [17] This was to fulfill what was spoken through Isaiah the prophet: "He Himself took our infirmities and carried away our diseases."

Jesus healed Peter's mother-in-law from an undisclosed illness. With a simple touch of the hand, this incident is presented as commonplace. The healing was instantaneous and effective. The woman got up and began to serve with no apparent delay of time needed to regain her strength!

The Lord also healed many others—casting out demons and curing sicknesses. In each case He simply spoke a word. Such is the absolute authority He held over both demons and human health. This shouldn't surprise us who, with hindsight, know Him to be God in the flesh. But for the Jews these things needed substantiation from OT Scripture. So Matthew, the author, quotes Isaiah 53:3 to show these things identify Jesus as the Messiah.

Rather than seeing these as confirmatory signs, some Christians today assert that passages like this mean we also can see great healings now—if we simply have enough faith. Such an interpretation might seem reasonable—and exciting! But biblical history and honest observation speak otherwise.

First, although it is clear that *at that time* many were healed, this was not the case for the entire ministry of Jesus on earth. Sometimes He performed few miracles because of unbelief (13:58).

Second, while it is clear that early in the church's existence the apostles performed many miracles (Acts 5:14-16), things changed over time. Paul himself was not healed of his "thorn in the flesh" (2 Cor. 12:7-9). Hardly would any conclude the great apostle lacked faith (see Acts 14:9-10). As referenced in an earlier devotional, he left Trophimus sick in Miletus and recommended Timothy take "a little wine" to relieve his ailment.

Third, if we Christians were given this power to miraculously heal all who have enough faith, then we should easily be able to empty hospitals of at least all Christians!

Lord, You are the great Healer, and I come to You with all my difficulties. I trust You whether You heal me nor not, for You are the authority over all my life.

Extreme Discipleship

Matthew 8:18-22

[18] Now when Jesus saw a crowd around Him, He gave orders to depart to the other side of the sea. [19] Then a scribe came and said to Him, "Teacher, I will follow You wherever You go." [20] Jesus said to him, "The foxes have holes and the birds of the air have nests, but the Son of Man has nowhere to lay His head." [21] Another of the disciples said to Him, "Lord, permit me first to go and bury my father." [22] But Jesus said to him, "Follow Me, and allow the dead to bury their own dead."

Volunteers, be warned! Discipleship is not for the fainthearted. While the multitudes received the general teaching about righteousness and the kingdom of God, those who actually wanted to become followers of the Lord Jesus Christ, what we call "disciples," were faced with demanding requirements. Jesus never downgrades the standards; in fact, the nature of His requirements send the message that following Him demands being absolutely devoted to Him.

As a scribe, the man in this passage was well aware of the concerns others would have had concerning an imposter Messiah. He was eager to break out of the group. Think of the resistance and risk of being identified with this new Teacher! This attitude would stand him in good stead as a candidate for discipleship, it would seem. Jesus presented a watershed moment for this man's life with a simple statement.

Building on the common idea that a disciple actually committed to living like the master he follows, Jesus simply pointed out the living condition that He, as the Master, was accustomed to—lacking the normal comforts of home. Being a disciple meant living the life of an itinerate preacher. No record is given of the scribe's response, which does not portend well for him, especially in light of the responses of others recorded in the Gospels.

Another "disciple" came with similar aspirations to follow Him, but Jesus speaks of the choice he had to make to do so. I don't think the Lord was forbidding His followers from attending a parent's funeral any more than He encouraged literal eye-gouging (5:27). Rather, His statement is best interpreted by His own words in 10:37 where He asserted that, "He who loves father or mother more than Me is not worthy of Me." His basic message of discipleship was this: "Follow Me, but count the cost!" Again, we don't know whether this second man continued to follow. We do know that many of His "disciples" did stop following the Lord when His teaching went below the surface needs (John 6:60, 66). Serious is the warning, "Count the cost."

Lord, I confess my often weak and double-minded commitment to You and Your cause. You are worthy of my absolute, undivided loyalty—no matter the cost.

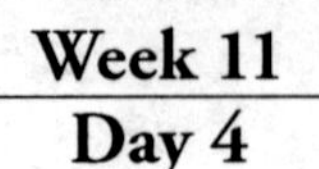

Week 11
Day 4

A Remarkable Man

Matthew 8:23-27

23 When He got into the boat, His disciples followed Him. 24 And behold, there arose
a great storm on the sea, so that the boat was being covered with the waves; but
Jesus Himself was asleep. 25 And they came to Him and woke Him, saying, "Save
us, Lord; we are perishing!" 26 He said to them, "Why are you afraid, you men of
little faith?" Then He got up and rebuked the winds and the sea, and it became
perfectly calm. 27 The men were amazed, and said, "What kind of a man is this,
that even the winds and the sea obey Him?"

The story before us is neither about a storm nor the disciples' fears. Nor is it really about a miracle. Rather, it is about the question, "What kind of man is this?" The overriding purpose of the events recorded in the Gospels, particularly the miracles of Jesus, was to bring His followers, and we readers of the gospel accounts, to confront this big question: "Who is Jesus, really?"

The storm was sufficiently fierce that even these sea-hardened fishermen were fearful, thinking death was inevitable. The Lord of creation, whom they had not yet recognized Him to be, was the "kind of man" who was sleeping like a baby. He was not bothered in the least. The disciples, in illogical desperation, interpreted this as a lack of care. He could have at least provided an extra set of hands in the dire circumstances. Maybe He was exhausted from dealing with people, but it seems a bit of a stretch that the disciples would have interpreted His lack of action in that way. What sort of man could have slept in such circumstances? One who didn't care, they thought.

Jesus, roused from His slumber, did two things: He rebuked His followers, characterizing them as "men of little faith." That's who *they* were! Then He turned and rebuked the winds and the sea. The calm that followed left the men almost speechless. Their second query was the right one. Jesus had already demonstrated with His many healings that He cared for people. Was He now demonstrating that He could command nature? They were slowly learning.

The application is obvious, but one that needs to be rehearsed frequently in our lives. When life is difficult and God is silent, it is not because He does not care. There are two questions we must always ask ourselves. First, am I a person of faith? Is that characteristic of me in what may seem like hopeless circumstances in life? The second question is related but focuses more on God. Do I really believe Jesus is the God of creation who can, in His wisdom and timing, command the elements, the demons, physical illness—the very things causing my difficulties?

Lord, I believe; help my unbelief (Mark 9:24). Thank you that You are mightier than anything or any situation that forces itself on me.

Control Over Demons

Matthew 8:28-29

28 When He came to the other side into the country of the Gadarenes, two men who were demon-possessed met Him as they were coming out of the tombs. They were so extremely violent that no one could pass by that way. 29 And they cried out, saying, "What business do we have with each other, Son of God? Have You come here to torment us before the time?"

One of Jesus' trips into Gentile territory was to the eastern shore of the Sea of Galilee. The place was near a town called Gadara. His ostensible reason for coming here was to avoid the crowds (v. 18). As with all His activities, there were various levels of motivations, but one could argue that He had a predetermined appointment with two violent, demon-possessed men who made their home in a graveyard.

Whereas Mark and Luke mention only one demon-possessed man in their parallel accounts of this story, Matthew tells us there were two. This is not a problem or contradiction; it just reflects a common phenomenon when different people relate the same incident. One might say, "I saw John today" but leave out the fact that John was with Mary at the time. Another might give a fuller account, "I saw John and Mary today." Both are correct.

While those in the boat wrestled with what kind of man Jesus might be, the demon-possessed men had no doubt. The men appeared to be insane yet were violent and living in a graveyard. Still, they had the perspicuity to recognize who Jesus really was, namely "the Son of God!"

The demons spoke through the men, and they were more concerned with their own well-being. Obviously they didn't care about the men they possessed, and they didn't care to worship the Son of God. They were completely surprised (and maybe even offended!) by Jesus' intrusion into what seemed to be their claim on humanity. At the least, they appealed to a notion that it was not yet time for the judgment (see Jude 6). They also knew Jesus to be their ultimate Judge and Sovereign, who would assign them to everlasting torment (see 25:41). There is coming a time when Satan himself and all his demons will be banished forever into the lake of fire (Rev. 20:10), never to haunt mankind again. Until then the demonic world is limited by God's permissive will, as we are about to see in this passage.

Father, thank you that Your power and authority reign over all that is evil in the world. I rest in Your ultimate control of my circumstances.

Weekend Reading

Saturday – Proverbs 11
Sunday – Psalms 44–48

Personal Reflections

A Fearsome Authority

Matthew 8:30-34

[30] Now there was a herd of many swine feeding at a distance from them. [31] The demons began to entreat Him, saying, "If You are going to cast us out, send us into the herd of swine." [32] And He said to them, "Go!" And they came out and went into the swine, and the whole herd rushed down the steep bank into the sea and perished in the waters. [33] The herdsmen ran away, and went to the city and reported everything, including what had happened to the demoniacs. [34] And behold, the whole city came out to meet Jesus; and when they saw Him, they implored Him to leave their region.

Swineherding is a sure sign that this incident took place in Gentile territory, for Jews would never be involved in that particular form of farming. Pigs were "unclean" to the Jews—that is, not fit for sacrifices or for food, according to the Mosaic law. Interacting with such people would have been beneath a good, law-abiding rabbi's repertoire of good deeds. But encounters with Gentiles were not out of the ordinary for *this* Rabbi (John 4), nor was dealing with demoniacs (cf. Matthew 4:24).

A few notes of interest should be observed. First, while humans often fail to submit to Jesus, these demons readily recognized His authority over them. Exorcism was a foregone fact; they just hoped to modify the method. So they asked permission to inhabit the herd of pigs. Second, their request to be sent into the swine seems odd at first. Bible scholars suggest that disembodied demons seek material experience. Inhabiting pigs is better than having no body at all to possess. This could support one interpretation of Genesis 6:1-4 where the "sons of God" refers cryptically to fallen angels which cohabited with the "daughters of men," resulting in the God's judgment in the worldwide flood. Demons, spiritual beings, aspire to human experience.

The third interesting feature of this incident is that after being possessed, the herd of swine ran into the water—another strange thing, unless under God's direction the demons were being consigned to a watery judgment similar to the great flood. (See also Matthew 12:43, where a cast-out spirit traveled through "dry" or "waterless" places before returning to the body originally possessed.) Demons apparently fear water, which is possibly symbolic of God's judgment. These, to be sure, are conjectures, but good alternative interpretations are lacking.

Fourth, the pig farmers had more of a concern for their loss of livelihood than for the healing of the two demoniacs. They begged Jesus to leave, probably to avoid any further loss of income.

Lord, You came to free people from bondage. Help me to focus more on people than on my income or standard of living.

Week 12
Day 2

Faith and Forgiveness

Matthew 9:1-2

[1] Getting into a boat, Jesus crossed over the sea and came to His own city. [2] And they brought to Him a paralytic lying on a bed. Seeing their faith, Jesus said to the paralytic, "Take courage, son; your sins are forgiven."

Messiah Jesus crossed back into familiar territory, the land to which He was called. His going into Gentile lands was a foretaste of the gospel spreading to the four corners of the world (Acts 1:8), but that was not His immediate or primary goal. He needed to focus on preaching the gospel of the kingdom first to the Jews. Through them the world would be reached. The promise to Abraham in Genesis 12:1-3 was that his descendants would be great and that they would be a blessing to the world. This is the grand theme of God in the Bible—to reach the lost world through the Jewish people, the descendants of Abraham, the father of faith (cf. Galatians 3:6-9).

"His own city" refers to Capernaum, the home base for His ministry (4:13), not Nazareth where He grew up, nor Bethlehem, His birthplace. Some men brought a paralyzed individual to Him. This is possibly the same incident referred to in Mark and Luke, in which a man was let down on a stretcher through the roof, above where Jesus was teaching a standing-room-only crowd. Matthew's abbreviated rendition focuses our attention on four succinct things. First, Jesus saw their faith. The one thing that highly impressed Him was not their good works, nor their doctrinal beliefs (as important as those things are). Rather, what caught His attention and favor was their faith. God always responds to faith. Hebrews 11:6 puts it this way, "Without faith it is impossible to please Him, for he who comes to God must believe that He is and that He is a rewarder of those who seek Him." It follows then that faith is what God is looking for. It is what pleases Him.

Second, Jesus challenges the man to "take courage." We are reminded of David, who "encouraged himself in the LORD his God" (1 Sam. 30:6 KJV). Other translations put it this way: David "drew strength from the LORD his God." The idea is that, like David, this paralyzed man who had faith now needed the courage to act in spiritual strength. This is the sum and substance of what it means to *encourage*. And Jesus urges the man to do just that.

Third, Jesus refers to him as *son* or literally *child*, intimating a tender relationship. (This truth is further developed in the NT, in passages such as 1 John 3:1). Finally, Jesus proclaims forgiveness to the man—to the consternation of the scribes, scholars in the Mosaic law (9:3).

Father, by faith I know that You are my spiritual Father, but I often lack the courage to act on that faith. Thank you for encouraging me with this account.

The Glory of Forgiveness

Matthew 9:3-8

[3] And some of the scribes said to themselves, "This fellow blasphemes." [4] And Jesus knowing their thoughts said, "Why are you thinking evil in your hearts? [5] "Which is easier, to say, 'Your sins are forgiven,' or to say, 'Get up, and walk'? [6] "But so that you may know that the Son of Man has authority on earth to forgive sins"—then He said to the paralytic, "Get up, pick up your bed and go home." [7] And he got up and went home. 8 But when the crowds saw this, they were awestruck, and glorified God, who had given such authority to men.

Jesus claimed to have authority that belongs only to God, and the Jewish scholars of that time objected. Their fine parsing of the text of the OT, along with their honed manipulation of biblical truth, led them to reject Jesus' actions as blasphemous. In their way of thinking, when Jesus forgave the paralyzed man's sins, He was claiming to do something only God could do and was therefore committing blasphemy. Make no mistake—Jesus' contemporary detractors knew exactly what He was presuming for Himself (never mind present-day assertions by critics that Jesus never claimed to be God). Jesus unabashedly identified objections to this as "thinking evil," not just misunderstanding.

The issue at heart is one of authority: *Did* Jesus have the authority to forgive sins? He Himself responds by appealing to demonstration and logic, as follows. He healed the man of paralysis in plain sight, for all to see. This was an undeniable, verifiable, eye-witnessed fact. Such a thing is humanly impossible.

There are two ways now to explain Jesus' argument. The first is that physical healing is the more difficult thing for a human to accomplish because it would be impossible to fake. Yet saying "your sins are forgiven" does not lend itself to tangible proof. It is easy to simply *say* it, because no one could objectively verify it one way or the other. The other way to consider this is that physical healing is much easier for God than forgiving sin. In the one case, it simply took a verbal statement. In the second case, it required the death of incarnate God Himself. At different levels, both aspects of the argument lead to the same conclusion—that Jesus did have the authority on earth to forgive sins.

The healed man simply got up and went home to carry on life as God intended. The crowds were "awestruck," for they recognized that God was at work in Jesus. Their belief in Him, however, had not yet advanced to the point of recognizing Him as Messiah, for they recognized only His authority to heal. That's what awed them, not His ability to forgive sins.

Father, in Your wisdom and love You do not always heal me of my physical problems. But You have taken care of my greatest problem by forgiving me all my sin! Someday in glory I will be healed of the physical as well!

Sinners and Followers

Matthew 9:9-13

[9] As Jesus went on from there, He saw a man called Matthew, sitting in the tax collector's booth; and He said to him, "Follow Me!" And he got up and followed Him. [10] Then it happened that as Jesus was reclining at the table in the house, behold, many tax collectors and sinners came and were dining with Jesus and His disciples. [11] When the Pharisees saw this, they said to His disciples, "Why is your Teacher eating with the tax collectors and sinners?" [12] But when Jesus heard this, He said, "It is not those who are healthy who need a physician, but those who are sick. [13] But go and learn what this means: 'I DESIRE COMPASSION, AND NOT SACRIFICE,' for I did not come to call the righteous, but sinners."

From a demon-possessed man to a paralytic and now to a Jewish turncoat, Jesus showed no prejudice or partiality. The demoniac's townspeople begged Him to leave; the paralytic was told to go home; but the tax-collector was invited to become a follower. The demon-possessed man was a Gentile; the paralytic, a social outcast; but Matthew was a man of influence, judging by the apparent size of the guest list to his "Meet Jesus" party.

How poignant is the immediacy of his response to Jesus' request and the speed of his invitation to others! He continued on to eventually write a book inviting people to know Jesus—namely, the Gospel According to Matthew, the writing we are now studying. Matthew did not hesitate to identify his preconversion lifestyle and, as a tax-collector, his explicit association with "sinners." His occupation did not endear him to his compatriots. Rome compelled people, like Matthew, from the subjected nations to do the dirty work of collecting from the Roman tribute (taxes) from their own people. Tax collectors were to forward the required sums to the government, but often opportunistically collected more than Rome required, skimming off the excess for themselves. The people were helpless to object, for the collectors enjoyed Roman protection. Tax collectors were despised as traitors by their countrymen, but not by Jesus, the Messiah.

As usual, the Pharisees were critical of what Jesus was doing. The Lord's first response was to state that these were the kind of people He had come for—the spiritually sick (v. 12) and sinners (v. 13). Second, He reminded these men that ritualistic worship which did not reflect genuine loving care for God and men had always meant little to God. The implications of this response struck at the Pharisees' arrogant hearts.

O Father, I am no different from Matthew, a spiritually sick individual, a sinner whom the Lord Jesus Christ has called to follow Him. Thank you.

New Way for New Life

Matthew 9:14-17

[14] Then the disciples of John came to Him, asking, "Why do we and the Pharisees fast, but Your disciples do not fast?" [15] And Jesus said to them, "The attendants of the bridegroom cannot mourn as long as the bridegroom is with them, can they? But the days will come when the bridegroom is taken away from them, and then they will fast. [16] But no one puts a patch of unshrunk cloth on an old garment; for the patch pulls away from the garment, and a worse tear results. [17] Nor do people put new wine into old wineskins; otherwise the wineskins burst, and the wine pours out and the wineskins are ruined; but they put new wine into fresh wineskins, and both are preserved."

Following the Sermon on the Mount, the incidents we have seen so far showcase our Lord's dealing with a variety of responses to His message. Now comes the questioning from the disciples of John the Baptist. To be sure, it must have been difficult to see some of their own fellow disciples abandon John to follow Jesus. Maybe they were jealous. Maybe they were proud of their aesthetic accomplishments. Maybe they were just overly zealous for John. As late as Acts 19—about 20 to 25 years later—we discover some of John's disciples who had not yet heard of the Holy Spirit and had not been baptized as followers of Christ. This was long after both John and Jesus had died. Their lack of knowledge is surprising in light of John's ministry focus of pointing out the One who would baptize believers with the Holy Spirit (3:11).

Old ways die hard; there will always be those who want to hold on to old ways of doing things. Symptomatic of this principle is John's disciples' issue with the freedom of Jesus' disciples to not fast, while they themselves did fast.

Jesus first addresses the immediate concern: in the same way that groomsmen don't fast while the groom is present, neither should followers of Christ fast while He is still present. Then Jesus addresses the larger issue of letting go of the old ways of the Law and embracing the new life in Himself. He uses two analogies: putting a patch of new cloth on an old garment, and putting new wine in an old wineskin. Not a good idea in either case. The writer of Hebrews expands on this. "There is a setting aside of the former commandment because of its weakness and uselessness (for the Law made nothing perfect), and … there is a bringing in of a better hope, through which we draw near to God. … Jesus has become the guarantee of a better covenant" (Heb. 7:18-19, 22).

Father, help me live in the light of Jesus' way and not hold onto the ritualistic requirements of the Mosaic law.

Weekend Reading

Saturday – Proverbs 12
Sunday – Psalms 49–54

Personal Reflections

Healing by Interruption

Matthew 9:18-22

[18] *While He was saying these things to them, a synagogue official came and bowed down before Him, and said, "My daughter has just died; but come and lay Your hand on her, and she will live."* [19] *Jesus got up and began to follow him, and so did His disciples.* [20] *And a woman who had been suffering from a hemorrhage for twelve years, came up behind Him and touched the fringe of His cloak;* [21] *for she was saying to herself, "If I only touch His garment, I will get well."* [22] *But Jesus turning and seeing her said, "Daughter, take courage; your faith has made you well." At once the woman was made well.*

Christ's reputation continued to grow with more and more people seeking Him for healing. An "official" now comes to Jesus with a concern for his daughter. The original Greek does not specifically identify the sphere over which he ruled, but he was probably, as the NASB indicates, a synagogue leader. Like Nicodemus (John 3), this man was one of the few who approached the Lord on favorable, though secret, grounds. Unlike the case with Nicodemus, we don't know if this man was a Pharisee or a Sadducee (the two main religio-political parties of the Jews). What we do know is that he had a need and was intentional in seeking Jesus' help to meet that need.

His faith is evident. He believed Jesus could heal his daughter just by laying a hand on her. Reminiscent of the Roman centurion (8:5), the *faith* of this official is the focus. In contrast with Jesus' dealings with the centurion (8:10), however, Jesus makes no comment about this man's faith. When Gentiles showed faith, Jesus marveled, but with Jewish people, faith was expected.

At the ruler's request, Jesus started toward the ruler's home to help the child. While on the way, the compassion of Christ, which shows no favoritism, changed His plans. Another individual's need intrudes into the story. This one was a woman with a bleeding problem—a uniquely feminine problem, in her case a particularly distressing one. Obviously she was not homebound but able to be about in public, at least making the effort to find Jesus in the midst of a crowd.

While the official sought the touch of the Master's hand on his daughter, this woman herself sought to touch *Him*. She had complete confidence in what might be considered the "passive power" of the Lord. Jesus rewarded her faith with miraculous healing. She took the initiative, and He healed her immediately. The Lord's healing was not confined to specific rituals, formulas, or techniques. The constant was faith.

Lord, You have left me with certain difficulties and ailments so that my faith will grow. I don't want formulas or techniques. I want to touch You by faith.

Healing from Death

Matthew 9:23-26

[23] When Jesus came into the official's house, and saw the flute-players and the crowd in noisy disorder, [24] He said, "Leave; for the girl has not died, but is asleep." And they began laughing at Him. [25] But when the crowd had been sent out, He entered and took her by the hand, and the girl got up. [26] This news spread throughout all that land.

While the woman with the bleeding problem reached out and touched the Lord (as seen in yesterday's reading), in this part of the story He comes to reach out and touch a dead girl. God is not confined to a set procedure for healing. So often we want Him to fit in a box, to be predictable. But the Lord will not be reduced to a formula.

In a masterful stroke of storytelling, Matthew records for us the contrast of perspectives. The girl, from the human standpoint, was dead. Of this the official had been quite certain. Yet from the perspective of the Divine Healer, she was simply "asleep." Both perspectives are true. They just focus on different levels of truth. Yes, death is a reality, contrary to the beliefs of some (such as adherents of the Christian Science group, who believe that death is illusory). We live in a real, though fallen, world which is not simply a product of our imagination or lack of faith. Death is real. Yet Jesus knew death for the girl was only brief, so He used a more appropriate word for her state, namely, *sleep.* In other words, Jesus saw not an illusion of death, but the temporariness of death.

The atmosphere in the house went from disorder to disrespect. The music reflected the mourning customs of the day; the disorder echoed the confusion that death always brings. Jesus' words were not euphemistic nor a ludicrous denial of reality, as some who were present thought. Their lack of faith in Christ prevented them from seeing God at work.

Jesus, in simplicity and calmness, took the girl's hand, and she got up. That's all it took. He brought order from disorder. Where the fallen, sinful world had wreaked its havoc, He brought peace, stilling the noise, like a storm on the Sea of Galilee. Death no longer had its sting. This was a foretaste of what was to come, the permanent healing when believers are raised again at Christ's return.

A friend of mine, after experiencing remission from cancer which ultimately took his life, used to say, "All healing here is temporary. In the end, we all die. There is only one permanent healing." Every "temporary" healing is to be enjoyed as a blessing now and a reminder of better things to come!

Lord, the touch of Your hand gives me hope. Sickness and death remind me that the best is yet to come. I am so glad that here and now is not all there is.

The Blind and the Mute

Matthew 9:27-34

*27 As Jesus went on from there, two blind men followed Him, crying out, "Have
mercy on us, Son of David!" 28 When He entered the house, the blind men came up
to Him, and Jesus said to them, "Do you believe that I am able to do this?" They
said to Him, "Yes, Lord." 29 Then He touched their eyes, saying, "It shall be done
to you according to your faith." 30 And their eyes were opened. And Jesus sternly
warned them: "See that no one knows about this!" 31 But they went out and spread
the news about Him throughout all that land. 32 As they were going out, a mute,
demon-possessed man was brought to Him. 33 After the demon was cast out, the
mute man spoke; and the crowds were amazed, and were saying, "Nothing like
this has ever been seen in Israel." 34 But the Pharisees were saying, "He casts out
the demons by the ruler of the demons."*

Jesus continued His healing ministry, and despite His frequent admonition against telling anyone about these events, news about Him spread (see 9:26). While He desired the good news of the message of the kingdom to be spread, He wanted the miraculous events downplayed. One could say these healed men were disobedient, but this might be forgivable because of the enormity of their experience. For a blind person to regain sight was a big deal, far more than "seeing people" could ever realize! Regardless, the stories of His miraculous powers circulated.

At that time, the Lord wanted to forestall the inevitable showdown with the religious leaders. Verse 34 says, "His time was not yet." Be that as it may, some observations are in order regarding the passage before us.

First, the two blind men asked for *mercy*, the initial and most basic form of request to God. The core problem for humanity is separation from Him because of rebellion. A request for mercy reflects a tacit admission of our problem and our need. In truth, mercy is the only hope a sinner has in approaching God, because he deserves nothing at all from his Creator, the God he has spurned.

Second, faith is required (vv. 28-29, see also Hebrews 11:6). If we, in faith, ask for mercy, God will reward us with an answer. This leads to the third observation: giving sight to the blind men was a sign of God's mercy. Along with the healing of the demonized man (the symptom of which was muteness), Jesus demonstrated His power over the most basic of human senses and abilities: to see and to communicate. Clearly, the Lord came to restore our ability to see (spiritually) and to speak (to communicate and give God praise as we ought). The crowds were amazed, but the Pharisees seethed.

Lord, help me see clearly what You are doing in my world and to use my mouth to give You the praise and glory You deserve.

Week 13
Day 4

Compassion-Driven Evangelism

Matthew 9:35-38

35 Jesus was going through all the cities and villages, teaching in their synagogues and proclaiming the gospel of the kingdom, and healing every kind of disease and every kind of sickness. 36 Seeing the people, He felt compassion for them, because they were distressed and dispirited like sheep without a shepherd. 37 Then He said to His disciples, "The harvest is plentiful, but the workers are few. 38 Therefore beseech the Lord of the harvest to send out workers into His harvest."

Matthew begins to shift focus from the crowds to the few—the Twelve who followed Jesus the most closely. Chapters 1 through 4 were the introduction of Christ to the world. Chapters 5 through 7 comprise the Sermon on the Mount. Chapters 8 and 9 view the Lord's ministry to the multitudes. Our present passage forms a transition into His discipleship ministry with the Twelve.

By this time, the disciples had observed Jesus in numerous situations, so seeing His compassion was nothing new. But now it becomes a backdrop for a foundational stage of Christian discipleship—having the heart of the Master. The ministry of Christ was one of compassion for the "felt needs" of people. The early post-resurrection disciples embraced this mindset (see for example, Acts 4:32-35 and Galatians 2:10). Christ is still mindful of human suffering today.

The word *compassion* means to "feel with" another. It differs from empathy in that while the latter is an emotion, the former is an impetus to action. James 2:15-16 makes it clear that empathy not leading to active compassion renders faith useless and dead. Discipleship, following the example of Christ, means doing something hands-on about the human needs of others.

The larger vision of discipleship, though, is to see more than just the felt needs. The *real need* of lost people is that they are without divine guidance in their lives, like sheep without shepherds. The needs go deep—inner distresses and discouragements in life. What people need is a good Shepherd, One who willingly lays down His life for the sheep in order that they might have abundant life (John 10:10-11).

Discipleship requires faith to see, in the faces of the nonbelieving world, that there is a harvest ready for reaping, that peoples' lives are not as complete and put together as they seem on the surface. There are relatively few who are willing to take up the challenge to reap the harvest, however. Those who already recognize the need should pray for more to share the burden of reaching the lost with the life-changing message of Christ.

Father, help me have the same compassion the Lord Jesus has for the lost. Bring more Christians to discipleship to help in this mission.

Authoritative Discipleship

Matthew 10:1-2a

[1] Jesus summoned His twelve disciples and gave them authority over unclean spirits, to cast them out, and to heal every kind of disease and every kind of sickness. [2] Now the names of the twelve apostles are these...

The naming of the Twelve begins a time of intense discipleship training, preparing the harvesters He spoke about at the end of the last chapter. These men had been following Him for some time, but now it was time for them to begin emulating the Master. He gives them authority to cast out demons and perform healings. They had seen the Lord doing this on multiple occasions (see 8:16, 28; 9:32-34). They were to wield the same authority, delegated as it was, that the centurion recognized in Jesus (see 8:9). Being a disciple involves doing what the Master does—by His authority!

Out of the multitude who had followed Jesus, He handpicks twelve men. Why these and not others? There were clearly differing levels of response to the Lord's ministry. The apostle John tells us when Jesus' teaching began to focus on commitment, the multitude abandoned Him. Only the Twelve continued on (see John 6:66-69). The Lord is on the constant lookout for those willing to commit to Him. They are the ones He selects for discipleship.

There were many "secret" believers, particularly some religious leaders who accepted His teachings but were afraid of the Pharisees (see John 12:42). Their commitment was low compared to the Twelve who openly followed Christ. Nicodemus was one such secret follower, coming by night to seek an audience with Christ. He admits, "Rabbi, we know that You have come from God as a teacher; for no one can do these signs that You do unless God is with him" (John 3:2). Joseph of Arimathea was another secret follower. But he, along with Nicodemus, quietly removed Jesus' body from the cross for a proper burial (John 19:38-39). There were others, including Cleopas, one of the two on the road to Emmaus who was devastated by the death of Jesus (Luke 24:18), and his wife, who witnessed Christ's crucifixion (John 19:25). Following His resurrection and ascension, the committed followers numbered about 120 (see Acts 1:15).

But Jesus gave the Twelve special training because of their unique task. They were to be the authorized agents of Jesus, His personally appointed witnesses (see Acts 1:8). They were promised perfect recall (John 14:26; 16:13) and supernatural guidance. Their teachings about the life and ministry of Jesus were foundational to the early church (Acts 2:42).

Lord, thank you for ensuring that Your teachings would continue to spread long after You ascended, and that Your apostles were faithful in passing them on.

Weekend Reading

Saturday – Proverbs 13
Sunday – Psalms 55–59

Personal Reflections

The Mission Personnel

Matthew 10:2-4

2 Now the names of the twelve apostles are these: The first, Simon, who is called Peter, and Andrew his brother; and James the son of Zebedee, and John his brother; 3 Philip and Bartholomew; Thomas and Matthew the tax collector; James the son of Alphaeus, and Thaddaeus; 4 Simon the Zealot, and Judas Iscariot, the one who betrayed Him.

The first four apostles were two sets of brothers, all fishermen. The gospel writers all introduce Peter first. He was the most vocal of the Twelve, often speaking for the group, such as when he proclaimed faith in Christ as the Son of God (16:16). He, along with James and John, form a sort of "inner circle." Jesus brought them into special confidence during three remarkable situations: the Mount of Transfiguration (17:1), the healing of a ruler's daughter (Mark 5:35), and Jesus' temptation in Gethsemane (Mark 14:33). The apostle Paul (whom God called to be an apostle after Christ returned to heaven) later described Peter, John, and Jesus' half-brother James as "pillars" in the Jerusalem church (Gal. 2:9).

Peter's important role, in particular, can be seen in Paul's reference to him as "the apostle to the circumcised" in contrast to Paul's apostleship "to the Gentiles" (Gal. 2:8). Though Peter played a crucial role, the other apostles did not considered him preeminent. In fact, Paul opposed Peter at one point, "because he stood condemned" (Gal. 2:11) for the sin of duplicity.

James held the distinction of being the first of the disciples to be martyred (Acts 12:2). This was not the same James prominent in the church of Acts 15, the half-brother of the Lord and the author of the epistle of James. (Evidently the latter was not a believer in Jesus until after Christ rose from the dead.) John, of course, became the writer of the gospel of John and three epistles bearing his name. He referred to himself as the "beloved disciple" (John 21:7). Tradition tells us he was the only apostle not to suffer a martyr's death. John died in old age following a period of exile on the island of Patmos.

Of the other nine men, Andrew is recognized as the first evangelist, having invited his brother Peter to meet the Messiah (John 1:40-41, see also John 12:22). Philip introduced Bartholomew to Jesus (see John 1:45, where the latter is called Nathanael). Thomas, of course, is well known for doubting the others' testimony of the resurrection. Matthew is the author of the present gospel account, followed by three disciples about whom we know little, if anything. Judas is listed last.

Lord, just as these men carried on Your message and mission, impress upon my soul the importance of joining them in the same glorious task.

A Mission Commission

Matthew 10:5-8

[5] *These twelve Jesus sent out after instructing them: "Do not go in the way of the Gentiles, and do not enter any city of the Samaritans;* [6] *but rather go to the lost sheep of the house of Israel.* [7] *And as you go, preach, saying, 'The kingdom of heaven is at hand.'* [8] *Heal the sick, raise the dead, cleanse the lepers, cast out demons. Freely you received, freely give."*

After calling out the Twelve, the Lord Jesus sends them on the first of two short-term mission trips. They had now spent some time following Christ, observing and learning *from* Him; now was their time to attempt ministry *for* Him. He instructs them where to go, what to say, and what to do. This will prepare them for when He will no longer be with them. When that time comes, He will give them a new Resource, the Holy Spirit, whom Jesus will later describe as "another Helper" (Greek, *paraklētos*), who will bring them into perfect recall of all Jesus was teaching them (John 14:16, 26). In the meanwhile, they have the Master training them, and they will return to Him after accomplishing the task.

First, their task was to preach to the Jews. This does not imply that God shows favoritism, but rather that God's master plan, as given to Abraham, is still intact: first, reach the descendants of Abraham (the Jews) and then, through them, reach the rest of humanity (the Gentiles).

Second, the disciples were to communicate the same message Jesus preached: "The kingdom of heaven is at hand." God's plan has remained unchanged: to bring about His own rule to the earth, to restore what was lost in the garden of Eden when Adam and Eve rejected God's ways. His purpose in creating humans in the first place was to display His majesty and glory to the creation made in His image. He desires us to willingly recognize Him as the Sovereign Creator, and ourselves as His craftsmanship made for His enjoyment. Our greatest joy is found in serving Him with open hearts and minds. When that happens, the kingdom of heaven is indeed present.

But we live in a fallen world, initiated when the first human abdicated his rightful place in God's order of things. The result is separation both from God and from life as He designed it. Sickness and death have become the bane of life ever since. The Twelve were given power to address these human frailties, the same way Jesus had been doing, and their actions would be signs validating the arrival of the kingdom of heaven.

Lord, impress upon me the responsibility to pass on the good news that the kingdom of heaven is at hand. You are looking for people to turn back to God.

A Mission Strategy

Matthew 10:9-13

[9] "Do not acquire gold, or silver, or copper for your money belts, [10] or a bag for your journey, or even two coats, or sandals, or a staff; for the worker is worthy of his support. [11] And whatever city or village you enter, inquire who is worthy in it, and stay at his house until you leave that city. [12] As you enter the house, give it your greeting. [13] If the house is worthy, give it your blessing of peace. But if it is not worthy, take back your blessing of peace."

The instructions Jesus gave the disciples included financial arrangements for their short-term trip: they were not to take along provisions. Their needs would be supplied by the people to whom they were sent. This was implied in the hospitality when one stayed in another's home.

A number of observations of this passage are in order. First, their support was not a right, simply a promise. The needs of those who "work" in the Lord's service would be met by those to whom they ministered. Scripture clearly teaches that a person in full-time ministry should be supported in his ministry (Luke 10:7). But the Lord here focuses not on the disciples' right to be supported—rather, that their work was *worthy* of support. Even Paul makes the point of foregoing his "right" to support so that the gospel would not be hindered (1 Cor. 9:6-11). Paul applied to himself what he taught others—that God would supply all his need according to His riches in glory (Phil. 4:19). This is a far cry from the modern-day practice of pastors negotiating a salary or missionaries asking for support. Christ and Paul never appealed for financial support, yet God met their needs as appropriate. (See Philippians 4:10-20 for Paul's attitude about his financial support in ministry.)

Second, attention should be given to those people who are "worthy" of the message. In the context of Jesus' ministry this refers to those open to the message. They would naturally invite the messengers (i.e. the disciples in this case) into their homes. In the ancient Near East, hospitality was highly regarded and practiced as a way of accepting strangers and their cause. That is why Christians are instructed in the Word not to invite false teachers into their homes (3 John 1:9-10) in support of *their* cause.

Third, disciples should spread the gospel broadly but focus on those who demonstrate open hearts. Go where the audience is receptive.

Lord, as I serve You sacrificially, direct me to those with hearts open to Your message of salvation. This is what really matters.

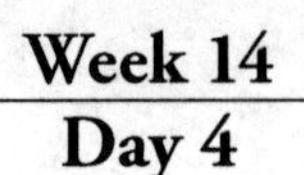

Week 14

Day 4

A Mission Rejected

Matthew 10:14-15

[14] *"Whoever does not receive you, nor heed your words, as you go out of that house or that city, shake the dust off your feet.* [15] *Truly I say to you, it will be more tolerable for the land of Sodom and Gomorrah in the day of judgment than for that city."*

Terse words from the mouth of the Savior! Some would rather think of a "gentle Jesus, meek and mild," a liberal, a do-gooder, tolerant of all people and their views. To some, His words here just don't match their image of Him. Some would prefer a Christ who excels at teaching and lives a generic ethical code that all religions apparently espouse to an institutionalized, self-righteous, hellfire-and-damnation kind of Christianity. The pendulum can swing to both extremes. But Jesus cannot be tamed in that sort of way.

His uncompromising message doesn't waver, and the consequences of rejecting it are enormous—a point He drives home with the disciples. As we have seen, following Christ involves spreading His message. Jesus says here that when people reject them outright because of His message, they should pronounce judgment and move on. In the case of the Twelve, He gave them the symbolism of shaking off the dust of their feet against the unreceptive. Whatever we do today to symbolize this, the point is that we shouldn't consider unfruitful witnessing a defeat. Instead, we should recognize that the person rejecting our message is under God's condemnation.

The Bible sometimes uses the imagery of Sodom and Gomorrah to symbolize God's fierce judgment. Jesus does not shrink from the comparison here—that those who reject His message will receive far greater condemnation. In a world where people so easily form profanity by linking the word *God* and the word damn, it's ironic that those two words in reality describe the havoc God will wreak on those who take His Name or His justice so lightly.

In this one statement, Jesus cuts across the entrenched, popular philosophies of our day—tolerance and pluralism. First, His message is unique, and rejection of it is not a matter of personal preference. Religions of the world that reject Jesus as the Messiah, God in the flesh, fall under His judgment. Second, warnings about God's judgment are not the domain of backward fundamentalists, nor are these warnings to be discarded as scare tactics. Jesus cared enough about people to warn us all of the consequences of rejecting His message.

Lord, I confess that I have bowed to the pressures of tolerance and pluralism in our world. If I love my neighbors, I need to warn them.

A Mission Enablement

Matthew 10:16-20

[16] *"Behold, I send you out as sheep in the midst of wolves; so be shrewd as serpents and innocent as doves.* [17] *But beware of men, for they will hand you over to the courts and scourge you in their synagogues;* [18] *and you will even be brought before governors and kings for My sake, as a testimony to them and to the Gentiles.* [19] *But when they hand you over, do not worry about how or what you are to say; for it will be given you in that hour what you are to say.* [20] *For it is not you who speak, but it is the Spirit of your Father who speaks in you."*

Being a disciple is not for the fainthearted. Jesus' message does not sound like a tract that says, "Come and discover God's wonderful plan for your life." Rather, being a follower of Jesus Christ is more like being part of a commando team sent to infiltrate a lost world with the message, "The kingdom of heaven is at hand." In one regard, the disciples were at a disadvantage, like sheep in the midst of wolves. The battle plan seems weak, unless one realizes that the Master who was sending them was the One who stilled the wind and waters with a word and who caused demons to tremble in His presence. Jesus Himself would one day be like a lamb led to the slaughter, so He conveyed to His followers the same *modus operandi* He Himself lived by.

The life and mission of discipleship will invoke conflict and persecution. It cannot be avoided. People will resist the message and messengers. The desire to follow Christ will outweigh fears of rejection. The disciples will be more concerned whether their apologetics will hold up—that is, their ability to defend the message when it comes under attack. The message of Christ goes completely contrary to all other philosophies, cultures, and religions, so the usual reaction from others will be negative, often hostile. Christ's message can be clearly understood through eyes of faith in Him. But it will seem intellectually untenable to non-believers. Still, it will strike a nerve because the message of Christ calls people to repentance from their rebellion against their Creator God.

Jesus assured His disciples that when the time comes, the appropriate words will be given. Those answers will not come primarily through intellectual prowess or theological training (helpful as these may be), but by the Spirit of God working within them and through them. It is a "God thing," as some people put it. The disciples' role is simply to follow the Lord's command, go out to a lost world, and become a ready vessel through which the Spirit can work. This requires simple obedience and faith. That's all.

Lord, thank you for the promise of Your Spirit to speak through me in reaching a lost world that desperately needs You.

Weekend Reading

Saturday – Proverbs 14
Sunday – Psalms 60–65

Personal Reflections

The Persecution of Discipleship

Matthew 10:21-23

[21] "Brother will betray brother to death, and a father his child; and children will rise up against parents and cause them to be put to death. [22] You will be hated by all because of My name, but it is the one who has endured to the end who will be saved. [23] But whenever they persecute you in one city, flee to the next; for truly I say to you, you will not finish going through the cities of Israel until the Son of Man comes."

Many homes—even otherwise pious families—have divided when one member becomes a follower of Christ. Both in Jesus' day and now, when a family struggles with someone whose life has been radically transformed by the Lord Jesus, tensions arise and animosity seeps in. This is frequently true when anyone "changes religions." But with Christian conversion, a person does not just change religions or churches. He exchanges a life for a life—his for Christ's. Add to that the new disciple's desire to share the message with his family, and conflict becomes inevitable.

In some parts of the world, and in some segments of history, this persecution often turns violent. Christians are ostracized simply because of their devotion to Christ. Jesus gives fair warning of this: if a person desires to follow Him, he had better accept these terms of discipleship. He must count the cost. Discipleship is not a passing fad, or just the religious thing to do. Discipleship includes a willingness to sacrifice one's personal safety and security for the task of spreading the news about Jesus Christ and His kingdom.

At the same time, there is no glory in unnecessary persecution, as a sort of "spiritual masochism" or martyr complex. In the case of the Twelve on their first missionary expedition, if they encountered opposition in one town, they were to simply go to the next, *posthaste*. To continue preaching to adamantly opposed audiences would not further the kingdom effort. Jesus told them to search for those who would listen. There was little time to be waylaid by useless endeavors. Their goal was to reach all the cities of Israel before Jesus arrived (presumably referring to His triumphal entry). We may assume they completed the task because of the comments the two disciples on the road to Emmaus made to the risen Lord. They expressed their surprise that anyone would *not* have been "aware of these things" (Luke 24:18)—that is, the message of the kingdom, and then the crucifixion of its king.

Lord, give me the strength to stand up under persecution and the wisdom to know when to move on.

The Expectation of Persecution

Matthew 10:24-27

[24] *"A disciple is not above his teacher, nor a slave above his master.* [25] *It is enough*
for the disciple that he become like his teacher, and the slave like his master. If
they have called the head of the house Beelzebul, how much more will they malign
the members of his household! [26] *Therefore do not fear them, for there is nothing*
concealed that will not be revealed, or hidden that will not be known. [27] *What I*
tell you in the darkness, speak in the light; and what you hear whispered in your
ear, proclaim upon the housetops."

Expect persecution, Jesus tells His disciples. If He as their Master experienced it, then they as His students would as well. A significant part of discipleship is living with and embracing the constant tension of walking out of step with the world. It is the nature of the thing. The message of Christ is inflammatory. It forces people to make a decision: either live for Christ or reject Him. One or the other! If one rejects the Truth, then one must also find a way to suppress the Truth.

There is no neutral ground when it comes to Christ, despite the sophisticated detachment of the pseudo-intellectuals and academics of this world. In Jesus' time, the very religious leadership—the experts in the OT Scripture, the ones you would expect would have welcomed God Himself come in the flesh—were the very ones who persecuted the Lord. They attributed His miraculous efforts to the work of Satan. (*Beelzebul* was the name of a pagan god, meaning "lord of the dung heap." In ancient times people commonly attributed names of enemy deities to evil forces.)

Jesus measured His words, teaching according to what the disciples could handle depending on their stage of growth in discipleship at any given time. He didn't tell them at the beginning about expected persecution. But as they grew in their understanding of and commitment to Him and His mission, He took them deeper now—to the point of telling them about the resistance they would experience. They would not have been ready to hear this before, and, in fact, many quit following Christ when opposition came.

In speaking soberly about what to expect, the Lord challenges them not to fear any adverse surprises. The writer of Hebrews says, "Nothing in all creation is hidden from God's sight. Everything is uncovered and laid bare before the eyes of him to whom we must give account" (Heb. 4:13 NIV). Having nothing to fear, they should go and proclaim the message of Jesus and not hold back.

Lord, thank you for clueing me in ahead of time. I don't have to fear the unknown because I already know there will be opposition. I accept that, Lord.

Discipleship Takes Courage

Matthew 10:28-31

[28] *"Do not fear those who kill the body but are unable to kill the soul; but rather fear Him who is able to destroy both soul and body in hell.* [29] *Are not two sparrows sold for a cent? And yet not one of them will fall to the ground apart from your Father.* [30] *But the very hairs of your head are all numbered.* [31] *So do not fear; you are more valuable than many sparrows."*

Reprising His earlier teaching concerning God's care for the disciples compared to His care for birds (6:26), Jesus soothes the natural anxiety that arises in the face of their formidable task of witnessing. The prospect of going on without Jesus daunted them. On one level, they had seen some of the opposition Jesus had endured. In that time, it was dangerous to incur the anger of the religious establishment because they had the power to excommunicate people from Israel's spiritual community. But Jesus boldly took them on. He knew who He was. And He was certain of His relationship with the God of Abraham, Isaac, and Jacob. The disciples were becoming enlightened about both of these truths, but that didn't immediately translate into their own boldness. Thus Jesus knew their need for encouragement.

On another level they had not yet seen the full extent of persecution they might expect. Jesus' own torture and death were still future, and the disciples little realized their commitment to witness for Him would lead to their own physical persecution as well. Historians tell us that ten of them did, in fact, experience martyrdom (John died in old age; Judas committed suicide). It bears repeating that discipleship is not for the fainthearted!

Jesus' training at this juncture points toward the ultimate cost of persecution—losing one's life. But He lifts His disciples to a higher perspective. The real fear is not physical death or those who can cause it. The greater issue is eternal death in hell. Some commentators today think this refers to Satan, but the better understanding is that God is the One who destroys "both soul and body in hell." He is the One who has prepared hell for Satan and his followers (25:41). Those who reject Christ will join them there forever.

The ones who reject the message of the disciples are the ones who need to fear. As for the disciples, their fear is unfounded; they are Jesus' personally chosen men. If God takes care of sparrows, He will certainly take care of these men who have sacrificed all to follow Him. Even if torture or death is their destiny here on earth, God's care extends into heaven for eternity.

Lord, thank you for Your encouragement to look for my security not in this earthly realm, but in the extended dimension of heaven.

Discipleship Demands Loyalty

Matthew 10:32-33 (part 1)

[32] *"Therefore everyone who confesses Me before men, I will also confess him before My Father who is in heaven.* [33] *But whoever denies Me before men, I will also deny him before My Father who is in heaven."*

Discipleship is about loyalty. If one is to become like his master, then one must publicly identify with his master. As Jesus continues to train the Twelve, He sternly zeroes in on the crux of the matter. This is no business for Sunday-only Christians. There were some, including Nicodemus (John 3:1; 19:39) and Joseph of Arimathea (John 19:38), who were "secret" adherents to the teachings of Jesus. But their fear of others eclipsed their open identification with the Lord. It is true that such believers can accomplish some things for the Lord, as these two men did in giving Jesus' body a proper burial. However, Jesus was recruiting for a higher calling.

In Jesus' day, and in the years following the birth of the church, being identified with Christ and His revolutionary teachings invariably brought persecution. There was a real cost in being a disciple of Christ. Jesus alerts them to this in the next few verses. Presently in North America and many parts of the world, particularly Christianized countries, publicly identifying oneself as a Christian is not hazardous to one's health. That is because the term *Christian* often conveys a culturally acceptable or institutionalized form of Christianity far removed from real discipleship. There is no risk, no test of loyalty in calling oneself a Christian in such cultures. However, in our Western culture, "Christian" often carries with it an unflattering political connotation!

In other areas of the world, disciples of Christ *do* suffer and die because of their identification with Christ. They take these words of Jesus seriously. What does this mean for the rest of us? How can we distinguish our loyalty to Christ? The answer is that we are called by Jesus to be identified with *Him,* not with a movement or a religion or a philosophy of life. Though "Christian" has been used for 2000 years, the term is only recorded in the Bible three times (Acts 11:26; 26:28; 1 Pet. 4:16). It meant "Christ-like" or "little Christ." And the term was originally used as an epithet, a short, quick way of identifying those people who had become followers of Christ. Eventually it became institutionalized, in the same way many things in the checkered history of the church have. Today we need to recovered that meaning. Some have adopted the self-reference, "I am a follower of Jesus Christ." This is more to the point.

Lord, I want to live my life so that others will see by my actions and know by my words that I am Your follower, a true "Christ-like" one.

The Cost of Discipleship

Matthew 10:32-33 (part 2)

[32] "Therefore everyone who confesses Me before men, I will also confess him before My Father who is in heaven. [33] But whoever denies Me before men, I will also deny him before My Father who is in heaven."

Theologians battle over two main interpretative views of what Jesus was teaching here. Some would say that Jesus is referring to those of His followers who, at some point, deny Him, presumably under persecution. In this view, Jesus Himself will deny that person before God, and therefore that person will lose his salvation. This, it is believed, provides a motivation to confess Christ openly. Those who hold this view present other Scripture to support their view. Each step of the way, disciples need to walk in obedience and loyalty lest they forfeit their salvation.

A different (in fact, opposite) interpretation is that Jesus here is still in the process of disclosing what discipleship is all about, weeding out those who are not truly His followers. He is not speaking to the issue of salvation but of counting the cost of discipleship. There is no point in deluding oneself about being a follower of Christ if one is not willing to identify with the Master. At this stage, being called a "disciple" was not synonymous with being "saved" and having eternal salvation. Christ had not yet died, and they knew nothing of His coming substitutionary atonement. Further, as we have pointed out before, at times His teachings became so difficult that many of His so-called disciples turned back from following Him (e.g., John 6:66). Judas provides the clearest example of one who was called a disciple but clearly was not. In John 17:21 Jesus called him "the son of perdition." It was not a matter of Judas being saved then losing his salvation. His betrayal was prophesied well in advance of his life. Further, passages such as Romans 8:28-39 and many others show that those who place their faith and trust in the finished work of Jesus Christ on the cross are secure for all eternity.

We believe that this second interpretation better fits the whole tenor of the NT. So how should we apply this text? First, the public identification that Jesus speaks of, in context of His earthly mission, was baptism "in the name of the Father and the Son and the Holy Spirit." Those who refuse are essentially ashamed of identifying with Christ. Not that baptism is required for salvation, but refusal of it calls into question a person's sincerity of faith. The importance of identifying with Christ continues then into our daily living.

Lord, show me ways today that I may identify with You. Show me how I can honor You in an ungodly world. Give me an opportunity to speak Your name.

Weekend Reading

Saturday – Proverbs 15
Sunday – Psalms 66–69

Personal Reflections

The Priority of Discipleship

Matthew 10:34-39

[34] "Do not think that I came to bring peace on the earth; I did not come to bring peace, but a sword. [35] For I came to SET A MAN AGAINST HIS FATHER, AND A DAUGHTER AGAINST HER MOTHER, AND A DAUGHTER-IN-LAW AGAINST HER MOTHER-IN-LAW; *[36] and* A MAN'S ENEMIES WILL BE THE MEMBERS OF HIS HOUSEHOLD. *[37] He who loves father or mother more than Me is not worthy of Me; and he who loves son or daughter more than Me is not worthy of Me. [38] And he who does not take his cross and follow after Me is not worthy of Me. [39] He who has found his life will lose it, and he who has lost his life for My sake will find it."*

Often Jesus says things in startling ways, and this is one of those passages. He draws attention to one of the ramifications of being a disciple. The ultimate purpose of Christ's coming was to bring about the kingdom of God. His *immediate* purpose was to restore God's image bearers to the Creator—to reunite sinful human beings with the God from whom they are estranged. One effect of His purpose was that those restored image bearers would gain abundant and eternal life (John 10:10). Another ramification was the disunity that would ensue between those who came to faith and those who did not.

The choice to follow Christ strikes at the heart of every other relationship. A genuine believer in Him will catapult the Lord to first place in priority, even over the most fundamental relationships of life—family connections. Jesus, using hyperbole, put it as bluntly as possible in verse 37. To get this order wrong is to completely miss the point of the discipleship. Campus Crusade for Christ has, for years, illustrated this with a circle representing our lives. Drawn at the center is a throne. Inside the circle are written various important things, such as family, career, self, school, and money. If any of these are on the throne, everything else degenerates into disarray and confusion, each vying for supremacy. But if Christ is on the throne, all is in balance around the throne.

So, many people today focus on "finding themselves," not realizing that is the wrong goal. The Lord calls us to "lose" ourselves for His sake. In doing that we can actually live out the meaning and purpose for which God created and saved us. Christ calls us to an all-or-nothing commitment. Giving Him first place is the way we can we experience the kingdom of heaven *now*.

Lord, I humbly submit to Your lordship in my life and place You first above everything else in my life, including family and friends.

The Reception of Discipleship

Matthew 10:40-42

[40] *"He who receives you receives Me, and he who receives Me receives Him who sent Me.* [41] *He who receives a prophet in the name of a prophet shall receive a prophet's reward; and he who receives a righteous man in the name of a righteous man shall receive a righteous man's reward.* [42] *And whoever in the name of a disciple gives to one of these little ones even a cup of cold water to drink, truly I say to you, he shall not lose his reward."*

So far, discipleship training has focused on the task and its difficulty. In these final statements of the disciples' preparation, Jesus' words take on a more encouraging tone. First, He reminds them that they are His ambassadors—nothing more, nothing less. The intended goal of their mission as disciples is for people to receive Christ. Of course, for this to happen people must receive the disciples. However the end goal is not the disciples' prominence but Christ's.

Second, the reception of the message is, in fact, the disciples' reward. The true desire and ultimate satisfaction is seeing others receive the message about Christ and, receiving Him, to become His followers as well. This truth is not limited to the Twelve. He applies it progressively to

You (the Twelve) → a prophet → a righteous man → a disciple → little ones.

What is true for Jesus' immediate disciples is also true for the prophets, who by definition, simply proclaimed a message from God. While some may feel this applies only to a certain class of people in full-time ministry, Jesus also applies it to "a righteous man." Others feel this applies to a certain kind of "spiritual" Christian, possibly identified in Matthew's own community as he was writing this gospel account. However, Jesus had already called His followers to a high standard of righteousness (5:20). He progresses to applying this to disciples. This group might be seen as a broader category than the previous three designations. But we rather think Jesus is not making so fine a distinction as some may want to impose on the passage. In fact, the implication is that these are all "little ones" in the sense that they are simply representatives of the "Big One," namely, Jesus. Certainly all disciples are dismissed by the world in that the world persecutes them and rejects their message. The disciples are belittled in that sense. Jesus' point is that those who go out representing Him and those who receive them will be rewarded!

Lord, I look for no other reward than to see lost sinners receiving You and becoming faithful disciples. It doesn't get any better than that!

Conflict and *Withdrawal*

The Doubts of Discipleship

Matthew 11:1-6

[1] When Jesus had finished giving instructions to His twelve disciples, He departed from there to teach and preach in their cities. [2] Now when John, while imprisoned, heard of the works of Christ, he sent word by his disciples [3] and said to Him, "Are You the Expected One, or shall we look for someone else?" [4] Jesus answered and said to them, "Go and report to John what you hear and see: [5] the BLIND RECEIVE SIGHT and the lame walk, the lepers are cleansed and the deaf hear, the dead are raised up, and the POOR HAVE THE GOSPEL PREACHED TO THEM. [6] And blessed is he who does not take offense at Me."

Matthew has outlined the *Introduction of the King* (chapters 1–4) and the *Character of the Kingdom* (chapters 5–10). This last section finished with Jesus' preparing the disciples to spread the teaching about the kingdom (11:1). Now the focus turns to the *Conflict and Withdrawal of the King* (chapters 11–18).

In setting the stage for this new section, Matthew includes a surprising parenthesis about John the Baptist in prison. The herald of Christ, once supremely confident in his identification of the Lord, had begun to doubt. The experience must have been quite harsh and unrelenting to shake a robust man like John to the core of his faith. So he sends one of his own disciples to Jesus with a question: Are you really the Messiah, or did I get it wrong? As Joni Eareckson Tada points out, "We believe in the light, but we are so quick to doubt in the darkness." This was John's darkness.

While on the one hand we might malign John for his lack of faith, we must also recognize he took his doubts to the right place! Jesus sent John this answer: follow the evidence to where it leads. The prophets long before had laid down the evidence for identifying the Messiah: the blind, lame, and deaf would be healed (e.g., Isa. 35:5; 61:1). Jesus was doing those very things! John would have known all this, but most likely he just needed to be reminded and encouraged. As the Baptizer, he was larger than life, but he was still subject to the feebleness of the human spirit. Suffering has a way of preying on faith. Faith must be bolstered, but not just through words. To the chagrin of modern-day skeptics, Jesus didn't verbally affirm that He was the Messiah. That would have proved nothing. The evidence of His miracles demonstrated who He was. That was enough for John, and it should be enough for us. We too must follow where the evidence leads.

Lord, I want to always take my doubts to You when my Christian walk becomes difficult and I face persecution. Forgive me for doubting.

Week 16
Day 4

The Ruggedness of Discipleship

Matthew 11:7-10

[7] *As these men were going away, Jesus began to speak to the crowds about John, "What did you go out into the wilderness to see? A reed shaken by the wind?* [8] *But what did you go out to see? A man dressed in soft clothing? Those who wear soft clothing are in kings' palaces!* [9] *But what did you go out to see? A prophet? Yes, I tell you, and one who is more than a prophet.* [10] *This is the one about whom it is written, 'Behold, I send My messenger ahead of You, who will prepare Your way before You.'"*

John the Baptist was now languishing in jail, wondering if he had misidentified the Messiah. This did not bode well for the message that the kingdom of heaven was "at hand." We don't know if his disciples in the previous section brought his concerns to Jesus publicly or privately. Regardless, news of John's predicament must have spread like wildfire among the throngs following Jesus. If John was shaken in his faith, others must have had second thoughts as well about the message, and ultimately about Jesus Himself.

Just as John had testified at the beginning concerning Jesus, Jesus now returned the favor, testifying about him. He stressed the importance of John's role, using a series of rhetorical questions meant to eliminate false perceptions. The Baptizer had not just made noises in the desert of his own concoction. His obvious goal was *not* to find a comfortable career that led to a luxurious life. Quite the contrary. His activities led to incarceration. The kingdom of heaven, about which he preached, was not about palaces and nice clothes (subtle references to his own primitive attire and abode).

John was a prophet and, as Jesus described, "more than a prophet." He was prophesied in Malachi 4:1 as the coming herald of the Messiah. Matthew, as usual, he records the emphasis Jesus placed on the fulfillment of Scripture. Jesus' essential maxim was: go where the evidence and Scripture leads. Jesus Himself was fulfilling the OT picture of the Messiah, and now as that One, He endorses John. Where does this point toward, if not to the Messiah?

With Jesus now ministering among the people, John's formal assignment was finished. His imprisonment served at least two purposes: First, it was an example of Jesus' teaching that there would be trials for His followers, and second, disciples need to continually go back to Scripture to strengthen their faith.

Lord, when times get difficult, please remind me, as You did John and Your first-century followers, to go back to Your written Word to strengthen my faith.

The Greatness of Discipleship

Matthew 11:11-15

[11] "Truly I say to you, among those born of women there has not arisen anyone greater than John the Baptist! Yet the one who is least in the kingdom of heaven is greater than he. [12] From the days of John the Baptist until now the kingdom of heaven suffers violence, and violent men take it by force. [13] For all the prophets and the Law prophesied until John. [14] And if you are willing to accept it, John himself is Elijah who was to come. [15] He who has ears to hear, let him hear."

Continuing His commentary, Jesus calls John the Baptist the greatest of all men up until that point (obviously excluding Himself from comparison). Just as Mary, the earthly mother of Jesus, was the most exalted of women, John was the greatest of all men. Mary was the vehicle through whom Jesus entered the world. John was the vehicle through whom Jesus was introduced to His people as their Messiah. Prophets before then had predicted Messiah's coming, but John pointed unambiguously toward Jesus.

John's place was not *within* the kingdom; rather, it was *prior to* the kingdom. Jesus asserted that the least *in* the kingdom is greater than John. Believers have the privilege of knowing Christ personally, being redeemed and baptized in the name of the Father, Son, and Spirit. We can point even more unambiguously toward Jesus, seeing a more complete picture of Him and His redemptive work. John had only a partial view.

Verse 12 has been variously interpreted (and translated), but suffice it to say this new movement of God in bringing the kingdom of heaven would not come about peacefully. John's own incarceration demonstrated that, and he himself had difficulty grasping it—certainly not the stuff for timid discipleship!

When Jesus said that John was Elijah (v. 14), He qualified it with "if you are willing to accept it." He knew this would be difficult for some to comprehend. In fact, Malachi 4:5 prophesied that Elijah would return as a forerunner before the "great and terrible day of the Lord." Jesus, though, applies this metaphorically to John. Before John's birth, the angel of the Lord had told his father, Zechariah, that John would minister "in the spirit and power of Elijah" (Luke 1:17). John himself, when he began his wilderness ministry, was specifically asked about his identity, and he always denied he was Elijah himself (John 1:21). The thrust of Jesus' comment was to point out that John fulfilled the role of Elijah, which the Jews believed would signal the Messiah's coming. In other words, "This is what you have been waiting for, the sign you have been looking for."

Father, what a privilege You have given us to share the person of Jesus Christ, Your Messiah. This is a role greater than what the prophets had. Thank you.

Weekend Reading

Saturday – Proverbs 16
Sunday – Psalms 70–73

Personal Reflections

The Fickleness of Unbelief

Matthew 11:16-19

16 "But to what shall I compare this generation? It is like children sitting in the market places, who call out to the other children, 17 and say, 'We played the flute for you, and you did not dance; we sang a dirge, and you did not mourn.' 18 For John came neither eating nor drinking, and they say, 'He has a demon!' 19 The Son of Man came eating and drinking, and they say, 'Behold, a gluttonous man and a drunkard, a friend of tax collectors and sinners!' Yet wisdom is vindicated by her deeds."

The contrasting lifestyles of John and Jesus proved troublesome to the Jews at large. Springboarding from His teaching to the disciples about John's prominence among all the prophets and the greater position of believers in the kingdom, Jesus turns His comments to those who refuse His message and John's. The Jewish leaders held sway, as leaders do in all social or religious institutions, either openly or subtly controlling people's behavior. Jesus likened their responses to childish whining—and that neither He nor John would dance to their tune.

Jesus, in using the term *generation*, refers to the Jewish people, as a whole, who would not accept His teachings. Yet God has always had His remnant of believers. A similar situation seems to be reflected in the institutional church today. Some criticize Christians who are too extreme in their devotion to righteousness. These critics say we should be able to enjoy temporal pleasures without puritanical guilt. And they marginalize old convictions as legalistic. Others judge those who enjoy freedom from legalism for conforming to fleshly worldliness and giving themselves over to the wanton pleasures of sin.

The fact remains, based on the examples of John and Jesus, that there is a place for different lifestyles and applications of kingdom living. John was not a participant of the kingdom of heaven per se. But it is clear from Scripture that there is a time and place for disciplines of the flesh. Being a disciple means self-discipline! For example, Paul, that great preacher of grace, sometimes fasted (Acts 13:2). Yet Christians are to live in liberty, as Jesus did, not shackled by the whims of others and their interpretations of the law.

There is a time for refraining and a time for enjoying the good things God provides. Christians debate things such as the use of wine, forms of entertainment, and fashions. Certainly Scripture addresses these things (see 1 Corinthians 8–9 and Romans 14). But our behavior should not be controlled by the opinions of others.

Lord, help me to gain my convictions from the Word of God and be certain of the things I believe and practice.

Week 17
Day 2

Warnings of Unbelief

Matthew 11:20-24

[20] Then He began to denounce the cities in which most of His miracles were done, because they did not repent. [21] "Woe to you, Chorazin! Woe to you, Bethsaida! For if the miracles had occurred in Tyre and Sidon which occurred in you, they would have repented long ago in sackcloth and ashes. [22] Nevertheless I say to you, it will be more tolerable for Tyre and Sidon in the day of judgment than for you. [23] And you, Capernaum, will not be exalted to heaven, will you? You will descend to Hades; for if the miracles had occurred in Sodom which occurred in you, it would have remained to this day. [24] Nevertheless I say to you that it will be more tolerable for the land of Sodom in the day of judgment, than for you."

Continuing the denunciation of "this generation," Jesus sharpens His rhetoric by targeting specific cities where most of His miracles apparently took place. Having told John the Baptist to observe the evidence of Jesus' identity as Messiah, He now denounces those who had an abundance of these signs but still rejected the One to whom they pointed. His vitriol escalates, and He proclaims two "woes" and a warning of judgment. He concludes with the ultimate and acerbic insult: comparing the contemporary Gentile cities of Tyre and Sidon with Sodom of OT infamy.

We observe a number of sobering points. First, the authentication of Christ was inextricably linked to His miraculous workings. These set Him apart from the many imposters—then and now—who proclaim themselves to be the Messiah. Second, the person and message of Jesus Christ is not a "take it or leave it" proposition. The consequences of rejecting Him are enormous.

Third, hades (virtually synonymous with *hell*) is a real place and, despite excessive fearmongering of past generations, there is still a place today for warnings about the reality of this place of torment. Being a Christ imitator (for that is what a disciple is) demands that we do as He did—namely, warn non-believers of the very real next-world consequence of this-world rejection of Christ. As unpalatable as that may seem in our tolerance-promoting society, our love for the lost compels us to warn them.

Fourth, judgment is meted out according to the amount of light (revelation) received. Sodom did not receive as much light as the Galilean cities, so its judgment will not be as severe. This is no great comfort to Sodomites because "more tolerable" judgment is still judgment, and hades is still hades. The point is that Chorazin, Bethsaida, and Capernaum should be warned!

Father, give me the courage as well as the compassion to warn my nonbelieving friends and associates about the destiny I so want them to avoid.

Intimacy with God

Matthew 11:25-28a

25 At that time Jesus said, "I praise You, Father, Lord of heaven and earth, that You have hidden these things from the wise and intelligent and have revealed them to infants. 26 Yes, Father, for this way was well-pleasing in Your sight. 27 All things have been handed over to Me by My Father; and no one knows the Son except the Father; nor does anyone know the Father except the Son, and anyone to whom the Son wills to reveal Him. 28 Come to Me ..."

Intimate prayer with the Father was characteristic of the Son. Here we catch a glimpse into the kind of thing He prayed. (See John 17, the longest recorded prayer of Jesus.) The Son praises the Father for His way of revealing the truth Jesus has been talking about. God's revelation of truth does not come through scientific inquiry or philosophical reasoning and debate. Anyone can comprehend it—even the least intelligent, symbolized here as infants.

On the one hand, everyone is given what we call *general* revelation about God, that which can be learned about Him through the observation and study of nature (see Romans 1:18-20). *Special* revelation, on the other hand, is that knowledge about God which can only be known through the written Word of God. More specifically, the true knowledge of God the Father can only be found in Jesus Christ, the Living Word of God.

His prayer reveals to us profound truth, namely the unique connection between the Father and the Son. This is seen in three ways. First, the Father has given all things to the Son. The apostle Paul comments on this: "All things have been created through Him and for Him" (Col. 1:16; see an expansion of this teaching in the context of verses 5-20). What belongs to the Father belongs to the Son. Creation is the Father's gift to His Son.

Second, only the Son really knows the Father. The Greek word for *know* refers to an intimate knowledge that goes beyond simple awareness of someone. It can refer to the relationship of a man and woman, being united as one flesh. More than this, it is the kind of understanding and insight that comes from living with a Person for eternity, rooted in an eternal love relationship. John succinctly records Jesus saying, "I and the Father are One" (John 10:30). Third, this is two-way knowledge: the Son has the same knowledge of the Father as the Father has of the Son—reflexive, responsive, reciprocal.

Amazingly, the Lord invites us into this relationship. Upon finishing His prayer, He says, "Come to Me ...." (See also John 17:21.)

Lord, thank you for inviting me to become part of the inner circle of fellowship, into the love relationship between You and Your Father.

Week 17
Day 4

Resting in Jesus

Matthew 11:28-30

[28] *"Come to Me, all who are weary and heavy-laden, and I will give you rest.* [29] *Take My yoke upon you and learn from Me, for I am gentle and humble in heart, and* YOU WILL FIND REST FOR YOUR SOULS. [30] *For My yoke is easy and My burden is light."*

One of the most comforting and encouraging passages in Scripture is found here. The invitation for all—non-believers or believers—is reminiscent of Isaiah's words, "Ho! Everyone who thirsts, come to the waters; and you who have no money come, buy and eat. Come, buy wine and milk, without money and without cost" (Isa. 55:1).

At the time of Jesus' ministry, Roman subjugation constantly reminded the people of Israel of their disfavor with God. They were not *experiencing* God's promise to their ancestor Abraham that his descendants would possess the land in the fullness of God's blessings. Since returning from the Babylonian exile, life had been difficult. It had not yet risen to Davidic or Solomonic glory.

The Pharisees' remedy to the national problem was to intensify the keeping of the Law, hoping to find renewed favor with God and gain His full blessings. Then, as God's covenant people, they could live autonomously in the land.

Another group, the Essenes, believed the rulers of Israel were to blame for the nation's woes. As they considered themselves to be God's genuine and faithful remnant, they withdrew to the Judean wilderness to lead an austere life of strict adherence to extensive religious and communal rules—an intensification of the Mosaic law.

Others, called zealots, determined that frequent uprisings against Roman rule, led by messianic-type characters, were the only remedy for Israel. All of these were efforts to deliver the Jews from the weariness, failure, and guilt that weighed them down.

Everyone is under the yoke of someone or something. For the Jew it was the yoke of Rome or the yoke of the Law. But Jesus called people to come and rest in Him. Paradoxically, He offered the best of all yokes—rest at the deepest level. Even though the emancipation of the nation was yet future, personal rest could be attained then and there.

The world today labors under the judgment of God, the uncertainty of life, and the oppression of sin. Life apart from the Creator becomes weary and increasingly meaningless. (Read the book of Ecclesiastes.) The invitation is still there for all. The choice is to follow Jesus or to follow something else.

Lord, I find my rest in You. Though life is difficult, You are the best of all masters. You comfort and encourage me when all around me is in turmoil.

Compassion in the Law

Matthew 12:1-8

[1] At that time Jesus went through the grain fields on the Sabbath, and His disciples became hungry and began to pick the heads of grain and eat. [2] But when the Pharisees saw this, they said to Him, "Look, Your disciples do what is not lawful to do on a Sabbath." [3] But He said to them, "Have you not read what David did when he became hungry, he and his companions, [4] how he entered the house of God, and they ate the consecrated bread, which was not lawful for him to eat nor for those with him, but for the priests alone? [5] Or have you not read in the Law, that on the Sabbath the priests in the temple break the Sabbath and are innocent? [6] But I say to you that something greater than the temple is here. [7] But if you had known what this means, 'I DESIRE COMPASSION, AND NOT A SACRIFICE,' you would not have condemned the innocent. [8] For the Son of Man is Lord of the Sabbath"

The Pharisees were infuriated by Jesus' reinterpretation of the Sabbath law. This law was one of the unique practices that gave Jews a sense of pride in being set apart as God's people. They kept the Sabbath holy by not working on that day. In their quest to prove fidelity to God, they fiercely debated how the fourth commandment was to be kept. In particular, the Pharisees disallowed the casual picking of grain on Saturdays. This kind of minutia worked against the very purpose for which the Sabbath was given. God meant it as a blessing, not a law for its own sake.

When the Pharisees criticized the disciples' infraction of the Sabbath law, Jesus responded by directing them to King David's example. The Jews recognized David as the archetype of godliness, the one whose name was given to the Messiah (i.e., "Son of David"). But Jesus points out that David sidestepped the Sabbath law because of his emergency situation. He was famished, running for his life, so he ate food otherwise disallowed to him. No one would dare question his high regard for God's Law (see Psalm 19), yet David deemed it permissible to supersede the Law in one area for a higher concern in another area.

Jesus poignantly asserts that He Himself, as the Son of Man, is the Lord of the Sabbath. His interpretation of the Sabbath law therefore trumps that of the Pharisees. The general application is that at times the ethical code in the Word of God may result in conflicting situations, where obeying one command may supersede obeying another command. Compassion should be a determining factor in our resolution of these tensions. It *was* permissible for the disciples to pick grain and eat it as they walked through the fields on the Sabbath. The Pharisees had it all wrong.

Lord, help me to know the difference between true fidelity versus legalistic practices. Help me to know, understand, and extend Your compassion to others.

Weekend Reading

Saturday – Proverbs 17
Sunday – Psalms 74–77

Personal Reflections

Compassion Trumps Legalism

Matthew 12:9-16

9 Departing from there, He went into their synagogue. 10 And a man was there
whose hand was withered. And they questioned Jesus, asking, "Is it lawful to heal
on the Sabbath?"—so that they might accuse Him. 11 And He said to them, "What
man is there among you who has a sheep, and if it falls into a pit on the Sabbath,
will he not take hold of it and lift it out? 12 How much more valuable then is a man
than a sheep! So then, it is lawful to do good on the Sabbath." 13 Then He said to the
man, "Stretch out your hand!" He stretched it out, and it was restored to normal,
like the other. 14 But the Pharisees went out and conspired against Him, as to how
they might destroy Him. 15 But Jesus, aware of this, withdrew from there. Many
followed Him, and He healed them all, 16 and warned them not to tell who He was.

Continuing on the theme of Sabbath observances, the issue of healing on that day takes center stage. Jesus had amassed a large following, and the Pharisees were irritated and jealous, looking for any reason to accuse Jesus of purposefully breaking the Mosaic law, thus discrediting Himself. Skilled in one-upmanship and manipulation, the Pharisees baited Jesus, using a physically deformed man as a pawn in a chess game of religiosity. The location was a synagogue, so they must have felt comfortable in their usually controlled environment, and they made the first move. "Is it lawful to heal on the Sabbath?" they asked.

If Jesus said yes, He would be breaking the Law. In their view, healing came under the category of work and therefore would desecrate the Sabbath. If Jesus said no, He would have shown Himself inconsistent, since He had already asserted it was permissible to glean grain on the Sabbath. Furthermore, it would have shown that the compassion which Jesus preached was subjugated by the Law.

In a masterful move, Jesus points out that anyone would have the sense to rescue an animal from danger on a Sabbath—so how much more, then, to rescue a man from physical infirmity? His answer is a direct hit: "It is lawful to do good on the Sabbath." Then, without delay, Jesus heals the man.

At this, the Pharisees went berserk, immediately making plans to get rid of Him. Jesus withdrew to safety but continued to preach and heal. His popularity continued to grow. But He cautioned His followers not to banter about His identity, for He did not want to unnecessarily encourage the persecution.

Lord, thank you that You are a compassionate God. Help me not to capitulate to the pressure toward legalism and manipulation of others. Also, help me not to coerce others to follow my interpretations as a means of controlling them.

Week 18

Day 2

Messianic Predictions Fulfilled

Matthew 12:17-21

[17] This was to fulfill what was spoken through Isaiah the prophet: [18] "Behold, My Servant whom I have chosen; My Beloved in whom My soul is well-pleased; I will put My Spirit upon Him, And He shall proclaim justice to the Gentiles. [19] He will not quarrel, nor cry out; Nor will anyone hear His voice in the streets. [20] A battered reed He will not break off, And a smoldering wick He will not put out, Until He leads justice to victory. [21] And in His name the Gentiles will hope."

Following his penchant for presenting the life and ministry of Jesus as fulfillment of OT prophecy, Matthew, guided by the Holy Spirit, quotes a messianic passage from the book of Isaiah—the longest quotation in Matthew. Some have stumbled over the differences in wording (in English Bibles) between Isaiah 42:1-4 and this quote. But this was not uncommon in the NT use of OT passages. We can attribute it to a number of factors. The OT was written in Hebrew and translated into Greek (called the Septuagint, or LXX) well before the time of Jesus. Matthew's quotation reflects the Septuagint, commonly used in Palestine during those days. Our English Bibles render the Hebrew OT and the Greek NT (which relies on the Greek Septuagint for quotes from the OT). Add to this some ambiguity in the meaning of some of Isaiah's words, and we can easily understand the translational variations. Matthew provides for us an interpretation and application of the messianic prophecy, and thus a faithful translation of the meaning of Isaiah, even though the wording isn't exactly the same.

Matthew zeroes in on several characteristics of Jesus the Messiah, as prophesied by Isaiah: (1) He would be a Servant. (There are several "Servant Songs" in Isaiah's prophecy). Jesus affirmed His servanthood in His own words, "The Son of Man came not to be served, but to serve." (2) He was loved of God. The reader of this gospel will remember the Father saying to Jesus, "This is My Son, whom I love." (3) God would be pleased with Him. (4) He would be anointed by the Spirit of God, empowering Him for service. (5) He would be all about justice. Finally, someone fulfills Micah 6:8 and does what is just! (6) He would have a concern for all people, not just Jews. (7) He came not to argue but to perform the will of God. He wasn't just a philosopher looking for a debate. (8) He'd be gentle and tender, One to whom anyone can go for comfort (cf. 11:28-30). (9) In the end, His justice will win out. (10) In Christ the fulfillment of the Abrahamic promise will come—namely, blessing to all the nations. What a sweeping depiction of the character and mission of Christ! Isn't He wonderful!

Lord, what a wonderful Savior You are! I praise and worship You for all You are and do.

The Messianic Mission Validated

Matthew 12:22-29

22 Then a demon-possessed man who was blind and mute was brought to Jesus, and He healed him, so that the mute man spoke and saw. 23 All the crowds were amazed, and were saying, "This man cannot be the Son of David, can he?" 24 But when the Pharisees heard this, they said, "This man casts out demons only by Beelzebul the ruler of the demons." 25 And knowing their thoughts Jesus said to them, "Any kingdom divided against itself is laid waste; and any city or house divided against itself will not stand. 26 If Satan casts out Satan, he is divided against himself; how then will his kingdom stand? 27 If I by Beelzebul cast out demons, by whom do your sons cast them out? For this reason they will be your judges. 28 But if I cast out demons by the Spirit of God, then the kingdom of God has come upon you. 29 Or how can anyone enter the strong man's house and carry off his property, unless he first binds the strong man? And then he will plunder his house."

Today's reading shows the Pharisees' growing hostility toward Jesus. We saw in 10:25 a hint that they had started associating Christ with Beelzebul. Here, the bold charge emerges into the open. The occasion was an exorcism and the crowd's wildly approving response, attributing the status of "Son of David" to Jesus. Or at least they were asking the question expecting (perhaps gingerly) a favorable answer. The Pharisees, who considered themselves the guardians of the Law and Jewish way of life, were incensed with what they saw. Finally, they laid their cards on the table, audaciously pronouncing their judgment about Christ. There was desperation in their tone, a sort of panic to stem the tide of the crowd's thinking that Jesus was the Messiah.

So, they declared blatantly that Jesus was in partnership with the devil. It's important to note that even Jesus' detractors did not deny that a miracle had taken place. Peter refers to this in his description of Jesus in the great Pentecost speech: "Men of Israel, listen to these words: Jesus the Nazarene, a man attested to you by God with miracles and wonders and signs which God performed through Him in your midst, just as you yourselves know" (Acts 2:22). The miracles that Jesus performed were not stories made up by parties who favored Him. His miracles were undeniable to all at that time.

Jesus told the Pharisees that their objections were ludicrous. The logic was inescapable. How could He cast out demons by the power of Satan? That would be inherently self-defeating. On the contrary, His actions demonstrated that the kingdom of God had definitely come. There is no other rational explanation!

Lord, thank you for leaving the historical witness of Your wonderful, confirmatory works. They demonstrate that You really were the Messiah.

The Unforgivable Sin of Unbelief

Matthew 12:30-32

30 "He who is not with Me is against Me; and he who does not gather with Me scatters. 31 Therefore I say to you, any sin and blasphemy shall be forgiven people, but blasphemy against the Spirit shall not be forgiven. 32 Whoever speaks a word against the Son of Man, it shall be forgiven him; but whoever speaks against the Holy Spirit, it shall not be forgiven him, either in this age or in the age to come."

The Lord had been attacked openly by the Pharisees, and now He turned the tables. He warned His detractors that they had better get on board with His mission. There was, and is, no neutral position. The direst posture is to *not* be *with* Jesus, tantamount to being *against* Him.

This passage has caused considerable debate among Christians today. Is it possible for a Christian to commit an unforgiveable sin? Can he lose his salvation? In answering these questions, we must note the context. Jesus was responding to Pharisees who had just attributed the exorcism He performed to the devil rather than to the Holy Spirit. They were not criticizing the Holy Spirit but were rejecting the only authenticating signs which could prove that Jesus was the promised Messiah. They asserted that He received His power and authority from the serpent of Eden.

Ironically, this satanically endowed power and authority is precisely what the wilderness temptation of Christ was all about. The tempter wanted Jesus to act independently of God the Father and to worship Satan instead! The deceiver had apparently been successful in convincing the Pharisees that that is exactly what had happened. Satan appears in subtle ways, trying continuously to oppose Christ every step of the way.

The unique circumstances of this interchange demonstrate that, at the primary level, committing the "unforgiveable sin" could only occur during Jesus' earthly ministry, at the time of His authenticating miracles. There was no other path to forgiveness of their sins if they rejected the proofs of who Jesus was.

Today, the only unforgiveable sin occurs when a person rejects the Spirit's conviction of who Christ is. To curse God when things are going badly is not an unforgiveable sin. Even to use His name in vain is not beyond God's forgiving reach. But rejection of Christ through unbelief is unforgivable, for there is no other way to salvation (Acts 4:12). And to die in that state puts a person beyond God's forgiveness. A Christian, by definition as one who has accepted Christ, cannot be guilty of committing the unforgiveable sin.

Lord, I do not want to dishonor Your name in any way. Help me recognize the evidence of Your work in my life, so I can give You all the glory.

Words Reveal the Heart

Matthew 12:33-37

[33] "Either make the tree good and its fruit good, or make the tree bad and its fruit bad; for the tree is known by its fruit. [34] You brood of vipers, how can you, being evil, speak what is good? For the mouth speaks out of that which fills the heart. [35] The good man brings out of his good treasure what is good; and the evil man brings out of his evil treasure what is evil. [36] But I tell you that every careless word that people speak, they shall give an accounting for it in the day of judgment. [37] For by your words you will be justified, and by your words you will be condemned."

Conduct reveals character. Jesus here speaks wisdom as if by proverbs. There is no greater indicator of the state of a person's heart than what comes out of his mouth. Even seemingly insignificant words, carelessly spoken, testify to the inner thinking of a man.

Jesus' words hold true, first of all, for Himself. His outward comment—"You brood of vipers, how can you being evil ...?"—shows His inner thinking concerning His detractors. He has passed judgment based on their outward behavior. The Pharisees (who had just accused Him of satanic power and authority) were intrinsically evil in their hearts despite their outward "good show" of religiosity. This should be as obvious as concluding from the shape and taste of an apple that the tree from which it was picked is truly an apple tree. The words spoken by a person lead us to draw certain conclusions regarding the character of his heart. In the case of Pharisees, Jesus simply followed the evidence (the fruit) to where it led (the heart).

In this immediate context we can apply the principle "conduct reveals character" to the reactions of people to Jesus and His miracles. Such comments uncover his or her heart concerning Jesus. When one asks, "Could this be the Son of David?" (v. 23), we may assume his heart is open to the evidence of Jesus' true identity. When one "speaks a word against the Son of Man" (v. 32), he reveals the evil state of his heart. It can be no other way. How often do we object when others form an opinion or judgment about us based on something we say but then allow ourselves this same prerogative? We hear their words and conclude certain things.

Jesus projects this principle forward to the judgment seat of God. The things we have said will be held up as evidence of our inner intentions as we stand before a holy God whose word "judges the thoughts and intentions of the heart" (Heb. 4:12). Our words and our heart are not just "incidentally" connected. That is why people have a hard time forgetting our careless words.

Lord, my tongue is like a wildfire (James 3:5). Help me not to take my own words lightly but to follow them where they lead—to my heart.

Weekend Reading

Saturday – Proverbs 18
Sunday – Psalms 78–79

Personal Reflections

Week 19
Day 1

Thirsting for Signs

Matthew 12:38-45

[38] Then some of the scribes and Pharisees said to Him, "Teacher, we want to see a sign from You." [39] But He answered and said to them, "An evil and adulterous generation craves for a sign; and yet no sign will be given to it but the sign of Jonah the prophet; [40] for just as JONAH WAS THREE DAYS AND THREE NIGHTS IN THE BELLY OF THE SEA MONSTER, so will the Son of Man be three days and three nights in the heart of the earth. [41] The men of Nineveh will stand up with this generation at the judgment, and will condemn it because they repented at the preaching of Jonah; and behold, something greater than Jonah is here. [42] The Queen of the South will rise up with this generation at the judgment and will condemn it, because she came from the ends of the earth to hear the wisdom of Solomon; and behold, something greater than Solomon is here. [43] Now when the unclean spirit goes out of a man, it passes through waterless places seeking rest, and does not find it. [44] Then it says, 'I will return to my house from which I came'; and when it comes, it finds it unoccupied, swept, and put in order. [45] Then it goes and takes along with it seven other spirits more wicked than itself, and they go in and live there; and the last state of that man becomes worse than the first. That is the way it will also be with this evil generation."

The Pharisees, joined by the scribes, wouldn't give up. As their trump card, they demand a sign from Him to validate His teaching. The irony of this is inescapable. Jesus had been giving them signs all along, but now they want it on their terms, reminiscent of Satan's challenge in the desert to control how and when Jesus performed the miraculous. Jesus responded, saying they show the signs of being an "evil and adulterous generation."

The only further sign Jesus would give to satisfy their demand would be His death and resurrection, pictured in the story of Jonah. However, this would be a sign of judgment on Israel. Jesus and His message are far greater than Jonah and his message. So this is a warning! Just as the Queen of Sheba came to Solomon for wisdom, they ought to take heed to His teachings because the Lord is greater than she was. These stories form the backdrop of Israel's punishment for rejecting that which is greater!

Jesus finishes His diatribe with a parable. Israel is like a demon-possessed man, and the Messiah is now present to free them from their captivity to sin. Since they refuse to repent, their end will be worse than their beginning, which Jesus pictures as the demon returning with others more wicked than itself. In contrast to their earlier accusation that Jesus is in partnership with Satan, He implies *they* are!

Lord, You don't need to prove Yourself to me. Your death and resurrection are enough proof that You love me. Everything else is extra blessing.

Week 19

Day 2

An Unashamed Brother

Matthew 12:46-50

46 While He was still speaking to the crowds, behold, His mother and brothers
were standing outside, seeking to speak to Him. 47 Someone said to Him, "Behold,
Your mother and Your brothers are standing outside seeking to speak to You."
48 But Jesus answered the one who was telling Him and said, "Who is My mother
and who are My brothers?" 49 And stretching out His hand toward His disciples,
He said, "Behold My mother and My brothers! 50 For whoever does the will of My
Father who is in heaven, he is My brother and sister and mother."

Jesus has just warned of the consequences of rejecting His authenticating works. Now He uses family terminology in referring to those who truly get His message, the ones willing to do as God directs rather than continuing to rebel. This incident is pregnant with application for today.

First, God shows no respect for a person's earthly pedigree. Christ gave no deferential treatment to His earthly family, here identified as His mother and brothers. So, too, being born into a Christian home, living in a Christian culture, even attending a Christian church, wins no points with God. What matters is whether or not a person does the will of God. Second, when a person becomes a follower of Christ, he becomes part of the spiritual family of God.

Third, exercising faith is the first step in doing the will of God. The very words in Scripture related to how to be saved from sin are commands: "Believe on the Lord Jesus Christ and you will be saved" and "This is My beloved Son, listen to Him." They are imperatives. This does not mean faith and repentance are "works" that earn salvation, as though they contain some source of merit. Believing is a simple response to God's command and the first step in doing His will.

Fourth, Mary, His earthly mother, did not command special respect from Christ. Although she was "blessed among women," she is not to be worshiped. Jesus places her on the same level as all others. Nowhere in Scripture are we ever encouraged to pray to her or see her as a "co-redemptrix" or a mediator between man and God. "There is one God, and one mediator between God and men, the man Christ Jesus" (1 Tim. 2:5). In order for her to be part of the spiritual family of God, she too had to do the will of God. She too was a sinner, for she prayed, "My spirit has rejoiced in God *my Savior*" (Luke 1:57).

Fifth, Jesus had siblings (half-brothers), which means that Mary did not remain a virgin after His birth. This is the most natural understanding of the word *brothers* in verses 46-47, despite the fact that it can sometimes be used to refer to relatives. Jesus uses *brothers* now to describe His disciples.

Lord, thank you for not being ashamed to call me "brother" (Heb. 2:11).
As when I first believed, I desire to continue walking in the Father's will.

A Seed Thought

Matthew 13:1-9

[1] That day Jesus went out of the house and was sitting by the sea. [2] And large crowds gathered to Him, so He got into a boat and sat down, and the whole crowd was standing on the beach. [3] And He spoke many things to them in parables, saying, "Behold, the sower went out to sow; [4] and as he sowed, some seeds fell beside the road, and the birds came and ate them up. [5] Others fell on the rocky places, where they did not have much soil; and immediately they sprang up, because they had no depth of soil. [6] But when the sun had risen, they were scorched; and because they had no root, they withered away. [7] Others fell among the thorns, and the thorns came up and choked them out. [8] And others fell on the good soil and yielded a crop, some a hundredfold, some sixty, and some thirty. [9] He who has ears, let him hear."

Parables convey truth powerfully but cryptically in story form. So Jesus concludes this parable with "He who has ears, let him hear." It is a challenge to go below the surface. Following the dialogue between Jesus and the Pharisees, this particular story contains a powerful message about the various responses to His ministry.

In this story a farmer is planting seed in the fashion of a sower walking along, casting out seed by hand from his seed bag. The seed falls on various kinds of ground. Certain principles apply when interpreting parables. The main principle is to look for the central thought and not get hung up on the details. In this parable, for example, there is no thought about the relative amount of seed falling on the different kinds of soil or whether the farmer was careless where he sowed. We disagree with some people's interpretation that Christians should sow the word of God broadly because only one quarter of it will fall on hearts that are like the good ground. This is unwarranted and misses the focus of the parable.

Jesus had attracted quite a crowd, despite acid objections of the religious leaders and Jesus' confrontation regarding their spiritual errors. The actions of the crowds showed they were not letting the opinions of their religious leaders deter them from hearing was Jesus had to say. This grassroots following of Christ was growing (albeit, it proved to be short lived), and the Pharisees and scribes were becoming quite worried.

Because of the crowd size, Jesus moved to a boat, a better vantage point for communicating the story. Jesus was sitting (the common position for a rabbi when teaching), and the crowd was standing on shore, accepting His teaching as authoritative.

Lord, help me to have ears to hear Your teachings clearly. I want to understand both the surface meanings as well as the nuances. Please take me deeper.

Week 19

Day 4

Why Parables?

Matthew 13:10-17

[10] And the disciples came and said to Him, "Why do You speak to them in parables?" [11] Jesus answered them, "To you it has been granted to know the mysteries of the kingdom of heaven, but to them it has not been granted. [12] For whoever has, to him more shall be given, and he will have an abundance; but whoever does not have, even what he has shall be taken away from him. [13] Therefore I speak to them in parables; because while seeing they do not see, and while hearing they do not hear, nor do they understand. [14] In their case the prophecy of Isaiah is being fulfilled, which says, 'YOU WILL KEEP ON HEARING, BUT WILL NOT UNDERSTAND; YOU WILL KEEP ON SEEING, BUT WILL NOT PERCEIVE; [15] FOR THE HEART OF THIS PEOPLE HAS BECOME DULL, WITH THEIR EARS THEY SCARCELY HEAR, AND THEY HAVE CLOSED THEIR EYES, OTHERWISE THEY WOULD SEE WITH THEIR EYES, HEAR WITH THEIR EARS, AND UNDERSTAND WITH THEIR HEART AND RETURN, AND I WOULD HEAL THEM.' [16] But blessed are your eyes, because they see; and your ears, because they hear. [17] For truly I say to you that many prophets and righteous men desired to see what you see, and did not see it, and to hear what you hear, and did not hear it."

Jesus did not use parables to make the truth more plain through storytelling. If that were the case, the disciples would not have had to ask Him why He used that method of teaching. It would have been obvious. He made the truth difficult to understand for those who lacked a receptive heart, or "whoever does not have," to quote Jesus exactly. But to the disciple, the "whoever has," Jesus reveals the "mysteries," or the insight of the parables, as He is about to do in this case.

Happy are those who see and understand, the ones who "get it." But "getting it" requires two things: (1) revelation from God, for spiritual truth cannot be known apart from Him, and (2) reception by the individual, for God will not give more truth to those who reject what they have already been given. Hebrews 11:6 echoes this: "He who comes to God must believe that He is and that He is a rewarder of those who seek Him." That's what Jesus meant by "For whoever has, to him shall be given, and he will have an abundance."

The Jews had a veil over their eyes, so to speak. Some had hardened hearts that prevented their understanding. Others, including the prophets and angels, longed to know more. Peter echoed this: "It was revealed to them [i.e., the prophets] that they were not serving themselves, but you, in these things which now have been announced to you through those who preached the gospel to you by the Holy Spirit sent from heaven—things into which angels long to look" (1 Pet. 1:12). In Christ, the truth is revealed to those who believe and obey.

Lord, thank you for revealing to me Your truth. Help me to obey and put into practice what I already know, so that You will reveal more to me.

Sowing Broadly

Matthew 13:18-23

[18] "Hear then the parable of the sower. [19] When anyone hears the word of the kingdom and does not understand it, the evil one comes and snatches away what has been sown in his heart. This is the one on whom seed was sown beside the road. [20] The one on whom seed was sown on the rocky places, this is the man who hears the word and immediately receives it with joy; [21] yet he has no firm root in himself, but is only temporary, and when affliction or persecution arises because of the word, immediately he falls away. [22] And the one on whom seed was sown among the thorns, this is the man who hears the word, and the worry of the world and the deceitfulness of wealth choke the word, and it becomes unfruitful. [23] And the one on whom seed was sown on the good soil, this is the man who hears the word and understands it; who indeed bears fruit and brings forth, some a hundredfold, some sixty, and some thirty."

Jesus' explanation of the parable of the sower is straightforward. There are four different responses when the word of God is communicated. Isaiah 55:1 tells us, "My word ...which goes forth ... will not return to Me empty, without accomplishing what I desire, and without succeeding in the matter for which I sent it." Yet here in this parable, Jesus tells us that sometimes the word of God—His message to us—is thwarted, "empty," it seems. How can this be? The answer lies in understanding the purpose of God's word.

The word of God has a dual purpose: to produce fruit (as is clear in this parable), and to reveal the condition of people's hearts. In this last sense, the word does not return to Him empty. "For the word of God is living and active, sharper than any double-edged sword, it penetrates even to dividing soul and spirit, joints and marrow; it judges the thoughts and attitudes of the heart" (Heb. 4:12). Jesus, in this parable, said His message will reveal hearts, four kinds.

Keep in mind that parables are designed to hide truth from those resisting Christ and to reveal it to His disciples. Therefore, this parable is part of Jesus' discipleship training program. So what is the message to His disciples? It is this: they need a sober, balanced understanding of how people will respond to the message when they preach it. They can expect that some will reject it out of hand! Others will become believers, but their faith dies out because it is superficial or choked by temptations of life. But (and this is good news for the disciples), some *will* receive the message and go on to become fruitful disciples of Christ. And that prospect is what encourages a disciple to keep sharing his faith.

Lord, help me not to be picky about where I sow Your word, and help me find those whose hearts are open to the good news, that I might share it with them.

Weekend Reading

Saturday – Proverbs 19
Sunday – Psalms 80–85

Personal Reflections

The Genuine and the Spurious

Matthew 24:24-30

[24] Jesus presented another parable to them, saying, "The kingdom of heaven may be compared to a man who sowed good seed in his field. [25] But while his men were sleeping, his enemy came and sowed tares among the wheat, and went away. [26] But when the wheat sprouted and bore grain, then the tares became evident also. [27] The slaves of the landowner came and said to him, 'Sir, did you not sow good seed in your field? How then does it have tares?' [28] And he said to them, 'An enemy has done this!' The slaves said to him, 'Do you want us, then, to go and gather them up?' [29] But he said, 'No; for while you are gathering up the tares, you may uproot the wheat with them. [30] Allow both to grow together until the harvest; and in the time of the harvest I will say to the reapers, "First gather up the tares and bind them in bundles to burn them up; but gather the wheat into my barn."'"

Determining who is a genuine believer and who is not is difficult, even for those who have been enlightened. That principle is the subject of this second parable of our Lord. The seed represents the word of God and the wheat represents those in whose life the word produces spiritual results. (See the previous parable of the sower and the seed.) Historians tell us that tares looked very much like wheat. They represent unbelievers who act like believers and play the part well. This parable contains several key lessons about the kingdom. First, the community of believers will include some unbelievers. Israel, during the exodus had its "rabble"; the church has its unbelievers. Second, the presence of unbelievers is Satan's ploy to thwart the work of God.

Third, unbelievers are like tares sucking nutrients from the soil and thus hindering the growth of genuine wheat. They have the potential for hindering spiritual growth in the church.

Fourth, Christians should not obsess with creating a pure church that contains no unbelievers. Efforts to do so will inadvertently result in some true believers (albeit ones that may not meet the contrived spiritual qualifications of human judgment) being put out of the fellowship. At times a believer may need to be excommunicated from the fellowship because of a serious, rebellious, immoral lifestyle. But the goal of such actions is not purification of the church. Rather, it is restoration of the believer to true fellowship through the "shock treatment" (see 1 Corinthians 5).

Fifth, God will take care of the purification process at the end ("harvest" time), so we need to leave it to Him. His judgment is absolutely righteous.

Lord, help me be gracious to all, showing Your love, so that those around me who are not true believers might recognize You as Lord and Savior.

Abundance of Parables

Matthew 13:31-35

31 He presented another parable to them, saying, "The kingdom of heaven is like a mustard seed, which a man took and sowed in his field; 32 and this is smaller than all other seeds, but when it is full grown, it is larger than the garden plants and becomes a tree, so that THE BIRDS OF THE AIR *come and* NEST IN ITS BRANCHES." *33 He spoke another parable to them, "The kingdom of heaven is like leaven, which a woman took and hid in three pecks of flour until it was all leavened." 34 All these things Jesus spoke to the crowds in parables, and He did not speak to them without a parable. 35 This was to fulfill what was spoken through the prophet: "*I WILL OPEN MY MOUTH IN PARABLES; I WILL UTTER THINGS HIDDEN SINCE THE FOUNDATION OF THE WORLD."

This series of parables is often referred to as the "kingdom parables" because they all begin with, "The kingdom of heaven is like ..." The Lord Jesus used analogies to explain the new order He was bringing. In our reading today we find two more of these parables. The first compares the kingdom to a mustard seed, which was the smallest of the seeds cultivated in Jesus' day. The kingdom, like a mustard seed, had an inauspicious beginning, but when it takes full effect, it becomes quite significant. In fact, when the kingdom fully arrives, it will provide for all who come to it. In down-to-earth language, the community of God's people to outsiders seems like an insignificant social organization for weak people. But when a person comes to faith, then the community of God's people becomes a welcome rest, like a tree birds flock to for shade. And the teachings of God's written Word become the repository of truth which eclipses all other sources of teaching.

The second parable compares the kingdom with leaven (yeast), which is hidden out of sight in flour but permeates and affects the whole batch of flour. Again, the kingdom has an inauspicious beginning, but it will permeate all of life. This is true for believers (in the primary sense) but also for unbelievers who are ultimately affected as the gospel goes out into the whole world.

Matthew, inspired by the Holy Spirit, points out that this method of teaching in parables was prophesied in the OT (Ps. 78:2). Jesus' teachings were hidden from those who were antagonistic toward Him but uncovered to His followers. At times, the church may seem ineffective and the number of true believers relatively small, but the kingdom of heaven is slowly permeating the whole world. Someday we will see that "heaven and earth are full of His glory."

Lord, help me understand with faith Your message to me today. May I see the pervading influence of Your kingdom in this broken-down, fallen world.

Divine Separation

Matthew 13:36-43

36 Then He left the crowds and went into the house. And His disciples came to Him
and said, "Explain to us the parable of the tares of the field." 37 And He said, "The
one who sows the good seed is the Son of Man, 38 and the field is the world; and as
for the good seed, these are the sons of the kingdom; and the tares are the sons of
the evil one; 39 and the enemy who sowed them is the devil, and the harvest is the
end of the age; and the reapers are angels. 40 So just as the tares are gathered up
and burned with fire, so shall it be at the end of the age. 41 The Son of Man will send
forth His angels, and they will gather out of His kingdom all stumbling blocks, and
those who commit lawlessness, 42 and will throw them into the furnace of fire; in that
place there will be weeping and gnashing of teeth. 43 Then the righteous will shine
forth as the sun in the kingdom of their Father. He who has ears, let him hear."

At the request of His disciples, Jesus clarified what the parable of the wheat and tares meant (vv. 24-30). Why did He not just tell the plain truth clearly the first time? The answer is that parables showed up those who wanted to learn truth and those who did not. Those with open hearts were drawn to Christ; the Pharisees, with few exceptions, were not. As Simeon predicted, "This Child is appointed for the fall and rise of many in Israel...and a sword will pierce ... to the end that thoughts from many hearts may be revealed" (Luke 2:34-35).

The sower in this story is the Lord. The seed, as distinguished from an earlier parable, represents the people whom Jesus sends out into the world ("the field"). The devil sows the tares, which represent evil people mixed in among those sent into the world. Jesus calls them stumbling blocks and people who are lawless. Certainly, Judas was a "tare" among the disciples. But the religious leaders also were tares, stumbling blocks for the nation.

The focus of the story is on the ultimate destination of true believers and false believers. The latter will suffer what is described as an extremely painful punishment. Called *hell* in other parts of the NT narrative, this destination is a real place characterized by fire. There is no indication that Jesus meant this to be other than a literal description. He does not describe utter annihilation, as some teach today, because "there will be weeping and gnashing of teeth," which indicates a living conscious experience. Someone has said that if there's no literal fire, there will be something worse.

On the other hand, those who are the true seed—the genuine followers of Christ who are seeding the kingdom of heaven into a lost world—will shine forth with the wonderful, life changing message of the King.

Lord, like a smooth, polished mirror, I want to reflect Your glory to a world in darkness desperately needing light. Help me not be a stumbling block.

God's Treasure

Matthew 13:44-52

[44] "The kingdom of heaven is like a treasure hidden in the field, which a man found and hid again; and from joy over it he goes and sells all that he has and buys that field. [45] Again, the kingdom of heaven is like a merchant seeking fine pearls, [46] and upon finding one pearl of great value, he went and sold all that he had and bought it. [47] Again, the kingdom of heaven is like a dragnet cast into the sea, and gathering fish of every kind; [48] and when it was filled, they drew it up on the beach; and they sat down and gathered the good fish into containers, but the bad they threw away. [49] So it will be at the end of the age; the angels will come forth and take out the wicked from among the righteous, [50] and will throw them into the furnace of fire; in that place there will be weeping and gnashing of teeth. [51] Have you understood all these things?" They said to Him, "Yes." [52] And Jesus said to them, "Therefore every scribe who has become a disciple of the kingdom of heaven is like a head of a household, who brings out of his treasure things new and old."

The last three of the kingdom parables continue the theme of distinguishing true believers from those who are not. As pointed out earlier, the basic rule for interpreting parables is to look for the main idea and not get hung up on details. Today's first parable focuses on the great lengths to which God will go to obtain a person for the kingdom. The analogy is that of a man who spares no expense to buy a field because of his discovery of a treasure hidden there.

The second parable conveys a similar message. The value God places on one soul is compared to finding a pearl of great value. The third parable portrays the painful consequences of not being a true member of the kingdom. In the end times a final judgment will clearly delineate between the righteous and the wicked. The Jews had thought of end-times judgment in terms of national restoration to prominence over the Gentile nations. But Jesus spoke in individual and personal terms. The poignant irony here is that according to His earlier teaching in the Sermon on the Mount, the standard of righteousness that God requires exceeds anything they had imagined: "For I say to you that unless your righteousness surpasses that of the scribes and Pharisees, you will not enter the kingdom of heaven" (5:20).

Those who are humble would come back to Jesus for a solution to the dilemma of how to enter the kingdom when the standard of righteousness is so high. The answer would give new understanding to old truths of Scripture. It would be like a person who "brings out of his treasure things new and old."

Lord, I am humbled to think how much You valued me, to spare no expense in "finding" me. Thank you that I do not have to face eternity outside of Your love.

No Faith, No Miracles, No Honor

Matthew 13:53-58

53 When Jesus had finished these parables, He departed from there. 54 He came to His hometown and began teaching them in their synagogue, so that they were astonished, and said, "Where did this man get this wisdom and these miraculous powers? 55 Is not this the carpenter's son? Is not His mother called Mary, and His brothers, James and Joseph and Simon and Judas? 56 And His sisters, are they not all with us? Where then did this man get all these things?" 57 And they took offense at Him. But Jesus said to them, "A prophet is not without honor except in his hometown and in his own household." 58 And He did not do many miracles there because of their unbelief.

Two things amazed the people who met Jesus: the wisdom of His teachings and the miraculous things He did. But their amazement brought two results: either people accepted Him or rejected Him. The majority rejected Him. Nowhere is this more obvious than when Jesus returned to the town in which He grew up. Instead of praising God for Jesus' teaching and miraculous deeds, they dismissed Him as an offense.

At this point, we note the record of Jesus' siblings. They shared the same earthly mother, but Joseph was Jesus' stepfather. Some people teach that the brothers and sisters were in reality cousins and that Jesus had no siblings. They assert that Mary remained a virgin all her life. Such people reason that the terms *brother* and *sister* can simply refer to relatives. However, this conjecture has no base. While it was prophesied that the Messiah would be born of a virgin (Isa. 7:14), there was no prophetic requirement that the mother would remain a virgin after the birth of Messiah. Furthermore, in today's passage Mary is called Jesus' mother, so the natural reading would conclude that the other individuals named were Jesus' actual siblings (half-brothers and half-sisters). It is clear that His own family did not accept the teachings and miracles of Jesus either.

The half-brother James came to faith sometime later and went on to be a leader in the early church. In Acts 15 we find him acting as the spokesperson for the Jerusalem council. In Galatians 1:19 he is referred to as the Lord's brother. In Galatians 2:9 Paul mentions him as one of the pillars of the church along with Peter and John. Also, he most likely was the author of the epistle of James. (He was not the apostle James in Acts 12.)

But because of the unbelief in Jesus' hometown at the time, He did not do many miracles there. And this situation gave rise to the adage, "A prophet is not without honor except in his hometown."

Father, help me not become so overly familiar with the Lord Jesus Christ that I fail to honor Him in all of my life.

Weekend Reading

Saturday – Proverbs 20
Sunday – Psalms 86–89

Personal Reflections

An Exemplary Model

Matthew 14:1-2

[1] At that time Herod the tetrarch heard the news about Jesus, [2] and said to his servants, "This is John the Baptist; he has risen from the dead, and that is why miraculous powers are at work in him."

After being rejected in His hometown, Jesus withdraws from there (14:13). The gospel writer gives us the occasion for this withdrawal: the report that John the Baptist had been executed by Herod the tetrarch (i.e., governor) over Galilee. His full name was Herod Antipas, and he was a son of Herod the Great—that insecure, would-be assassinator of the infant Jesus. The death of John, forerunner to Christ, cast a large shadow over the kingdom prospects.

John played the major role in introducing the ministry of Jesus, but then he quickly faded to the background. In chapter 4 he was arrested. And the report of his arrest led to Jesus' withdrawal back into Galilee. Chapter 9 finds some remaining disciples of John complaining that Jesus' disciples did not fast as they or the Pharisees did. John's disciples seemed to hold the Pharisees as role models rather than Jesus, indicating resistance to Christ Himself. Whether that is true or not, we do know this: some of John's disciples did not become disciples of Jesus but instead remained loyal to John, who was now in prison. Their growing discontent may have contributed to John's own doubting, as recounted in chapter 11. In fact, some of John's disciples did not stay around long enough after John's death to either witness or hear about the resurrection of Christ. Acts 19 records that when Paul preached the gospel to some of them, years later, they apparently had not fully accepted John's stance that "He [Jesus] must increase, and I must decrease" (John 3:30).

Now in our present passage we have a brief flashback to the events leading up to John's death. Herod had ordered John executed. He was sufficiently impressed with John that, in his mind, Jesus' miracles could only be explained one way: John had come back from the dead! This leads us to two observations. First, the miracles of Jesus were undeniable among His contemporaries, lending historical credibility to Matthew's record of Jesus' life. Second, John lived such an exemplary life that even in adverse circumstances, when he was subject to doubting, his enemies saw his life and Jesus' life as somewhat indistinguishable. He exemplified what Peter later taught: "Keep your behavior excellent among the Gentiles, so that … they may because of your good deeds, as they observe them, glorify God in the day of visitation" (1 Pet. 2:12).

Father, help me to live a life like Jesus' life so that whether I suffer adverse consequences for my faith or not, others see the resemblance.

Week 21
Day 2

A Foolish Decision

Matthew 14:3-12

3 For when Herod had John arrested, he bound him and put him in prison because
of Herodias, the wife of his brother Philip. 4 For John had been saying to him, "It
is not lawful for you to have her." 5 Although Herod wanted to put him to death, he
feared the crowd, because they regarded John as a prophet. 6 But when Herod's
birthday came, the daughter of Herodias danced before them and pleased Herod,
7 so much that he promised with an oath to give her whatever she asked. 8 Having
been prompted by her mother, she said, "Give me here on a platter the head of
John the Baptist." 9 Although he was grieved, the king commanded it to be given
because of his oaths, and because of his dinner guests. 10 He sent and had John
beheaded in the prison. 11 And his head was brought on a platter and given to the
girl, and she brought it to her mother. 12 His disciples came and took away the
body and buried it; and they went and reported to Jesus.

What a pathetic soap opera of discord in the Herodian family! The elements are typical, if not tragic: unfaithfulness, divorce, hatred, sexual immorality, revenge, fear, insecurity, and stupidity. The importance for the gospel account is that it provides some detail regarding the death of John.

Though the real reason for Herod arresting John is recorded obliquely in Scripture, we may surmise that John's stirring up considerable messianic excitement may have contributed to Herod's decision. Caesar held the rulers of Palestine accountable for keeping the unruly Jews in line—a nearly impossible task, given the Jews' tenacious, ancestral zeal. They were always on the precipice of rebellion against their overlords. Herod would have been quite nervous over John's message, "The kingdom of heaven is at hand!" Arresting him quelled a potential uprising.

Additionally, John's denunciation against sin and his calls to repent were like arrows finding an appropriate target in the cavalier behavior of Herod, who disregarded the Jewish laws of morality. But as our story today indicates, jail did not dampen John's prophet voice. Ironically, Herod was fascinated with John. Mark 6:20 records, "Herod was afraid of John, knowing that he was a righteous and holy man … and when he heard him, he was very perplexed; but he used to enjoy listening to him." Yet John did not stop denouncing Herod's marital situation.

The pathos of Herod's household resulted in John's grisly death. But it was too late to stop Jesus' movement. About Him John said, "He who is coming after me is mightier than I, and I am not fit to remove His sandals" (3:11).

Lord, help me to have the courage to root out sinfulness in my life. Any short-term benefit is nullified by the long-term consequences. Forgive my selfishness.

Week 21
Day 3

Ministry of Multiplication

Matthew 14:13-21

13 Now when Jesus heard about John, He withdrew from there in a boat to a secluded
place by Himself; and when the people heard of this, they followed Him on foot from
the cities. 14 When He went ashore, He saw a large crowd, and felt compassion for
them and healed their sick. 15 When it was evening, the disciples came to Him and
said, "This place is desolate and the hour is already late; so send the crowds away,
that they may go into the villages and buy food for themselves." 16 But Jesus said
to them, "They do not need to go away; you give them something to eat!" 17 They
said to Him, "We have here only five loaves and two fish." 18 And He said, "Bring
them here to Me." 19 Ordering the people to sit down on the grass, He took the five
loaves and the two fish, and looking up toward heaven, He blessed the food, and
breaking the loaves He gave them to the disciples, and the disciples gave them to
the crowds, 20 and they all ate and were satisfied. They picked up what was left
over of the broken pieces, twelve full baskets. 21 There were about five thousand
men who ate, besides women and children.

Often, Jesus retreated to spend time alone, only to be found by the throngs of people who wanted more of Him. This time He was motivated by the news of John the Baptist's death. While not afraid for His own life, the circumstances made it difficult for Him to continue His ministry in that locale at that time.

While large crowds seeking out Jesus would seem a good thing, the apostle John records Jesus' assessment: "You seek Me, not because you saw signs, but because you ate of the loaves and were filled" (John 6:23). In other words, their concerns were for their own "felt needs" and not for the kingdom of God. Yet, despite their self-serving motivations and intrusion on His "personal time," Jesus' compassion for them trumped His need for solitude.

He could have called down manna from heaven or turned rocks into bread, but rather than work unilaterally He engaged His disciples in the process of meeting the need. Instead of telling them the solution, the Master-discipler raised the problem to a different level, "You give them something to eat!" The disciples wanted Jesus to release the crowd to find their own food, but He wanted them to own the problem so they would appreciate the remedy.

In this story we discover profound lessons for discipleship. (1) Compassion should extend to all, not just those with pure motivation. (2) While personal time is necessary for reviving one's own spiritual vitality, it should never completely trump loving others. (3) We can accomplish far more than we imagine or think when we allow God to work through what we have.

Lord, I am so glad You have compassion on me when I struggle with my own selfishness. Help me become more centered on You than on my needs.

Week 21
Day 4

Incarnational Strain

Matthew 14:22-23

[22] Immediately He made the disciples get into the boat and go ahead of Him to the other side, while He sent the crowds away. [23] After He had sent the crowds away, He went up on the mountain by Himself to pray; and when it was evening, He was there alone.

Why would Jesus need to spend time praying if He Himself was God in the flesh? It seems like an anomaly to us, bound as we are by the natural world and logic. Jesus, the man, was the intersection between the infinite and the finite, deity and humanity Immanuel—God with us. At that juncture in the spiritual-physical warp in which God became a human being—the bridge between the spirit and the flesh—unusual phenomena happen. It should not surprise us, therefore, to find Jesus communicating with His Father, God communing with God.

We see this fellowship within God Himself as early as Genesis 1. God had repeatedly said, "Let there be …" in reference to such things as light, dark, land/water divisions, vegetation, and animals. But when He created humans, He said, "Let us make man in Our image." A central tenet of faith for Christians is the uniqueness of one God, yet a plurality within that One. Scripture teaches both monotheism (only one God, Deut. 6:4) and trinitarianism (three persons in one God—which the NT identifies as the Father, Son, and Holy Spirit). This is not a contradiction, as Islam charges, for Christians do not believe there are three gods in one god. Nor do we believe there are three persons in one person. There is one God who is revealed to us as three persons. Before and apart from creation, He was and is not alone. There is full and satisfying communion within God, independent of all else.

It is no small wonder, therefore, that there would be strain in the incarnation. Illustrating that strain, Jesus goes back continually to fellowship with His Father in prayer. This was one of the humbling, condescending aspects of God limiting Himself to the experience of being a man. While this may be difficult for our finite minds to comprehend, it is not an illogical contradiction. It speaks of the transcendence and "otherness" of God. His ways are above our ways and mysterious. Just as He had the normal human needs of food, drink, and rest, He also had the human-spiritual need of fellowship with, and guidance from, His heavenly Father.

The Son placed great importance on fellowshipping with the Father through prayer. In this area more than most, we need to imitate the Master.

Lord, I want to know You better. Even more, I want to spend time fellowshipping with You. Help me to pray more regularly.

Jesus, Our Helper

Matthew 14:24-27

[24] But the boat was already a long distance from the land, battered by the waves; for the wind was contrary. [25] And in the fourth watch of the night He came to them, walking on the sea. [26] When the disciples saw Him walking on the sea, they were terrified, and said, "It is a ghost!" And they cried out in fear. [27] But immediately Jesus spoke to them, saying, "Take courage, it is I; do not be afraid."

While Jesus prayed, the disciples sailed. He enjoyed the tranquility of quietness alone with His Father; they battled the tumult of a storm in the middle of the lake. Their vessel was taking a battering while Jesus was "recharging His batteries." What a contrast!

The disciples are not to be faulted for being out there, on a number of accounts. First, they were following their Master's instructions. Second, even seasoned fishermen could not always anticipate the sudden storms that often cascaded suddenly down on the Sea of Galilee. It will not do, though, to think that the storm took *Jesus* by surprise. He is the Lord of creation and could very well have planned the storm for that time in that place—to stage a faith lesson. Some might see this as the Lord, in His perfect foreknowledge, taking advantage of the natural order of things for the benefit of discipleship training. Regardless, nothing happens by chance, and everything works together according to God's plan.

At any rate, the disciples' progress slowed and the stress grew. It had been a long night, and now, between 3 a.m. and 6 a.m. ("the fourth watch"), they must have been bone weary from fighting the elements. The Sea of Galilee is not overly large, measuring roughly eight by thirteen miles, but shore was a long way off.

At that point Jesus came walking on the water (one of His most well-known miraculous feats). Other accounts indicate that He made like He was going to walk right past the boat. Nothing in the framework of those seasoned fishermen's experience could make sense of what they saw. They concluded it was an apparition of some sort. Terror struck. They screamed in panic. Jesus waited until that very moment to make His next move.

He spoke, and His message was this: no matter how dire the circumstances or fearful the experience, no matter how fruitless the efforts or hopeless it seems, the presence of the Lord and His "It is I" overrides all else. He is our peace, our protector. He is our shelter, fortress, and strong tower. He is our gyroscope, stabilizer, and trump card. Therefore, take courage!

Lord, help me see You in the midst of my troubled times and experiences. You overshadow all else. In You I have courage.

Weekend Reading

Saturday – Proverbs 21
Sunday – Psalms 90–95

Personal Reflections

Impetuous Faith

Matthew 14:28-31

[28] Peter said to Him, "Lord, if it is You, command me to come to You on the water."
[29] And He said, "Come!" And Peter got out of the boat, and walked on the water and
came toward Jesus. [30] But seeing the wind, he became frightened, and beginning to
sink, he cried out, "Lord, save me!" [31] Immediately Jesus stretched out His hand
and took hold of him, and said to him, "You of little faith, why did you doubt?"

Impulsivity has both an upside and a downside; Peter was a stranger to neither. His gaffs are well known. There was no guessing his thoughts or feelings at any moment. But calculation was not his strong suit. The upside is that where the timid hold back, those with impetuous faith move ahead.

Peter dared to engage his fears and boldly called out to what might be the Lord. First, he had to make sure it was the Lord out there walking on the water before taking another step. Second, he'd better be certain the Lord wanted him out there. Third, he figured he'd be safer out in the storm with the Lord than in the ship with eleven fearful, boat-hugging men.

The presence of Christ eclipsed his fears of the storm. One can only imagine the thoughts of the other men in the boat. Was Peter crazy? To a sailor, the safest place is in the boat. Even if it is sinking, wood still floats! Abandoning all tangible security must have seemed foolish. But Peter wasn't influenced by what others thought. To quote a well-worn comment on this incident, "If you want to walk on water, you have to get out of the boat!" Faith meant letting go of human securities and reaching to the Lord.

Yes, Peter began his faith-walk well, but he began to sink when he shifted focus off the Lord and onto the storm. Some say he only needed to believe that he had the ability to walk on water because, after all, the Lord believed he could do it. But that puts things backward. He walked on water as long as his eyes were on Jesus, as long as his faith was in Christ, not in his own self-confidence.

Peter cried for help and Jesus lifted him out with a rebuke, "You of little faith, why did you doubt?" Rebuke? Yes! But I'd rather be chastised for little faith than be ignored for having no faith. Some Christians don't experience the exhilaration of God's powerful presence because they are paralyzed by fear—fear of circumstances, of failure, of missing His "perfect" will. Peter failed, but he walked on water and the others did not! The old saying goes, "The only way to steer a parked car is to first get it moving." The same is true for faith-walking.

Lord, help me to know Your will and not get bogged down in seeking it.

Surprised by Sonship

Matthew 14:32-36

[32] When they got into the boat, the wind stopped. [33] And those who were in the boat worshiped Him, saying, "You are certainly God's Son!" [34] When they had crossed over, they came to land at Gennesaret. [35] And when the men of that place recognized Him, they sent word into all that surrounding district and brought to Him all who were sick; [36] and they implored Him that they might just touch the fringe of His cloak; and as many as touched it were cured.

After Peter and Jesus got back into the boat, everyone enjoyed the ensuing calm. But Peter had the inestimable experience of having walked on water *while* the storm was still raging. Peace comes when the Lord calms the believer in the adverse circumstances of life, but unprecedented victory bursts forward when a Christian faith-walks with the Lord *through* the adversity!

When it was all over the disciples were overwhelmed with new insight about Jesus. Was there any limit to what He could do? They concluded that He was no less than "God's Son." It wasn't that the disciples were articulating that Jesus is the second person of the Trinity (they came to understand that later). But they were now recognizing Him to be greater than a mere man. Some scholars have debated that the phrase may simply characterize Him as divine. What we do know is that this identification of Jesus was the challenge of Satan in the wilderness (Matthew 4), the admission of the demons at their exorcism (8:29), the inquisition of Caiaphas at Jesus' trial (26:63), and the startling declaration of the centurion at the cross (27:54). Only in the case of the disciples did this recognition invoke worship—due to God alone! There is no mistake—the disciples were beginning to see in Jesus the manifestation of God Himself.

While the disciples were following where the evidence led—recognizing who Jesus was—the crowds on shore saw Him simply as a healer. The contrast is unmistakable: the crowd who desired healing, the disciples who desired security, and Peter who desired to be with Christ in the storm.

The Sea of Galilee was also known as the Lake of Gennesaret, a name shared with a town on its southwestern shore near Bethsaida and Capernaum. The area was quite populous in that day, and the people there were familiar with Christ. Word got around and many came (and brought others) for healing. The frenzy was on, and people clamored to just touch His clothes. Graciously, He healed them. There was no denying that He cared about them, no matter how closely or distantly they followed Him. But unlike the Twelve, the crowds had not yet discerned who He really was—God's Son.

Lord, I choose to follow You, not just because of what You do for me, but also because of who You are. I worship You because You are the Son of God!

Resisting Legalism

Matthew 15:1-2

[1] Then some Pharisees and teachers of the law came to Jesus from Jerusalem and asked, [2] "Why do your disciples break the tradition of the elders? They don't wash their hands before they eat!"

Recent scholarship has brought to light some historical background regarding the rise of such pharisaical traditions. There was an inbred awareness and self-identity of the Jewish people that they were God's preeminent, chosen nation. The Lord had promised that all the nations of the earth would be blessed through Abraham's descendants. These promises were repeated to Isaac and Jacob. Coming into clearer focus in the time of Moses and Joshua, the promises of a special land and prominence among the nations motivated heroic action and loyalty to God. The Davidic dynasty was eventually established with the vision of benevolent rule over all the nations. The overarching ideal was to experience God's blessing in the land, influencing all peoples toward worship of Yahweh.

Over time, Israel rebelled and God repeatedly sent prophets warning them to repent and return to the Lord or He would punish them with defeat and captivity by another nation. This, in fact, happened—first by the Assyrians and subsequently by the Babylonians. After 70 years of exile in Babylon, they returned to the land, but Israel did not rise again to international prominence, nor did they become a blessing to the world. By the time of Jesus, some 400 years later, they had come under Roman domination. The nation had never fully returned from "spiritual exile," nor had they experienced the full blessings promised.

In time, people began asking what Israel could do to bring about God's blessings. Some, like the Maccabees, thought the solution was to rebel against their Roman overlords. So they led various insurrections they hoped would prompt God to send His Messiah and bring them to their rightful prominence. Others, like the Essenes, thought a complete withdrawal into a "purified" community (a remnant) was the solution. Then God would notice their faithfulness and raise that community to be the true Israel. Still others, wanting reform for the nation as a whole, determined the solution was to follow the Mosaic law more fastidiously. Then, they hoped, they would be found worthy of the Lord's blessings. The Pharisees were rooted in this latter group.

However well-intentioned were the precursors to the Pharisees, in time that thinking led to a stringent legalism which became impossible to keep. It became a tool of coercion and manipulation. And this is what was happening when they approached Jesus concerning ritualistic hand washing.

Oh Lord, in my zeal to follow You more closely, help me not to fall into rank legalism, using my convictions to coerce others to conform to my practices.

Duplicity Exposed

Matthew 15:3-9

[3] Jesus replied, "And why do you break the command of God for the sake of your tradition? [4] For God said, 'Honor your father and mother' and 'Anyone who curses his father or mother must be put to death.' [5] But you say that if a man says to his father or mother, 'Whatever help you might otherwise have received from me is a gift devoted to God,' [6] he is not to 'honor his father' with it. Thus you nullify the word of God for the sake of your tradition. [7] You hypocrites! Isaiah was right when he prophesied about you: [8] 'These people honor me with their lips, but their hearts are far from me. [9] They worship me in vain; their teachings are but rules taught by men.'"

Jesus reserved His harshest denunciation for those who maintained an ostentatious show of spirituality while lacking inner integrity. Simply put, this committee of Pharisees and "teachers of the law" accused Jesus of breaking their man-made traditions while they themselves were guilty of breaking God's commandments. This group, probably representing the Sanhedrin, made a big deal of the fact that Jesus and His disciples didn't wash their hands before they ate (vv. 1-2). Their concern was not for personal hygiene; they presumed that since Jesus and His disciples associated with common people who were presumed to be unclean, they must have become unclean themselves but took no care to ceremonially purify themselves before eating.

Jesus saw through their duplicity. He exposed it by pointing out that one of their traditions, specifically, broke the fifth commandment—to honor one's father and mother (Ex. 20:12). Honoring parents included caring for them in a material way when needed. Yet the Pharisees devised a ruling that allowed people to circumvent that obligation. This is how it worked: A man could set up a sort of spiritual trust fund in which he could earmark a certain part of his wealth as a gift to God. But these were resources that otherwise could have been used to support his parents. By declaring these things to be "corban" (Luke 7:11), which means "gift," the resources were no longer available to help the parents in need. With this legalistic loophole, they could avoid keeping the fifth commandment. Jesus identified this as a flagrant violation of what God intended. These people had elevated their traditions above His commands.

In a scathing rebuke, Jesus calls them hypocrites (the true object of Isaiah's stinging, prophetic condemnation). Their worship was completely devoid of spiritual value. Samuel's admonition reverberates: "It is better to obey than to sacrifice" (1 Sam. 15:22). We note that only Jesus has the right to accuse others of hypocrisy. He alone was without sin, and He alone know's men's hearts and minds.

Lord, help me see my own hypocrisy and confess it as sin.

Blind Guides of the Blind

Matthew 15:10-14

[10] Jesus called the crowd to him and said, "Listen and understand. [11] What goes into a man's mouth does not make him 'unclean,' but what comes out of his mouth, that is what makes him 'unclean.' " [12] Then the disciples came to him and asked, "Do you know that the Pharisees were offended when they heard this?" [13] He replied, "Every plant that my heavenly Father has not planted will be pulled up by the roots. [14] Leave them; they are blind guides. If a blind man leads a blind man, both will fall into a pit

The designation of clean or unclean has to do with what comes *out* of a person, not what goes into him. The Pharisees and teachers of the Law had it all wrong. Their hypocrisy had blinded them to the absurdity of their insistence on ceremonial washing before eating.

In the OT Law, the concept of being clean or unclean had to do with a person's fitness for entering into Israel's formal rituals. In order to worship God properly at the temple, a person had to be free of any unclean activity or state of being. For example, touching a dead animal or eating pork rendered a person unclean and required a prescribed course of cleansing in order to again become acceptable to God for worship. The Pharisees intensified the Law, applying it way beyond God's intention. The case in our passage provides an example of this. They assumed the following sequence: a person out in public presumably came into physical contact with unclean people or things, thereby rendering his hands unclean. Upon returning home and eating, his unclean hands would have made his food unclean. That unclean food, then, entering his body, would finally result in his becoming unclean and therefore unfit to participate in publicly worshiping God.

Jesus, however, undercut this teaching with a simple assertion: uncleanness was not a matter of what went into the mouth but what came out of the mouth. What hindered a person's worship was not outward things but the condition of his heart. He further exacerbated this slam against the Pharisees and scribes by publicly advising the people not to follow these leaders' teachings. He directly and completely denounced those who focused entiredly on outward behavior. They were "blind guides" leading the Jews astray.

For Christians, we can hear the echo of this warning in James's admonition: "Not many of you should presume to be teachers, my brothers, because you know that we who teach will be judged more strictly" (James 3:1).

Lord, help me focus on issues of the heart and not simply outward behavior. And help me likewise not to lead others astray through legalistic teaching.

Weekend Reading

Saturday – Proverbs 22
Sunday – Psalms 96–101

Personal Reflections

Dullness of Spirit

Matthew 15:15-16 (pt. 1)

[15] *Peter said, "Explain the parable to us."* [16] *"Are you still so dull?" Jesus asked them.*

By this juncture in the disciples' training, they should have been able to understand the parables of their Master. They had been slow to trust—"you of little faith" (14:31) and now were slow to learn—"Are you still so dull?" What caused the dullness? Did Jesus inadvertently select men of minimal IQs or with learning disabilities? Were they lacking in basic seminary education or some prior spiritual training necessary for understanding Jesus' deep theological and philosophical insights? The exchange Jesus had with Nicodemus negates those possibilities. Nicodemus was a highly educated Pharisee, and yet Jesus had good cause to say to him, "Are you the teacher of Israel and do not understand these things?" (John 3:10).

The issue is not deficiency of mental acuity but lack of spiritual acumen. The disciples' spiritual sensitivities had been seared by long years of living under religious legalisms foisted on them by the religious hierarchy. Life was measured, and the Sanhedrin (the ruling body of Israel's religion) was watching like "Big Brother." (Lest we blame all on the Pharisees and scribes, it must be noted that the common people of Israel, for the most part, followed along willingly with their faulty view of spirituality, embracing it as a way of life.)

Even after the church was endowed with the Holy Spirit, dullness in the spirit of believers continued. Paul admonished the Galatians, "You foolish Galatians, who has bewitched you, before whose eyes Jesus Christ was publicly portrayed as crucified? This is the only thing I want to find out from you: did you receive the Spirit by the works of the Law, or by hearing with faith?" (Gal. 3:1-2). The Jewish Christians likewise were rebuked, "Concerning him we have much to say, and it is hard to explain, since you have become dull of hearing. For though by this time you ought to be teachers, you have need again for someone to teach you the elementary principles of the oracles of God, and you have come to need milk and not solid food" (Heb. 5:11-12).

Not judging those early Christians too harshly, we must include ourselves in the same category of "slow to learn" as well. How often does the Lord give us insight into the ignorance we portrayed in the past? Wisdom recognizes that the present may be the past we one day look back on with humility! "For now we see in a mirror dimly, but then face to face; now I know in part, but then I will know fully just as I also have been fully known" (1 Cor. 13:12).

Lord, help me to grow in my understanding of Your Word. Human intellect alone is not enough; I need the enlightenment of Your Holy Spirit.

Week 23
Day 2

Dullness Overcome

Matthew 15:15-16 (pt. 2)

[15] *Peter said, "Explain the parable to us."* [16] *"Are you still so dull?" Jesus asked them.*

Despite our human foibles and limitations, we don't need to continue in a spiritually dull state. God has provided us with resources to aid our spiritual progress in knowing Him. First, the Lord has given us His Word. The psalmist says, "Your word is a lamp to my feet and a light to my path" (Ps. 119:105). A clear perspective on life based on instruction from the Word of God will help us live in the way for which God designed us. Without the Word, we constantly stumble about with a dulled sense of right and wrong, a lack of true spiritual discernment. The goal is not just to know truth, but to live it. That is why David prays, "Teach me Your way, O Lord; I will walk in Your truth; unite my heart to fear Your name" (Ps. 86:11).

But how does one go from "head knowledge," or the academic reading of God's Word, to really knowing it in a transforming way? It begins with a deep humbleness before the Creator God of the universe. Solomon put it this way: "The fear of the Lord is the beginning of knowledge" (Prov. 1:7), and "The fear of the Lord is the beginning of wisdom, and the knowledge of the Holy One is understanding" (Prov. 9:10). Knowledge and wisdom are rooted in a relationship with God, who is infinitely greater than us. He is not to be trifled with. His Word is not on the level of a self-help book. It is the communication of the One who created all, who is sovereign over all, and who will judge all. He is the One who *speaks* in the Scripture, and that is why we call it "God's Word." So we must take His Word seriously because we must take *Him* seriously. We will not escape spiritual dullness apart from that!

As Christians, we have an empowering resource in Christ. "But a natural man does not accept the things of the Spirit of God … he cannot understand them, because they are spiritually appraised. But he who is spiritual appraises all things, yet he himself is appraised by no one. For who has known the mind of the Lord, that he will instruct Him? But we have the mind of Christ" (1 Cor. 2:14-15). We have the mind of Christ teaching us from within! Peter adds, "His divine power has granted to us everything pertaining to life and godliness, through the true knowledge of Him who called us by His own glory and excellence" (2 Pet. 1:3). As we live out what we have in Christ, we experience the principle we read in Hebrews 5:14: "Solid food is for the mature, who because of practice have their senses trained to discern good and evil."

Lord, thank you for giving me Your Word and the mind of Christ. Help me to move beyond spiritual dullness to maturity in knowledge and wisdom.

Withdrawal Brings Hope

Matthew 15:21-22

21 Jesus went away from there, and withdrew into the district of Tyre and Sidon. 22 And a Canaanite woman from that region came out and began to cry out, saying, "Have mercy on me, Lord, Son of David; my daughter is cruelly demon-possessed."

The fact that Jesus withdrew for a fourth time does not mean He was fearful. Three times previously He had responded to events and attitudes by changing His location—when John the Baptist was arrested (4:12), when the Pharisees first began planning to destroy Him (12:14-15), and when the news arrived of John's execution (14:13). Now He retreated after His denunciation of the Pharisees. Each pivot point in His ministry potentially threatened to short-circuit the timing of the divine plan. When His half-brothers mockingly told Him to be more public in His efforts, He responded, "My time is not yet here" (John 7:5). That the timing of Jesus' death was orchestrated by the Father's sovereign plan cannot be denied. Peter, in his great message on the day of Pentecost, made this point: "This Man, delivered over by the predetermined plan and foreknowledge of God, you nailed to a cross by the hands of godless men and put Him to death" (Acts 2:23). Jesus' withdrawals were simply a means of controlling the tempo as the events unfolded.

Now the Lord made a rare excursion into Gentile territory, to the north, while the opposition's fervor settled down. His reputation preceded Him even beyond the boundaries of Israel. A woman there beat a path to Jesus' door and cried out, identifying Him as "Son of David," just as blind Bartimaeus would (Mark 10:47). This was an odd comment for a Gentile to make. Non-Jews generally did not recognize the historical importance of King David, or even the significance of the title which identified the dynastic right of Jesus to sit on David's throne. She must be numbered among the so-called "God-fearing Gentiles," such as the centurion of Matthew 8 or Cornelius of Acts 10:22. (See also 13:43; 17:4, 7). These were non-Jews believed in the God of the Jews but were not necessarily converts to the Jewish religion.

The woman's plea indicated that she had likely tried everything else to win freedom and relief for her daughter. In asking for mercy, she cast herself on the only One who could help. In this carte-blanche, tacit confession she recognizes she has no merit of her own. Whatever the cause of her misfortune, the need for a cure explained her humility in asking for mercy.

Lord, Your help in my life comes despite my falling short of holiness. Your mercies are new every morning; great is Your faithfulness (Lam. 3:21-23).

Week 23
Day 4

A God of Mercy

Matthew 15:22

[2] And a Canaanite woman from that region came out and began to cry out, saying, "Have mercy on me, Lord, Son of David; my daughter is cruelly demon-possessed."

Normally one calls out for mercy to another who has been offended or who is charged with carrying out justice. Why would the Canaanite woman ask Jesus, whom she had never met before, for this help? In those days most people believed that personal misfortune was the result of some sin or falling short of God's expectations. That is what Job's friends presumed. They said, "If you return to the Almighty, you will be restored; If you remove unrighteousness far from your tent" (Job 22:23). So if there was a difficulty, people would naturally conclude the person had not "returned to the Almighty." In other words, there was still sin in the person's life. So in this case, the woman or her child was assumed to be unworthy and in need of mercy.

In addition, any God-fearing Gentile would have recognized God's favor of the Jews and that Gentiles had no right to the promises or blessings of God. So in calling out for mercy she was admitting her status as an outsider. Nevertheless, she was hoping for some small favor, undeserved though it might be.

This woman recognized in Jesus a potential solution to the problem of her daughter being demon-possessed. Demonic activity was quite prevalent—not unexpected—during Christ's earthly tenure. At this watershed time of history, with the incarnate Son of God on the earth, Satan no doubt dispatched his troops in an unprecedented manner to resist the plan of God at every level. It should be pointed out that the Bible presents Satan and demons as being real, personal entities, not just figments of ancient mythologies. At times they do possess people, taking control of their lives. Clearly, the woman justifiably sought mercy, for this condition of her dear daughter was far beyond her capabilities to cure. Demon possession is not something one can cure by oneself.

What a picture of our situation! All humans have sinned and come short of God's standards (Rom. 3:23). Like this woman, we cannot cure our own condition, we cannot solve our own sin condition, and we do not deserve God's favor. There is only one hope—that God will be merciful to us, that He will forgive us on some other basis than our worthiness—His own.

Lord, I know that I don't deserve anything from You. You are a merciful God, and I thank you for forgiving me and setting me free from sin.

Apparent Hardness

Matthew 15:23-24

[23] But He did not answer her a word. And His disciples came and implored Him, saying, "Send her away, because she keeps shouting at us." [24] But He answered and said, "I was sent only to the lost sheep of the house of Israel."

Silence exacerbates deep anguish. In this case, the woman hollers even more loudly, maybe even obnoxiously. Propriety is not her concern. The disciples were so annoyed at her incessant badgering that they pleaded with Jesus to somehow get rid of her. Such callousness exhibited itself at another time when they (in particular, James and John) wanted to call down judgmental fire from heaven on the inhabitants of a Samaritan village which refused hospitality to Jesus and His entourage (Luke 9:54). Old prejudices die hard, and their animosity found little room for compassion for this poor mother. One can only imagine the horrors that gripped her heart and mind.

At first glance, Jesus appeared to share the disciples' hardness. But the ensuing discussion puts that notion to rest. In the end Jesus does show mercy. But first there is a point to be made.

Jesus' primary ministry focused on the Jews. God established that priority in His promise to Abraham—to bless him and his descendants, and then to bless the whole world through them (Gen. 12:1-3). The apostle Paul confirmed that priority when he wrote, "For I am not ashamed of the gospel, for it is the power of God for salvation to everyone who believes, to the Jew first and also to the Greek" (Rom. 1:16). If Jesus freely responded to all requests from the Gentiles for blessings that were to go first to the Jews, the master plan of salvation would have gone awry. The fact that He showed mercy to a Gentile during this rare venture outside of Jewish territory necessitated a reinforcement and clarification of that principle. At this point she had no claim on Jesus or the blessing of God. Jesus' initial silence was intended to make all parties aware of that—and thereby demonstrate that His mercy, when it was given, was truly given freely. This would be far above and beyond the original promise to Abraham, but yet was based on that promise. God would bless Gentiles in certain situations even apart from the Jews. Now, during the "church age," God continues to bless non-Jewish believers.

Fortunately the story does not end with Jesus' initial rebuff of the woman. But nothing can thwart God's sovereign plan. The higher purpose is never lost.

Lord, thank you that You are not controlled by the "tyranny of the urgent," even when You are silent during my crisis issue of the moment.

Weekend Reading

Saturday – Proverbs 23
Sunday – Psalms 102–104

Personal Reflections

Hope for Mercy

Matthew 15:25-28

[25] But she came and began to bow down before Him, saying, "Lord, help me!" [26] And He answered and said, "It is not good to take the children's bread and throw it to the dogs." [27] But she said, "Yes, Lord; but even the dogs feed on the crumbs which fall from their masters' table." [28] Then Jesus said to her, "O woman, your faith is great; it shall be done for you as you wish." And her daughter was healed at once.

Not put off by Jesus' silence, the woman continued pleading her case. The Lord answered tersely. (His tone would appear even more stern, understood within the context of Middle Eastern culture.) Jesus essentially told her that if He were to grant her request, that would be tantamount to throwing food from a child's plate into a dog's bowl. The woman didn't miss a beat. Even if she were like a dog, she reasoned, at least dogs eat whatever may fall off the table. In saying that, she's intimating that although she doesn't deserve anything from this Jewish healer, she can at least benefit from the blessings falling off the Jewish "plate."

The insight here goes deeper than the woman perceives. The Jews were, in fact, more like children who didn't want the food on the table—in effect, pushing the food, the blessings of the kingdom, off the table. There was plenty for the Gentiles because of the Jews' growing rejection of Christ. This episode shows that when the Jews did not respond to God's blessing and plan, He went outside of Israel to bring blessing to the Gentile world. In fact, after Christ's death and resurrection, and the Jews' continued rejection, God turned from the Jews and began dealing directly with Gentiles. The promise to Abraham, though, remains intact, for it was to the Jews first that the gospel had come. It was through the Jews that Jesus had come, and it was through this Jewish descendant of Abraham, that God would bless the whole world. Our story here of the Gentile woman is a preview of that very thing.

Jesus commends the woman's faith! She believed Jesus *could* heal her daughter; the only question was whether He would be *willing* to do it. The woman's only hope was in this Jewish teacher. As a Gentile, that was all she had. And it was good enough. Her child was healed of demon possession.

Another Gentile, the centurion whose young servant was dying (8:10), showed similar faith. And Jesus praised him as well. That is the kind of faith God is still looking for today.

Lord, I make no claims on You as though I deserve anything. I stand in Your grace and mercy, which is my only hope. I trust You.

Week 24
Day 2

Precious Souls

Matthew 15:29-31

[29] Departing from there, Jesus went along by the Sea of Galilee, and having gone up on the mountain, He was sitting there. [30] And large crowds came to Him, bringing with them those who were lame, crippled, blind, mute, and many others, and they laid them down at His feet; and He healed them. [31] So the crowd marveled as they saw the mute speaking, the crippled restored, and the lame walking, and the blind seeing; and they glorified the God of Israel.

Having left the crumbs under the table, Jesus reentered Jewish territory to serve up food, as it were, on top of the table to the "children." The feeding of the 4000 in these next verses (vv. 32-38) contrasts with the Canaanite woman of Syria who asked for the crumbs. The present section serves as a summary and transition between the two events, with meager details presented. After following the coastline of the Sea of Galilee southward, Jesus found a hill, climbed it, and sat down (the usual position for a rabbi when teaching), humbly taking that position on the ground rather than in the ornate confines of the temple. Jesus' main focus after His fourth "withdrawal" was to return to proclaiming to the Jews the kingdom of God.

Whether the crowds immediately followed Him or found Him after a period of time, the point is that they came not to hear Jesus teach but to get healed from various kinds of physical difficulties. The large gathering was not deterred by Jesus' sharpening criticism of the religious establishment, nor by their growing hostility toward Him. The potential for physical healing outweighed the religio-political correctness of their day.

The list of maladies is impressive: people who were maimed, those who couldn't walk, see, or speak. These were brought and laid at the feet of Jesus, appealing to nothing but His compassion. All diseases and physical difficulties being under His control, Jesus graciously healed them, even though He was concerned about more than their bodies.

We can easily infer that He cares for each Christian at a variety of levels despite our often mixed motives for coming to Him. He can handle it all graciously. Matthew Henry points out in his commentary that, in this story, we discover that "the souls of peasants are as precious with Him as the souls of princes." All that is required is the humility to go where He is.

When Pharisees saw His works, they blasphemed. But when this crowd saw His works, they marveled and glorified God. Henry again comments, "Miracles, which are the matter of our wonder, must be the matter of our praise."

Lord, You have taken care of many small needs in my life, even when You are concerned about far more important things. Thank you for being gracious.

An Appetite for Compassion

Matthew 15:32-33

[32] *And Jesus called His disciples to Him, and said, "I feel compassion for the people,*
because they have remained with Me now three days and have nothing to eat; and
I do not want to send them away hungry, for they might faint on the way." [33] *The*
disciples said to Him, "Where would we get so many loaves in this desolate place
to satisfy such a large crowd?" [34] *And Jesus said to them, "How many loaves do*
you have?" And they said, "Seven, and a few small fish."

This story of this miraculous feeding is similar to the one recorded in Matthew 14:13-21. In both we find Jesus having compassion on the multitude, engaging the disciples in solving the problem, miraculously feeding the people, and providing plenty of leftovers. In Matthew's gospel, we read of Jesus' concern that if the crowd were sent away, some may collapse with hunger on the way. The disciples saw only their limited resources. Interestingly, leaders often find themselves facing difficult situations where they lack sufficient resources for meeting the needs of those whom they lead. But if leaders try to absolve themselves of their responsibility by simply sending people away, that could be counterproductive to the needs of those very people.

In training the Twelve here Jesus engaged them by drawing their attention to the need and then posing a simple question. He did not ask for His own benefit. He knew the available provisions were meager. Rather, He wanted to emphasize to them how little He had to work with, so that in the end they would see His glory—how great He really was and is. As the Master Discipler, He was also teaching them a practical lesson: to look beyond their own abilities and resources and to engage God—a lesson they had obviously not yet learned.

The source of the meager available food remains anonymous, unlike in the story in John 6, where a boy's lunch was used to feed 5000. It is possible in this incident that the food came from one of the disciples. At any rate, someone had rationed his available supply so that while everyone else had exhausted theirs, he still had a little bit left. It is a great sacrifice for someone to part with his well-planned last meal when others do not make their own adequate provisions. Why did he give it? Did he alone remember what Jesus had done before with even less? Or did he simply trust the Master when asked for it? What we do know is that the Master needed it, so he willing gave it.

The crowd was smaller this time. But whether one or a million, God cares for every person who comes to Him.

Lord, let me not be so focused on my own needs, but let me be willing to give You what I have so that You can bless others through me.

God's New Math

Matthew 15:34-36

[34] *And Jesus said to them, "How many loaves do you have?" And they said, "Seven, and a few small fish."* [35] *And He directed the people to sit down on the ground;* [36] *and He took the seven loaves and the fish; and giving thanks, He broke them and started giving them to the disciples, and the disciples gave them to the people.*

This incident has a few lessons for us. First, God sometimes takes our hard work and the resources we have garnered for ourselves and uses them for something greater than just meeting our own needs. Second—and this is the flip side of the first—discipleship includes making our resources available to God. Both cut across our innate, fallen human nature, the propensity for self-centeredness.

We mentioned before the similarities between the two miraculous feedings—the 5000 of chapter 14 and the 4000 here. But contrasts are the catalyst for insights, so we observe the following differences. In the first case, the event took place in the evening; in the second, after three days of being with Jesus. Following the Lord sometimes requires sacrifice. Three days away from working the fields, fishing, or running the family business meant no income. Once healed, people could have just left to return to their employment, which leads one to believe they wanted more than healing. This, though, was a curious commitment, for most ended up abandoning Him, at least until after the resurrection. A mix of reasons may have been involved in their staying that long, not least of which was the superficial excitement at the many great things Jesus was doing and teaching. Maybe some people in this crowd were among the 3000 who later repented at Pentecost and were baptized!

In the first feeding, the disciples brought the problem to Jesus; in the second, Jesus brought the problem to them. Sometimes leaders see the problem but come up with poor solutions. Other times they just don't see the problem and need to be prompted by the Lord. Though we may see God work at one time in our life, that doesn't mean we always learn our lesson.

The number of loaves and fish multiplied in each incident differed. We must work with what we have. The size matters little to the Lord. In the first, Jesus blessed the food. (Note that the word *food* is in italics, which means there is no object of the verb *blessed* in the Greek. We could just as easily say that Jesus blessed *God*). In the second incident, Jesus "gives thanks." We, like Jesus, give thanks, recognizing that our meals ultimately come from God's supply to enable us to carry on our God-given mission in life.

Lord, help me never to take my food for granted but to see it as Your gracious provision for my physical health and strength to carry on.

A Provider Who Satisfies

Matthew 15:37-39

[37] And they all ate and were satisfied, and they picked up what was left over of the broken pieces, seven large baskets full. [38] And those who ate were four thousand men, besides women and children. [39] And sending away the crowds, Jesus got into the boat and came to the region of Magadan.

If there is one thing this story of the feeding of the 4000 tells us, it is that the works of Christ are satisfying. His provisions were not just adequate; there were leftovers, so no one went hungry. They were full. In another place, the people responded, "He has done all things well; He makes even the deaf to hear and the mute to speak" (Mark 7:37). This is reminiscent of the Queen of Sheba's reaction to seeing Solomon's wealth and hearing his wisdom: "I did not believe the reports, until I came and my eyes had seen it. And behold, the half was not told me. You exceed in wisdom and prosperity the report which I heard" (1 Kings 10:7). We today, in reading Matthew's gospel, are not even hearing half the story. For John says, "Many other signs Jesus also performed in the presence of the disciples, which are not written in this book" (John 20:30). We will spend all of eternity discovering the greatness of our Lord—and it will always satisfy! He truly is Jehovah Jireh, our Provider (Gen 22:14).

A few more contrasts are in order. In the first miraculous feeding, 5000 (plus women and children) were fed, in the second 4000 (plus women and children)—not quite as many people this second time. As was Jewish custom, crowd size was measured in terms of the number of adult males. However, the record shows a net loss of 1000—a 20 percent reduction. After the previous feeding of the 5000, Jesus intensified His teaching, saying that He Himself was the "bread of life" and that His followers must "eat His body and drink His blood" in order to have life. He was, of course, speaking figuratively, but His followers understood the level of commitment He was calling for, and "as a result of this many of His disciples withdrew and were not walking with Him anymore" (John 6:66). If Jesus had been a mere religious leader, then His challenge to the people was counterproductive. Many today would not present a challenge like this because of the potential of "losing" them. However, the loss of "numbers" was no surprise to Christ, nor did it affect His mission to preach the kingdom.

This story conveys the attitudes of gratitude, generosity, and sacrifice. It should also be noted that Jesus sent the crowd away. The miraculous was not to be expected every day. He still wants us to live out our lives responsibly.

Lord, help me not to compromise truth for outward appearances or even to emphasize largeness as the standard of success for my ministry.

Weekend Reading

Saturday – Proverbs 24
Sunday – Psalms 105–106

Personal Reflections

Reading the Signs

Matthew 16:1-4

[1] The Pharisees and Sadducees came up, and testing Jesus, they asked Him to show them a sign from heaven. [2] But He replied to them, "When it is evening, you say, 'It will be fair weather, for the sky is red.' [3] And in the morning, 'There will be a storm today, for the sky is red and threatening.' Do you know how to discern the appearance of the sky, but cannot discern the signs of the times? [4] An evil and adulterous generation seeks after a sign; and a sign will not be given it, except the sign of Jonah." And He left them and went away.

True to character, the religious leaders again attempt to corner Jesus. He had just returned from the north, having retreated there from the brewing hostilities in Israel with the Pharisees and Sadducees. Quickly finding Him, they demand miraculous proof of His spiritual credentials. Their "testing" of Jesus was designed for one purpose—to demonstrate He was a charlatan, an imposter. The test was this: someone who was truly the Messiah from God would be validated by supernatural events. If not, then the individual would prove to be fake; his words might be flowery, but ultimately they would be empty.

The irony of this is rich—if not pathetic—for in their own self-exalted wisdom, they did not know that the One they were confronting personified wisdom in the flesh. Jesus quotes to them a well-known proverb, namely the common wisdom for determining the weather forecast for a given day by observing the sky the night or morning before. He turns this proverb back on them: observe the signs you already have! Go where the evidence already leads! Jesus had been doing "signs" all along. Either the religious leaders had been blind (hardly a reasonable explanation) or they knew where the evidence led and were deliberately rejecting that conclusion. Nicodemus, himself one of them, admitted they did recognize who Jesus was: "Rabbi, we know that You have come from God as a teacher; for no one can do these signs that You do unless God is with him" (John 3:1-2).

At this point, Jesus pulled no punches. He pronounced judgment on those who still sought signs but rejected the signs already given. Only one sign remained for those who rejected the evidence of His life and ministry—the "sign of Jonah." Jesus had made this point before (12:39-40), intimating that the sign of Jonah referred to His death and resurrection. Paul affirmed this idea when he wrote, "For indeed Jews ask for signs and Greeks search for wisdom; but we preach Christ crucified, to Jews a stumbling block and to Gentiles foolishness" (1 Cor. 1:22-23).

Lord, help me not to chase after miraculous events trying to prove that You are real. You have already done enough in my life to show Your love to me.

Week 25

Day 2

On Guard Against Error

Matthew 16:5-12

5 And the disciples came to the other side of the sea, but they had forgotten to bring any bread. 6 And Jesus said to them, "Watch out and beware of the leaven of the Pharisees and Sadducees." 7 They began to discuss this among themselves, saying, "He said that because we did not bring any bread." 8 But Jesus, aware of this, said, "You men of little faith, why do you discuss among yourselves that you have no bread? 9 Do you not yet understand or remember the five loaves of the five thousand, and how many baskets full you picked up? 10 Or the seven loaves of the four thousand, and how many large baskets full you picked up? 11 How is it that you do not understand that I did not speak to you concerning bread? But beware of the leaven of the Pharisees and Sadducees." 12 Then they understood that He did not say to beware of the leaven of bread, but of the teaching of the Pharisees and Sadducees.

The stage for this incident is set by noting the disciples had forgotten to bring along food for their travels. They tended to be stuck on the tangible, physical aspects of life. By now they should have known their Master better. His normal way of teaching was to give new meaning to common words and concepts. It began with the Sermon on the Mount where He gave a grand reinterpretation of the Law. One would think that His frequent, "You have heard it said … but I say to you …" sayings would have sunk in. Today, as then, God's words are not easily understood by people of lazy faith.

Once again, the disciples' faith was on a slow learning curve compared with the faith of the Gentile centurion (8:10) and the Syrophoenician woman (15:28), both of whom Jesus commended. He expected more from His handpicked Jewish followers! He pointed out that twice He had fed a hungry multitude, and they had plenty left over. The disciples should not have had the slightest concern about their food. Had not Jesus taught them, "Do not worry then, saying, 'What will we eat?' … for your heavenly Father knows that you need all these things. But seek first His kingdom and His righteousness, and all these things will be added to you" (6:31-33).

They received their rebuke well, realizing that the leaven Jesus was warning about was the infectious, wrong teachings of the religious establishment. The warning is still relevant today. As Christians we need to be on constant watch for false teaching often hidden under the guise of dynamic preaching or large church attendance or even small, ingrown, "remnant"-focused groups.

Lord, I want to be alert for false teaching that creeps in through "Christian" broadcasting, publishing, and even the church. Help me to tell truth from lies.

Who Is Jesus, Really?

Matthew 16:13-14

[13] Now when Jesus came into the district of Caesarea Philippi, He was asking His disciples, "Who do people say that the Son of Man is?" [14] And they said, "Some say John the Baptist; and others, Elijah; but still others, Jeremiah, or one of the prophets."

The watershed moment of Jesus' training of the disciples had come. Up until this point, He had been teaching and doing many things that were clues to His identity. He had not said much in concrete terms, however. Being the Master teacher, He aimed to bring them to the point of discovery rather than teaching didactically.

The setting for this lesson was appropriate. Caesarea Philippi, about 150 miles north of Jerusalem at the northern extremity of Palestine, was so named by Herod's son Philip in honor of the reigning Caesar. It was the location of a shrine to the Greek god Pan as well. At this place, designed to honor both a pagan god and a deified Roman emperor, the Lord Jesus posed the poignant question about His identity.

In asking, "Who do people say the Son of Man is?" He was using His favorite designation for Himself (one He used thirty-one times in this gospel alone). He was not searching to "discover Himself" as though He were having an identity crisis. Nor was He checking the opinion polls, like a politician, to adjust His message for a greater following. Rather, as He had done in the feeding of the multitude, He was engaging the twelve disciples in the process of discovery.

The response of the disciples helps us understand the impact of Jesus' teaching then and helps us reflect on people's similar responses today. Some thought He was possibly John the Baptist, that he had escaped jail or even been raised from the dead (chapter 14). Many strange things had been happening since Jesus began preaching! And for many, that was a more palatable explanation of Jesus' miracles than the belief that the disciples were about to verbalize. Indeed, there was some support for that identification, for both Jesus and John preached, "The kingdom of heaven is at hand." And both preached a higher standard of morality.

Others thought Jesus was the prophet Elijah, warning the people to return Him. After all, Malachi had prophesied that Elijah would return (Mal. 4:6). Still others thought of Him as Jeremiah. Many religions today are comfortable calling Jesus a prophet. True, He *was* a prophet. But He was more, and that is precisely the conclusion to which He was bringing His disciples.

Father, help me to openly discuss Jesus with others and listen to what they believe about Him, so I can then share with them what I believe about Him.

Who Do You Think He Is?

Matthew 16:15-16

[15] He said to them, "But who do you say that I am?" [16] Simon Peter answered, "You are the Christ, the Son of the living God."

Turning to His disciples, Jesus asked the question most pivotal to everyone's spiritual journey. Nothing else matters much if we answer this question wrongly. Who do we say Jesus is? Everything hinges on that. It is foundational to all of life. Nothing can be assumed, not even with the disciples. In the OT, the question was, "Can God be trusted?" For example, when God promised Abraham that his descendants would be as numerous as the stars in the sky, the Scripture records, "Then he believed in the Lord; and He reckoned it to him as righteousness" (Gen. 15:6). The apostle Paul put it this way: "If you confess with your mouth Jesus as Lord, and believe in your heart that God raised Him from the dead, you will be saved …" (Rom. 10:9). The writer of Hebrews echoes this: "Without faith it is impossible to please Him, for he who comes to God must believe that He is and that He is a rewarder of those who seek Him" (Heb. 11:6). Faith in the God who presents Himself is central.

For the disciples, the moment of "coming out" had arrived. There is something about verbalizing a belief that crystallizes and solidifies it. To verbally communicate one's faith is like signing one's name on the dotted line, standing up and being counted. Yes, yes, I do believe. Jesus was inviting His disciples to cross the threshold. While He addressed the question to all of them, it was Peter who spoke up (though in all likelihood, his response was representative of the other eleven as well): "You are the Christ, the Son of the living God." Straightforward question, straightforward response—succinct and to the point. Jesus is the *Christ* (which, you remember, is the Greek term for the Hebrew word, *Messiah*). He was, and is, the Son of God, deity in human flesh. This statement did not mean that Jesus was less than fully divine, as some might assert. In fact, after Jesus claimed, "I and the Father are one" (John 10:30), the Jews tried to stone Him because, in their view, He was just a man making Himself out to be God (John 10:33).

Peter was sticking his neck out because calling a mere man God was punishable by death under Jewish law. It was a point of no return. No turning back now. No longer just followers of an earthly prophet, they were now committed to this man whom they believed to be God.

Lord, I believe You are Christ, the Messiah sent from God, manhood and deity combined in one individual. I trust You at the core of my being.

Peter Nailed It!

Matthew 16:17

[17] *And Jesus said to him, "Blessed are you, Simon Barjona, because flesh and blood did not reveal this to you, but My Father who is in heaven."*

Jesus affirmed Peter's confession. This often impulsive disciple answered correctly. His master, Jesus, was the Christ, the Son of the living God! Lest we give him undue credit, Peter did not figure this out by some superior intellect or reasoning ability. Rather, Jesus said this insight came through revelation. God had placed that knowledge into his mind. God had been revealing His Son all along, but few accepted that knowledge. Peter did!

This blessing reaches back to the Beatitudes in Matthew 4, where Jesus spoke eight times of blessing that depended on one's aspirations or life-faith circumstances. However, the biggest blessing is to correctly understandwho Jesus is. The word *blessed* means to be in a state of true happiness, a frame of life that supersedes all else. An illustration from the story of Nehemiah might help here. In the days of King Artexerxes, Nehemiah, the official cupbearer, approached the king in a very sad mood. He had approached the throne before but never in such a depressed disposition (Neh. 2:1-2). To do so could have incurred punishment. The idea was that any other troubles one might have should be completely eclipsed by the joyful experience of being in the king's presence.

In the same way, to have the joyful knowledge that Jesus is the Christ, the Son of the living God should completely and absolutely eclipse all else in life. It is because of this that the Beatitudes of Matthew 4 have substance and hope. We are blessed because, in Christ, the Son of God, ours "is the kingdom of heaven," we "shall be comforted," among other blessings.

A few textual notes are helpful. (1) Jesus calls Peter by his Hebrew name, *Simon*. As was sometimes the custom, people had a Greek name (in this case *Peter*) along with their Hebrew name. (2) *Barjona* comes from *bar*, which means "son of" and *Jonah*, his father's name. (3) The term *my Father* would have been an inappropriate way to refer to God in that day, the normal way being *Our* Father. Jesus uses this expression forty-four times in the gospels, implying a unique, personal relationship with God. No ordinary Jew would approach God with such familiarity. But, as the disciples came to realize, Jesus was no ordinary Jew. (4) The appeal to His Father in heaven reminds us of the Disciples' Prayer (6:9). It is from His position of governing the affairs of men that He has revealed to men the true knowledge of Jesus Christ.

My Father, thank you for causing me to be born into Your family and for adopting me as a son to be a fellow heir with the Lord Jesus, Your unique Son.

Weekend Reading

Saturday – Proverbs 25
Sunday – Psalms 107–111

Personal Reflections

Rock of Faith

Matthew 16:18 (part 1)

[18] *"I also say to you that you are Peter, and upon this rock I will build My church; and the gates of Hades will not overpower it."*

Does this verse indicate that Peter was the church's foundation and that he was given unique authority among the apostles? To both of these questions, we answer no. The name *Peter* in verse 18 comes from the Greek term *petros,* meaning "stone," whereas the term translated with the English word *rock* is *petra*—two different words. The natural understanding is that *petra* does not refer to *Peter* (*Petros*) but something else. In context, it would refer, instead, to the statement of faith Peter made in verse 16: "You are the Christ, the Son of the living God." That is the truth revealed by God, as indicated in verse 17. And that is foundational to everything else.

There is no record that the apostles themselves ever recognized Peter to have a preeminent position among them. In Galatians 2:9, Paul acknowledged James (the half-brother of Jesus), Cephas (another name for Peter), and John, equally, as "pillars" of the church at Jerusalem. Interestingly, Paul used Peter's Hebrew name, not the Greek name, *Petros.* When Paul later wrote to the Romans, the church had already been planted there, yet Paul made no mention of Peter in his letter. This would have been an extreme insult if, as the Roman church asserts today (on scant evidence), Peter founded the church there. In fact, in Galatians 2:11-13, Paul harshly rebuked Peter for hypocritical behavior. By his actions Peter was perpetrating the false doctrine that Gentiles needed to observe the Law in order to be justified before God. So Peter would be a fallible foundation for the universal church! Scripture clearly states, "No man can lay a foundation other than the one which is laid, which is Jesus Christ" (1 Cor. 3:11).

True, Ephesians 2:20 tells us the church was "built on the foundation of the apostles and prophets, Christ Jesus Himself being the cornerstone." There, the metaphor is used in a slightly different way. Jesus did not give us personally authored writings; instead, He gave His apostles perfect recall and authorized them to pass on His teachings (John 14:26; 16:13; Acts 1:8). The early church viewed apostolic teaching as foundational (Acts 2:42) precisely because it was the authorized teaching of Jesus. The foundational work was completed with the closing of the NT canon, and the church has rested on the apostolic teaching as the ultimate authority in matters of truth and faith ever since. Authority in the church is based not on an ecclesiastical, human hierarchy but on the infallible Word of God. In seminal form, that is the truth Peter confessed in Matthew 16:8.

Lord, thank you for that first articulation of faith. I too confess that You, Jesus, are the Christ, the Son of the living God.

Week 26
Day 2

The Church Will Prevail

Matthew 16:18 (part 2)

18 *"I also say to you that you are Peter, and upon this rock I will build My church; and the gates of Hades will not overpower it."*

Nowhere in Scripture do we find any indication that the apostles themselves understood Jesus' comment to mean that Peter was more important than the other apostles. Nor is there any indication at all that the role of apostleship was to continue through a process called "apostolic succession" beyond the Twelve themselves. But what we do see is the apostles leading the charge into Satan's territory, the world.

The picture in this verse is not one of the church bunkered down, pulling closed the doors of protection against the onslaught of the demonic world. Rather, Jesus foresees the church advancing into enemy territory against the very barriers of demonic influence. And the church *will* prevail because it is founded on the solid truth that "Jesus is the Christ, the Son of the living God," as Peter so aptly put it.

While Satan is the prince of the power of the air (Eph. 2:2) and the god of this age (2 Cor. 4:4), the church through the centuries has indeed made huge strides infiltrating the world system. The persecutions of Nero, for instance, did not prevail; the church only grew. By the fourth century, Christianity had become the dominant religion in the empire. The message about Christ is going out to people groups around the world, with missionaries, more than ever in history, translating, preaching, and discipling. Even in communist and Islamic countries, the message is penetrating deeply, despite severe persecution. The more the church is persecuted, the more it flourishes.

The battle continues to be waged to this very day. Yet the church's victory is not a passive one. The "Great Commission" is to go into all the world and make disciples of Christ (28:18-20; Mark 16:15). We are equipped for the spiritual battle with the armor of the Spirit (Eph. 6:10-17). We are given instructions on how to conduct the spiritual battle: "For though we walk in the flesh, we do not war according to the flesh, for the weapons of our warfare are not of the flesh, but divinely powerful for the destruction of fortresses. We are destroying speculations and every lofty thing raised up against the knowledge of God, and we are taking every thought captive to the obedience of Christ" (2 Cor. 10:3-5). No spiritual fortress will stand before the church! Above all, we must take our stand on the rock-solid truth that "Jesus is the Christ, the Son of the living God." There is no other foundation than this.

Father, thank you for revealing the Lord Jesus Christ to me. I believe that "we overwhelmingly conquer through Him who loved us" (Rom. 8:37).

Opening Doors

Matthew 16:19 (part 1)

[19] "I will give you the keys of the kingdom of heaven; and whatever you bind on earth shall have been bound in heaven, and whatever you loose on earth shall have been loosed in heaven."

We use keys to unlock and open doors. The Lord Jesus Christ Himself has "the keys of death and of Hades" (Rev. 1:18). And He uses similar and—in light of today's theological debates—controversial language as He gives Peter "the keys of the kingdom of heaven" and an ability to "bind" and "loose." What does this mean?

A basic principle for understanding the Bible is to let Scripture interpret Scripture—to let the clear passages help us understand the less clear passages. Can we find clarification for this in other passages?

After Christ's resurrection and Pentecost, we notice Peter having a time-limited prerogative to introduce the three main ethnic groups of the world (from the Jewish perspective) into the "kingdom," the community of believers. First, Peter was the primary spokesperson to the Jews at Pentecost (Acts 2:14-42), when the Holy Spirit came upon them in a distinctly phenomenal way. Peter "unlocked the door" of the kingdom for the Jews, who had, as a nation, rejected their Messiah. Second, Peter was present when the Samaritans received the Holy Spirit. The Samaritans, people of mixed Jewish and non-Jewish blood, were hated by the pure-blood Jews. The gospel message had already gone there through Philip. Although the new Samaritan believers had been baptized with water, the Holy Spirit did not fall on them until the apostle Peter (along with John) arrived (Acts 8:15-16)! This fact is not an incidental historical filler. Rather, apostolic presence validated the Samaritans' experience to be truly from God, something that would have otherwise been difficult for Jewish believers to accept. We might say that Peter was the "key agent" in unlocking the door to the Samaritans.

Acts 10 and 11 record the movement of the kingdom into Gentile lands, and Peter is again the key agent. He was "amazed that the gift of the Holy Spirit had been poured out on the Gentiles as well" (Acts 10:45). He then reported back to the church in Jerusalem. His personal witness was proof positive that the doors of the kingdom of God were open to all who believe, regardless of whether they were Jew or Gentile. There were not to be two or three different movements of God, but, rather, one unified church.

Peter fulfilled his role as the "keeper of the keys." Nowadays, anyone who comes to Christ by faith is saved and included into God's church.

Lord, thank you for opening the door to me and inviting me into Your kingdom. Please use me to help others see the open door and enter in as well.

Preserving the Message

Matthew 16:19 (part 2)

[19] *"I will give you the keys of the kingdom of heaven; and whatever you bind on earth shall have been bound in heaven, and whatever you loose on earth shall have been loosed in heaven."*

Binding and loosing was common language among first-century Jewish rabbis to refer to their interpretations of the Law. They were "binding" and "loosing" the meaning of the Scriptures. In time, the rabbinic teachings covering, roughly, 300 BC to AD 200 were written down in what is called the *Mishnah,* with further commentary in the massive and authoritative *Talmud.*

Jesus here gave His twelve disciples authority to disseminate the truth about Himself and His life after His departure. Indeed, this authority was validated on a number of fronts. After the resurrection, as recorded in Acts 1:8, Jesus authorized them this way: "You will receive power when the Holy Spirit has come upon you; and you shall be My witnesses both in Jerusalem, and in all Judea and Samaria, and even to the remotest part of the earth." In a sense this applies to all believers, but Christ was speaking first to the apostles (see Acts 1:2-7). The eleven saw the importance of the divine requirement for bringing the number back up to twelve, replacing Judas (Acts 1:16-26).

Further, at the initial formation of the church at Pentecost, "All the believers devoted themselves to the apostles' teaching." Their teachings served as the authorized recounting of Jesus' life and teachings. That is why Paul later wrote that the church is "built on the foundation of the apostles and prophets, with Christ Jesus Himself the cornerstone" (Eph. 2:20). Since the apostles could not be present everywhere as the church spread in the initial stages, God used prophets to communicate His truth. However, the ultimate arbiters of truth were the apostles, clarifying for believers which of the circulating stories and teachings were genuinely of Christ and which were not. In essence, they were "binding" and "loosing" the truth. They bore witness to what God had already determined to be truth (the Greek grammar is very specific about this in the verse).

After the apostles passed away, the immediate subsequent generations of Christians sought to preserve the authentic teachings of the apostles into an authoritative written collection, distinguishing what was genuine from what was not. The main criterion for including a document was whether it bore apostolic authority. If it did, the Christians treated it as authoritative. Today, Christians stand squarely on the foundation of Jesus Christ as reflected in the preserved teachings of the apostles, who were authorized to bind and loose the truth for us.

Father, thank you for preserving the teachings
of Your Son through the centuries.

Discreet Evangelism

Matthew 16:20

[20] Then He warned the disciples that they should tell no one that He was the Christ.

What's going on here? Weren't the disciples supposed to spread the word. Wasn't that the whole idea? As we've noted, this wasn't the only time Jesus censured the people who had significant interactions with Him. In Matthew 8:9, for example, He instructed the healed leper not to tell anyone Jesus had healed him but to go show himself to the priest (see also 9:30 and 12:16).

We find a clue in Matthew 17:9, where the Lord Jesus tells His disciples not to reveal what happened on the Mount until after the resurrection. There is a time for everything, including telling others about Jesus or particular aspects about the truth of Christ. In our passage today, Jesus had not finished training His disciples. They have come to a watershed moment, concluding the central truth of Jesus and His mission: He is the Christ, the promised Messiah, the Son of God. They didn't come by this easily, but had arrived at that conclusion without His stating it in point-blank terms. This is what we might call an inductive approach to training—one that leads them to discover for themselves the intended conclusion.

This was generally the Lord's approach to His teaching about Himself. Skeptics are quick to point out that He never claimed in unambiguous terms, "I am God." But He certainly encouraged people to come to that conclusion and never "corrected" people when they did. But if He were not God, it would have been monstrously blasphemous not to correct these assertions (John 8:53, 59; John 10:33).

Jesus was doing a bit of "time management" at this point. Things had to move forward on *His* schedule, not on the disciples' timetable. He knew the zeal and tendency of His disciples (especially Peter) to act impulsively. And He worked at containing their zeal because He knew it was not yet His "time" (John 7:6). He wanted people to arrive at the same conclusion as the disciples, and in the same way they did—by observing the signs and hearing His teachings.

Things would change after the Lord Jesus died, rose again, and left to be with His Father. That would be the time for full and open witness about His identity. At that time, and not before, they would be given not just permission but the authority to preach powerfully the message of Christ and identify fully with Him (28:18-20).

Lord, help me know when to talk freely about You to others and what to say. Also help me to be sensitive to what You are doing in their lives.

Weekend Reading

Saturday – Proverbs 26
Sunday – Psalms 112–118

Personal Reflections

Toward a Robust Faith–part 1

Matthew 16:21-23

[21] From that time Jesus began to show His disciples that He must go to Jerusalem, and suffer many things from the elders and chief priests and scribes, and be killed, and be raised up on the third day. [22] Peter took Him aside and began to rebuke Him, saying, "God forbid it, Lord! This shall never happen to You." [23] But He turned and said to Peter, "Get behind Me, Satan! You are a stumbling block to Me; for you are not setting your mind on God's interests, but man's."

The contrast does not get any sharper than the present circumstances. Peter had just been commended for his pivotal statement of faith, that Jesus was the Christ, the Son of the living God. Now Jesus rebuked Peter in the harshest possible terms. What do we make of this turnabout?

The disciples had just crossed the threshold of genuine faith in who Jesus was, and now He announced to them what seemed the absolute worst possible news. They had just taken a momentous, radical leap of faith. If they were wrong, they would have placed themselves under the curse of blasphemy, breaking the first commandment: "I am the Lord your God, You shall have no other gods before Me" (Ex. 20:2-3). Their new faith, right or wrong, carried eternal consequences.

Upon hearing of His impending death, they could take no more; the part about resurrection didn't register with them. Peter spoke up, censuring Jesus. Matthew, the inspired author, uses the word "rebuked." This death talk was not what Peter and the others had in mind when they confessed faith in Jesus as the Christ. They, along with most Jews, expected the Messiah to bring Israel into prominence over all the nations. That couldn't happen if Jesus died. Surely He must be wrong!

Peter says, "No, Lord." Peter would make sure it wouldn't happen! Loyalty personified, but misdirected. Peter was acting on human impulses. We human beings find it difficult to bring actions and attitudes in line with the implications of our faith. It takes time to learn to say, "Yes, Lord," to the seeming incongruities in our lives.

But what to us looks like contradictions are simply means for God to show His greatness. The disciples were now ready to be taken deeper in their faith, new as it was. Their childlike trust needed to become more robust. Jesus' harsh words established, early on, in the strongest possible terms, that to resist Christ is to side with the workings of Satan.

Lord, help me become more robust in my faith and not to abandon Your lordship when things seem contradictory.

Week 27
Day 2

Toward a Robust Faith–part 2

Matthew 16:21-23

[21] From that time Jesus began to show His disciples that He must go to Jerusalem, and suffer many things from the elders and chief priests and scribes, and be killed, and be raised up on the third day. [22] Peter took Him aside and began to rebuke Him, saying, "God forbid it, Lord! This shall never happen to You." [23] But He turned and said to Peter, "Get behind Me, Satan! You are a stumbling block to Me; for you are not setting your mind on God's interests, but man's."

Peter plays into Satan's hands—but not beyond the Lord's notice. At one level, we could assume Jesus is using a combination of metaphor and hyperbole, likening Peter to Satan as an extreme way to impress upon Peter and the other disciples the gravity of his actions. A man who has just declared faith in Jesus as the Christ, the Son of the living God should know better than to rebuke that same Jesus. The audacity of saying no to the Lord exceeds credibility. What an immediate turnaround!

At another level, the misunderstanding of the purposes of Jesus is stark. It is as though the only conclusion Peter could draw from Jesus' prediction of His death is that it would somehow signify God's displeasure and rejection of Him. To the Jews of that day, misfortune implied the judgment of God. Therefore, if it was true that Jesus was going to die, Peter's words would have been very appropriate. Literally, the words translated here, "God forbid it," could be rendered, "May there be mercy to you!" (See Hebrews 8:12 for a similar use of this word.) But Peter would have none of that; Jesus was not going to die.

The Lord gives the reason for His rebuke of Peter: a confusion of loyalty. Peter still had a prior loyalty to the human perspective. As such, he became a hindrance (stumbling block). Earlier (13:41-42), Jesus had indicated that stumbling blocks would be removed from the kingdom. Peter's actions were no light matter!

However, the reference to Satan takes on deeper significance. From the beginning the archenemy of Christ has been resisting the plan of God: the evil plan of Herod, the killing of the babies in Bethlehem, the temptation of Jesus in the desert. It should not surprise us that just when the disciples had come to recognize who Jesus really was (or, in the words of John 1:12, had "received Him") that the enemy would come to test that recognition and snatch away their fresh insight. Jesus' challenge to them showed the importance of what they now understood.

Lord, I believe in You. Thank you for Your rebukes; they keep me on track with Your plan and purposes. I don't want to side with Your enemy.

Surrendering All

Matthew 16:24

[24] Then Jesus said to His disciples, "If anyone wishes to come after Me, he must deny himself, and take up his cross and follow Me."

Watersheds provide the major pathways for water flowing down from mountains. The US Continental Divide is the ultimate watershed of North America; that rocky line divides rainwater runoff which ends up in the Pacific Ocean versus that which finds its way to the Atlantic. So also Matthew 16:13-26 provides the ultimate spiritual watershed of eternal proportions. The disciples have moved from being simply hearers of Jesus to being fully committed to Christ and His purpose. Other places in the Bible describe this divide as those who have spiritual life versus those who are spiritually dead, sons of the light versus sons of the darkness.

The disciples had proclaimed, in the words of Peter, "You are the Christ, the Son of the living God." They received their sobering rebuke, directed to the person of Peter, "Get behind me, Satan," for being at cross-purposes with Jesus. Now, springboarding on their statement of faith and that terse lesson of loyalty, they were ready for the core principle of discipleship.

Self-denial—ceasing to follow one's own natural inclinations and self-centeredness—is the only true way to follow Christ. Genesis 3:5-6 signaled this as the earthly struggle of humankind when Eve (along with Adam) took the fruit, thinking it would make them like God and therefore able to become independent of God. The concept is captured in Proverbs 14:12, "There is a way which seems right to a man, but its end is the way of death." Jeremiah 17:9 captures the stark reality: "The heart is more deceitful than all else and is desperately sick; who can understand it?"

To follow Christ means to diametrically oppose our innate core of rebellion against God. Jesus describes it as a denial of oneself. Like a condemned man who expresses his final submission to Rome in carrying his own instrument of crucifixion, disciples are those believers who willingly submit to Christ as Lord and Master, even to death. This only has meaning for those who have first come to Christ in faith.

"All to Jesus, I surrender, all to Him I freely give, I would ever love and trust Him, in His presence daily live... All to Thee, my blessed Savior; I surrender all." –Judson W. Van DeVenter

Losing to Gain

Matthew 16:25-26

[25] *"For whoever wishes to save his life will lose it; but whoever loses his life for My sake will find it.* [26] *For what will it profit a man if he gains the whole world and forfeits his soul? Or what will a man give in exchange for his soul?"*

Continuing the core principle of discipleship, Jesus presents the ultimate irony of life, the supreme paradox. He lays before them a truth that is completely incomprehensible to all but those who genuinely believe and trust in Him. This teaching, once embraced, is similar to what science hypothetically calls a wormhole between alternate universes. When a believer in Christ comes to grips with the Lord's teaching here, he is transformed. He has an entirely new way of looking at the world and of behaving in the world because he now actively lives in the "new to him" reality of submitting to the King and living out kingdom-of-heaven principles on earth.

The principle is simple in statement, but profound in application: To save one's life, one must lose it. The complementary truth is that if one loses his life for Jesus' sake, then he will, in fact, find it. Our contemporary world, ironically, has popularized the notion that individuals must find themselves. This is nothing new. Adam and Eve attempted that same thing in the garden, at Satan's behest. The serpent essentially said, "Go ahead and find yourself—apart from God. Before you can relate to the creator deity, you first must discover who *you* are." Such thinking places oneself above God—or at least equal to God—and leads to destruction. The Bible says it brings death—loss of who God made us to be.

Jesus, in this passage, says that the only way to live as God intended is to live for God, as revealed in Jesus, and *not* for oneself. What advantage is there if a person gets everything he desires here if it ultimately costs him his very own soul, the image of God placed in him? That would mean exchanging the most important thing for everything else—altogether worth far less.

Incessant messages constantly bombard us, urging us to live for ourselves. Even Christians sometimes slip into this superficial thinking. The psalmist struggled as well: "As for me, my feet came close to stumbling, my steps had almost slipped. For I was envious of the arrogant as I saw the prosperity of the wicked … until," he concludes, "I came into the sanctuary of God; then I perceived their end. Surely You set them in slippery places" (Ps. 73:2-3, 17-18).

Lord, I confess my self-centered tendencies. Help me continually find my life in You, seeking to live only for You and Your purposes for me.

The Son of Man Coming

Matthew 16:27-28

[27] "For the Son of Man is going to come in the glory of His Father with His angels, and WILL THEN REPAY EVERY MAN ACCORDING TO HIS DEEDS. *[28] Truly I say to you, there are some of those who are standing here who will not taste death until they see the Son of Man coming in His kingdom."*

Mark began his gospel account with "Jesus, the Son of God." Luke presented the angel announcing that "the holy Child shall be called the Son of God" (1:38). John's gospel account introduced John the Baptist saying, "I myself have seen, and have testified that this is the Son of God" (1:34), and Nathanael confessed, "You are the Son of God" (John 1:49). And, of course, in John 3:16 Jesus referred to Himself saying, "Whoever believes in [the Son] will not perish but have everlasting life." Yet in Matthew's gospel, Christ never referred to Himself as the "Son of God," preferring the alternate designation, *Son of Man.*

In Matthew's gospel, the description "Son of God" was used by others, namely Satan (4:3), the demons (8:29), the high priest (26:63), mockers (27:40), accusers (27:43), a centurion at the cross (27:54), and finally in the supreme confession of faith by the disciples (16:16). This is all in keeping with Matthew's purpose in writing, namely, leading the reader along inductively to reach the same logical conclusion the disciples did regarding who Jesus is, rather than Jesus' coming right out and saying it.

The use of *Son of Man* thirty-one times in Matthew emphasizes Jesus' humanity. But when used as a title, it would invoke in the Jews' minds the prophecy of Daniel: "I kept looking in the night visions, and behold, with the clouds of heaven One like a Son of Man was coming, and He came up to the Ancient of Days and was presented before Him" (Dan. 7:13). Jesus had already touched on the idea of the Son of Man returning (10:23) and was going to say more about it in chapters 24 and 25. The Son of Man will come to mete out God's justice, as appropriate, to each offense.

Jesus was now proclaiming that the return of the Son of Man, Christ Himself, was something they should anticipate within their own lifespan. This may have fueled their anticipation of the imminent political takeover so many were hoping for. As events unfolded, however, it would soon become clear that Jesus was referring to something else.

---

*Lord, while I look forward to Your return in glory, help me,
while waiting, to live my life here for Your glory.*

Weekend Reading

Saturday – Proverbs 1

Sunday – Psalms 119

Personal Reflections

A Morphed Moment

Matthew 17:1-2

[1] *Six days later Jesus took with Him Peter and James and John his brother, and led them up on a high mountain by themselves.* [2] *And He was transfigured before them; and His face shone like the sun, and His garments became as white as light.*

The six days must have been unbearable for the disciples. Ringing in their ears was the whirlwind sequence of events that boggled their minds. Following their huge expression of faith, they were hit with Jesus' prediction of His suffering and death, their first Satan-inspired failure, and the ramifications of what they had really gotten themselves into—a call to personal self-denial. They had six days to process this. (Luke's account indicates *eight* days elapsed, but this is not problematic. In the ancient world, different methods of counting time were used. Matthew was counting whole days, whereas Luke was most likely including partial days. Thus, from the first day to the last would have included two partial days plus the six intervening whole days.)

The event which then began to unfold in the gospel account would be a welcome "specimen" of the kingdom, a foretaste of infinitely better things to come. The call to discipleship would be so difficult that His disciples required supernatural motivation, and that motivation came in a vision of Christ glorified. Scripture encourages us to join the disciples in perceiving Jesus by faith. The writer of Hebrews, for example, exhorts us to "consider Him" and to "fix our eyes on Him" (Heb. 3:1, 12:1).

Jesus took along what has been called the inner circle: Peter, James, and John. Why just these three were included is left to conjecture. James was martyred in the early years of the church, and Peter and John became prominent in the early church. The venue for this event was a high mountain, away from the crowds and other disciples.

The Greek word used to describe what happened to Jesus is the word from which our English word *metamorphosis* comes. He was changed, similar to the way a caterpillar morphs into a butterfly. Just as the essence of the butterfly was contained in the caterpillar, so the essence of Christ's true nature was temporarily contained in a human body. The day would come—upon His resurrection from the dead and ascension back to His Father—when Christ morphed back into His full glory. (Paul captured this image in Philippians 2:6-11.) On the mountain, for an instant, the disciples caught a glimpse, a sneak preview, of that glory manifested.

Lord, when life gets hard, I want the proof of my faith "to be found to result in praise and glory and honor" when You are revealed (1 Pet. 1:7).

Week 28
Day 2

Heed Before You Proceed

Matthew 17:3-5

[3] *And behold, Moses and Elijah appeared to them, talking with Him.* [4] *Peter said to Jesus, "Lord, it is good for us to be here; if You wish, I will make three tabernacles here, one for You, and one for Moses, and one for Elijah."* [5] *While he was still speaking, a bright cloud overshadowed them, and behold, a voice out of the cloud said, "This is My beloved Son, with whom I am well-pleased; listen to Him!"*

The appearance of Moses with Jesus on the mountain brings to mind the time when Yahweh spoke to Moses on Mt. Sinai, covered with a thick cloud (Ex. 19:9). Suffice it to say, this vision of Christ in glory speaking with both the great Lawgiver and the great reformer of Israel's history signaled that God was about to embark on a new dispensation of dealing with His people. Its importance would rival—or surpass—God's giving of the Law and of God's calling His people back to the Law. This image of Christ reflects the OT imagery of God's presence in a cloud (for example, when His "presence," which the Jews called His *shekinah* glory, entered the tabernacle).

The voice from the cloud was clearly God the Father's. Notice that He did *not* say, "Listen to Moses and the Law"; any such reinforcement of the Law would only have prompted the people to work harder at being holy. Nor did He say, "Listen to Elijah, the prophet of warning and judgment." Jesus would clarify shortly that John the Baptist had completed that role. Rather, God focused on Jesus, and we learn much about the Father's thoughts about His Son in this short sentence.

First, God had something to say: "Listen to Jesus!" The rebuke to Peter is obvious, for he had other ideas about what needed to be done. The disciples needed to get a grip on the fact that instruction must come before action. It is better for one to heed before one proceeds (see 1 Samuel 15:22). This was a difficult lesson for Peter to learn.

God affirmed the conclusion the disciples had already arrived at based on the evidence: "This is My Son." The vision confirmed their faith. Further, the Father expressed His love and pleasure in His Son. If any of those three men had witnessed John baptizing Jesus, they would have heard a similar statement (3:17) and were now in a better position to appreciate its significance. As noted before, in that day, people believed that suffering meant a person was under God's judgment. Now, despite Jesus' prediction of His own death, God made it clear to them that Jesus was *not* under God's judgment. To the contrary, God was greatly pleased with Him!

Father, as You are pleased with Your "beloved Son," so too I am pleased with Him. What a wonderful Lord and Savior He is. I give You all my praise.

Praise God for Peter!

Matthew 17:6-9

[6] When the disciples heard this, they fell face down to the ground and were terrified.
[7] And Jesus came to them and touched them and said, "Get up, and do not be
afraid." [8] And lifting up their eyes, they saw no one except Jesus Himself alone.
[9] As they were coming down from the mountain, Jesus commanded them, saying,
"Tell the vision to no one until the Son of Man has risen from the dead."

Despite what should have given them tremendous hope, the disciples were engulfed with fear at the supernatural vision of Christ, Moses, and Elijah. The impact of this overwhelming experience had an enduring effect, seen in Peter's epistle, years later: "For we did not follow cleverly devised tales when we made known to you the power and coming of our Lord Jesus Christ, but we were eyewitnesses of His majesty. For when He received honor and glory from God the Father, such an utterance as this was made to Him by the Majestic Glory, 'This is My beloved Son with whom I am well-pleased'—and we ourselves heard this utterance made from heaven when we were with Him on the holy mountain" (2 Pet. 1:16-18).

Unless one is prepared to call Peter an outright liar, this provides evidence of the highest order of the character and ministry of Jesus. It would be extremely difficult to substantiate that all the disciples perjured themselves in giving false witness about Christ when, in fact, they were willing to suffer and be killed because of their belief that Jesus was the Christ, the Son of God. To claim they "mis-remembered" would be ludicrous in light of the consistency and early date of their testimonies. To say they were simply mistaken about such a serious thing would be to minimize, beyond credibility, the intelligence of these otherwise normal individuals, given the global movement they spawned. Finally, to infer they were deluded would mean that all who have subsequently believed their message were likewise deluded. That's hardly likely in view of the great minds that have embraced the apostolic teachings through the years.

Jesus told them to keep this event secret until after the resurrection. And they did. But after His ascension they did not fear to proclaim it widely. Today, we do not have living eyewitnesses, but we have the next best thing: the written, personal testimonies of eyewitnesses. Jesus planned for this when He commissioned the apostles, "You shall be My witnesses both in Jerusalem, and in all Judea and Samaria, and even to the remotest part of the earth" (Acts 1:8).

Lord, thank you for the faithful witness of the apostles and for all those through the ages who preserved their testimony for us today.

A Rejected Elijah

Matthew 17:10-13

[10] And His disciples asked Him, "Why then do the scribes say that Elijah must come first?" [11] And He answered and said, "Elijah is coming and will restore all things; [12] but I say to you that Elijah already came, and they did not recognize him, but did to him whatever they wished. So also the Son of Man is going to suffer at their hands." [13] Then the disciples understood that He had spoken to them about John the Baptist.

Completely missing the import of Jesus' prophecy of His resurrection, the disciples followed the Jewish thinking of the day that Messiah's coming would lead to the end times. Although there was much debate among various factions about the details, the Jews generally agreed that the next event anticipated by the OT prophets was the restoration of the kingdom to its rightful place as foremost among the nations. Before that, as the disciples pointed out, the scribes taught that Elijah must first come to restore everything (Mal. 4:5).

The appearance of Elijah along with Jesus and Moses would naturally play into that thinking. Some have suggested that Peter's idea of building tents (tabernacles) for the three reflects anticipation of the Feast of Tabernacles (or Booths) in Zechariah 14, which would presumably take place at the advent of kingdom restoration. Plainly put, Peter was confused, as he was later with some of the difficult teachings of the apostle Paul (2 Pet. 3:15-16). The perplexity is somewhat understandable because Elijah's brief appearance on the mountaintop could hardly be considered the ultimate fulfillment of the prophecy.

The Lord graced Peter with a gentle but firm response to his question. The fulfillment of the prophecy was to be found in John the Baptist, rather than the physical return of Elijah—at least for the present time. John was not a reincarnation of Elijah. Rather, Elijah was a picture, so to speak, pointing to or prefiguring the Baptist. God sent John to prepare the people for their Messiah by calling them to repentance. He fulfilled Malachi's prophecy in proclaiming the coming of the Christ.

Prophecy today is subject to many wild interpretations and bold predictions of specific fulfillments applied to contemporary events, often related to the Middle East. Such things make for exciting (if misguided) preaching. Prophecies were not given for our enjoyment but simply to challenge us to ready ourselves for the return of Christ.

Lord, help me to not have a morbid curiosity for minute details about prophecy. Rather, challenge me to love holiness and good deeds as I await Your return.

Driven to the Top

Matthew 17:14-18

[14] When they came to the crowd, a man came up to Jesus, falling on his knees before Him and saying, [15] "Lord, have mercy on my son, for he is a lunatic and is very ill; for he often falls into the fire and often into the water. [16] I brought him to Your disciples, and they could not cure him." [17] And Jesus answered and said, "You unbelieving and perverted generation, how long shall I be with you? How long shall I put up with you? Bring him here to Me." [18] And Jesus rebuked him, and the demon came out of him, and the boy was cured at once.

Having come down from their "mountaintop experience," Jesus, along with Peter, James, and John, reentered a trouble-filled, fallen world. We don't know what the other nine disciples were doing meanwhile, but we do know they had failed at an exorcism attempt, which precipitated this present account.

A man came to Jesus, pleading for mercy for his mentally deranged son. We note some pertinent features of the incident. First, the call for mercy revealed again the faulty belief that bad things happen to people because of their sin. Such was the premise of Job's "friends" in the OT account. Job's story, however, argues that not all suffering can be traced back to sin.

Second, nothing can be more heart-rending than a man pleading for his child. What parent hasn't repeatedly begged the Lord for his children as they go through the pains of living in a fallen world?

Third, all other issues of Jesus' identity aside, all that mattered was the father's hope that Christ could heal.

Fourth, the limitations of Christ's followers did not deter this father. He was not like some people today who slow down or abandon their quest to follow Christ because of the shortcomings of other Christ-followers. This man's need "drove him to the top"; nothing would stop him.

Despite all this, Jesus' responded in exasperation. In the end, we must remember, Jesus did heal the boy. But He also saw this as an example of people coming to Him only for His miracles and not following the evidence to where it leads—that Jesus is the Christ, the Son of the living God. This man didn't display *that* kind of attitude. So we can understand Jesus' response when we compare this fellow's action alongside the disciples' confession of faith. Yet the Lord's care for people, despite their ignorance or lack of faith, trumped His exasperation. He later demonstrated this patience and compassion on the cross when He prayed, "Father, forgive them, they don't know what they are doing."

Lord, I am so glad You care for me and my family's needs, but You are much more than that to me. I want to follow You more closely, day by day.

Weekend Reading

Saturday – Proverbs 2
Sunday – Psalms 120–130

Personal Reflections

A Certain Kind of Faith

Matthew 17:19-21

[19] Then the disciples came to Jesus privately and said, "Why could we not drive it out?" [20] And He said to them, "Because of the littleness of your faith; for truly I say to you, if you have faith the size of a mustard seed, you will say to this mountain, 'Move from here to there,' and it will move; and nothing will be impossible to you. [21] [But this kind does not go out except by prayer and fasting."]

The story of the young boy's healing raised two issues. First, as we saw in the previous meditation, it showed the unbelief of the general populace. Second, it showed the limitations of the disciples' faith, giving rise to Jesus' fundamental instruction that what matters is not the *size* or amount of one's faith but its *quality!* He taught this in a most memorable way by comparing their faith to a mustard seed, the smallest of the cultivable seeds at that time. If their faith were *that* size, it would be greater than what they had then. Yet that would still be small faith. In other words, the "littleness" of their faith was, in reality, no faith at all. It didn't even measure up to "small" faith.

In the parallel passage to this story (Mark 9:24), the father of the boy said, "I do believe, help my unbelief." So the point was not the *amount* of belief we have because we either have it or we don't. We may believe God for one thing but not another. With faith of any size there is no limit to what can be accomplished. (The concept of moving mountains was a proverbial expression in that day for doing great things.)

We need to note that Bible versions differ regarding the inclusion of verse 21, about the need for prayer and fasting in order to perform exorcisms (see the brackets placed around this phrase in the NASB above; see also 18:11). The reason for this is that most of the earliest Greek manuscripts do not contain this verse, but later manuscripts do. Scholars are divided, therefore, on whether the verse is authentic or was inserted by a copyist at some point. However, Mark 9:29 *does* contain the notion of the need for prayer and fasting, so the *concept* is authentic.

To the point, what was needed to move the mountain in question—the plight of this demon-possessed boy? Not *more* faith, but a certain kind of faith—a "prayer and fasting" kind of faith. Little faith accompanied by prayer and fasting can accomplish great things!

Lord, I do believe You in many areas of my life and have seen You do great things. But, in the thing I am facing today, "Help my unbelief."

Grief Unbearable

Matthew 17:22-23

[22] And while they were gathering together in Galilee, Jesus said to them, "The Son of Man is going to be delivered into the hands of men; [23] and they will kill Him, and He will be raised on the third day." And they were deeply grieved.

Regrouping with His disciples back in Galilee, His ministry staging area, Jesus continued preparing them for their advance into the neighboring province of Judea, and the city of Jerusalem in particular. He spoke of His betrayal, execution, and resurrection—events which were not just inevitable but part of the divine plan all along (see Acts 2:22-24). His words here were much the same as those He spoke earlier in Matthew 16:21, after Peter resisted with his famous "No, Lord," oxymoron. Now, however, Peter's resistance is replaced with extreme grief.

Matthew uses the Greek word for *grieved* here that he later uses to describe the disciples' reaction when Jesus revealed that one of them was a traitor. Each grieved that Jesus might think he was the one (26:22). The Lord used this same word to describe Himself during His struggle in the garden of Gethsemane, "My soul is deeply grieved, to the point of death" (26:38).

Strong words to convey strong feelings. Although further resistance would still come, the disciples' response to this information was more in line with Jesus' feelings. They were beginning to share in Christ's suffering, ultimately the precursor to the hope of resurrection. Indeed, this became an important theme in the apostles' ministry. Peter probably remembered well this experience when he wrote to his scattered readers, "To the degree that you share the sufferings of Christ, keep on rejoicing, so that also at the revelation of His glory you may rejoice with exultation" (1 Pet. 4:13). The memory of both the vision on the Mount of Transfiguration and Jesus' postresurrection appearances left an exciting hope Peter wanted to pass on to others.

Paul intimates a similar thought, "For just as the sufferings of Christ are ours in abundance, so also our comfort is abundant through Christ" (2 Cor. 1:5). This hope eclipses all suffering here on earth. "For momentary, light affliction is producing for us an eternal weight of glory far beyond all comparison" (2 Cor. 4:17). Paul so embraced this concept that he desired to " know Him and the power of His resurrection and the fellowship of His sufferings, being conformed to His death" (Phil. 3:10). One wonders if Paul's reference to being "untimely born" (1 Cor. 15:8) included missing out on the immediate sharing of Christ's sufferings while He went through them.

Lord, help me to not only accept the difficulties You have allowed in my life but to embrace them as opportunities to share in Your suffering.

Week 29
Day 3

Hooking a Tax Payment

Matthew 17:24-27

24 When they came to Capernaum, those who collected the two-drachma tax came to Peter and said, "Does your teacher not pay the two-drachma tax?" 25 He said, "Yes." And when he came into the house, Jesus spoke to him first, saying, "What do you think, Simon? From whom do the kings of the earth collect customs or poll-tax, from their sons or from strangers?" 26 When Peter said, "From strangers," Jesus said to him, "Then the sons are exempt. 27 "However, so that we do not offend them, go to the sea and throw in a hook, and take the first fish that comes up; and when you open its mouth, you will find a shekel. Take that and give it to them for you and Me."

Taxation is a permanent fixture in most civilizations, facilitating entire communities to fund those services which benefit all. The two-drachma tax was roughly equivalent to two denarii, typically two-days' wages for a common worker. It was exacted from all men twenty years and older to help maintain the temple in Jerusalem. The temple tax collector questioned Peter about whether Jesus was going to pay the tax. When they were in the house, Jesus discussed this with Peter. He wanted Peter to understand why He was going to pay it—and how.

The question at issue could have been framed this way: "Does this man Jesus support the Jewish religious system?" Certainly He had done much to raise the ire of the religious establishment and to incite the hopes of the populace. The question naturally arose about whether the temple, the great icon of the Jewish religion, was to be maintained. Early in His public ministry He had been understood (incorrectly) to predict that the temple would one day be torn down and replaced (John 2:19-22). So to the religious leaders, His attitude toward the temple must have appeared ambiguous.

As for the "why," Jesus spoke by way of analogy. Earthly kings do not tax their own children, those of royal blood. (Here He used the terms *customs* or *poll-tax,* which was exacted by Roman overlords and was thus a civil tax.) As Jesus was the Son God, He was exempt from taxation for the maintenance of His Father's house, the temple. The logic seemed straightforward. But not desiring to cause offense, Jesus ceded His privilege. And He provided the money in a miraculous but discreet way appropriate in this city, where people had previously rejected Him.

It should be obvious to even the casual observer that Jesus lived an austere life (2 Cor. 8:9); He never took money for "services rendered." He lived off the charitable gifts of a few (Luke 8:3). So He did not even have two days' wages to give. He dedicated His life and His death for others.

Father, let me have the attitude "which was also in Christ Jesus" (Phil. 2:5), that I might be humble, ceding my rights, so as not to offend others.

Week 29
Day 4

Emulating Humility

Matthew 18:1-6

1 At that time the disciples came to Jesus and said, "Who then is greatest in the
kingdom of heaven?" 2 And He called a child to Himself and set him before them,
3 and said, "Truly I say to you, unless you are converted and become like children,
you will not enter the kingdom of heaven. 4 Whoever then humbles himself as this
child, he is the greatest in the kingdom of heaven. 5 And whoever receives one such
child in My name receives Me; 6 but whoever causes one of these little ones who
believe in Me to stumble, it would be better for him to have a heavy millstone hung
around his neck, and to be drowned in the depth of the sea."

Pride of position dogged the disciples just as it so does Christians today. Title, rank, and privilege infiltrate the church when those God raises up to shepherd the local church transform the description of a spiritual gift into a title, such as *pastor* or *senior pastor*, thus propagating a superior rank of clergy among God's people. A far more appropriate (and higher) title of *brother,* which we all are privileged to own, is more suitable.

After having personally walked with the Master for so long, the disciples somewhat surprisingly entertained suspicious thoughts. How tenaciously the sinful nature of fallen humanity grips the soul! This was no time for a soft response from Jesus. If a person desired greatness, Jesus said, the pathway unavoidably traverses the realm of humility. This is the great paradox of discipleship, similar to the challenge Jesus laid on them earlier: "For whoever wishes to save his life will lose it; but whoever loses his life for My sake will find it" (16:25). Hard concepts require reinforcement!

First, entry into the kingdom of heaven requires that one become like a child—hardly a good starting point for ambitious position seekers. The visual illustration of standing an actual child before them was evocative. He began his teaching with "Truly I say to you," which was by then a familiar introduction giving weight to His teaching. He went on to say that childlike humbleness was not just for entry into the kingdom, but also for greatness in the kingdom.

On one level Jesus was speaking about valuing actual children. However, in context He seems also to be thinking about how we treat those who become *like* children in their humble attitude. Whoever receives one of them, also receives Christ. Therefore Jesus taught the disciples not only to avoid personal pride of position but also not to look down on those who emulate a humble childlike attitude. The consequences of rejecting this truth are great!

Lord, pride clings so easily to my soul. I come to You for You are "gentle and humble" and Your "yoke is easy" and Your "burden is light" (10:29-30).

Woe, I say, Woe!

Matthew 18:7-10

7 "Woe to the world because of its stumbling blocks! For it is inevitable that stumbling blocks come; but woe to that man through whom the stumbling block comes! 8 If your hand or your foot causes you to stumble, cut it off and throw it from you; it is better for you to enter life crippled or lame, than to have two hands or two feet and be cast into the eternal fire. 9 If your eye causes you to stumble, pluck it out and throw it from you. It is better for you to enter life with one eye, than to have two eyes and be cast into the fiery hell. 10 See that you do not despise one of these little ones, for I say to you that their angels in heaven continually see the face of My Father who is in heaven."

Continuing His warnings, Jesus adds force by starting with the word "woe." His teaching here is not to be trifled with! Further, His warning comes in a highly descriptive form, using a figure of speech called a *metonymy*: one thing used in the place of another. For example, when the psalmist wrote, "My lips shall praise you," he used the *lips* (the instrument of communication) in place of the person himself. This adds emphasis and color to the point being made. Similarly, Jesus used *feet* as a metonymy in place of the inner person who controls the feet. "But each one is tempted when he is carried away and enticed by his own lust. Then when lust has conceived, it gives birth to sin; and when sin is accomplished, it brings forth death" (James 1:14-15). So Jesus uses feet, hands, and eyes as metonymies as a dramatic way to refer to the person himself.

The terseness of His warning also comes through via His use of *hyperbole,* a rhetorical device that uses exaggeration to emphasize a point. The exaggeration in this case is to amputate any body part that causes us to stumble. The consequences are serious! Today we might apply His teaching this way: if using the Internet/TV/magazines causes a person to sin, he would do well to eliminate such things from his life altogether.

This message must have amazed Jesus' listeners, In the spiritual economics of Jesus, such maiming would actually be a good thing because it would avoid (in this hyperbolic way) God's judgment!

Coming full circle, Jesus added a final motivation for not stumbling children: they have a vital relationship with God. Jesus said children have a personal, angelic representative in the very presence of God. They have real souls, and to mess with them is to mess with God!

Lord, help me to be clear about the real priorities of life that come from a close walk with You and not to live by popular religious notions.

Weekend Reading

Saturday – Proverbs 3
Sunday – Psalms 131–136

Personal Reflections

The Thrill of the Find

Matthew 18:11-14

[11] ["For the Son of Man has come to save that which was lost.] [12] What do you think? If any man has a hundred sheep, and one of them has gone astray, does he not leave the ninety-nine on the mountains and go and search for the one that is straying? [13] If it turns out that he finds it, truly I say to you, he rejoices over it more than over the ninety-nine which have not gone astray. [14] So it is not the will of your Father who is in heaven that one of these little ones perish."

How precious are lost souls in Jesus' thoughts! This was a common theme in His ministry—and rightly so. The whole point of His coming was to reconcile us to our Creator God. Scholars debate the authenticity of verse 11 (17:21 also). The issue has nothing to do with the inerrancy of the Bible. Rather, it recognizes that some of the oldest Greek manuscripts do not include this verse though others (the preponderance of later ones) do include it. Discussing the relative merits of this issue goes beyond the scope of this devotional book. However, it is a moot point because the parallel passage in Luke 19:10 contains this verse, and no one disputes *its* genuineness. The purpose of Christ's coming was to "save that which was lost"!

Jesus pictures His mission as being like a sheep farmer who leaves his entire herd to go looking for one lost sheep. Some question the wisdom of leaving the vast majority untended, vulnerable and exposed, for the sake of recovering one. A key principle for interpreting parables, though, is to focus on the main point and not the incidentals. In Jesus' eyes, an individual is lost, and His concern for the masses extends only as far as His concern for the individuals who make up the masses. Because of this, we speak today of having a "personal relationship" with Christ and "individual salvation." The Lord seeks a personal connection with each of His creations, for we are all made in His image. No one lies outside the reach of His compassion.

Additionally, God's desire to save excludes no one. Peter made this point: "The Lord is not slow about His promise, as some count slowness, but is patient toward you, not wishing for any to perish but for all to come to repentance" (2 Pet. 3:9).

God is thrilled to save lost souls, for when each one "is found" and returns to his Creator, the Lord's emotional reaction can only be described as "joy." This is what the writer of Hebrews is getting at when he says, "Jesus … for the joy set before Him endured the cross, despising the shame …" (Heb. 12:2).

Lord, I am overwhelmed that You, the Creator of the universe, actually desire a relationship with me as though I were the only one!

Week 30
Day 2

A Primer on Conflict Resolution

Matthew 18:15-20

15 "If your brother sins, go and show him his fault in private; if he listens to you, you
have won your brother. 16 But if he does not listen to you, take one or two more with
you, so that BY THE MOUTH OF TWO OR THREE WITNESSES EVERY FACT MAY BE CONFIRMED.
17 If he refuses to listen to them, tell it to the church; and if he refuses to listen even
to the church, let him be to you as a Gentile and a tax collector. 18 Truly I say to
you, whatever you bind on earth shall have been bound in heaven; and whatever
you loose on earth shall have been loosed in heaven. 19 Again I say to you, that if
two of you agree on earth about anything that they may ask, it shall be done for
them by My Father who is in heaven. 20 For where two or three have gathered together
in My name, I am there in their midst."

"Conflict resolution" was paramount in Jesus' purpose of coming. The angels announced at His birth, "Peace on earth, good will toward men" (Luke 2:14)—peace with God, certainly, but also peace among men. Jesus presents a simple three-step outline for dealing with interpersonal issues. Speaking directly ("you"), He personalizes this teaching to apply to anyone who will hear Him.

Step one: go privately to the one who has sinned against you. Untold damage results when people ignore this and resort to gossip, innuendo, or passive-aggressive behavior. It takes courage to do what Jesus says here. Dysfunction is always easier in the short term, but it is disastrous down the road. It is not Christlike to simply ignore all offenses as though that were love. Honesty must prevail where relationships are concerned. Open and honest dialogue clears the way for communication and reconciliation.

Second, if step one does not work, take along one or two "witnesses." This may assume the "rightness" of your case, but godly and impartial witnesses can help mediate and resolve the issue. This may result in confession of sin (by either or both parties) and bring about reconciliation.

Finally, if the other person refuses to be reconciled, the issue should be brought to the church (literally, the "gathering" of God's people). This shock treatment ought to make the person realize that his sin affects the whole church and restoration is needed. If there is still no repentance, he is to be put out of the fellowship and treated as an outsider.

Much more is said about conflict resolution in Scripture (e.g. Luke 17:3; Gal. 6:1, 2 Thess. 3:15; James 5:19). Suffice it to say here that, as Jesus conveys, these matters carry divine authority when done by two or three acting genuinely in Christ's name and on His behalf (see also Matthew 16:19).

Lord, I confess how rarely I obey Your instruction here. Show me (remind me of) those relationships that have been breached and I will work for reconciliation.

A Forgiving Spirit

Matthew 18:21-22

[21] Then Peter came and said to Him, "Lord, how often shall my brother sin against me and I forgive him? Up to seven times?" [22] Jesus said to him, "I do not say to you, up to seven times, but up to seventy times seven."

Appropriately, building on His teaching about confronting or rebuking a sinning brother (and winning him back), Jesus exhorts His disciples to forgive lavishly. I say "appropriately" not because Jesus needs my endorsement but because this sequence of teaching reflects the overall mission of Christ: sin must be dealt with, but forgiveness is the goal. Where sin abounds, grace abounds more (Rom. 5:20). What is more gracious than forgiveness which follows rebuke?

If there is anything indisputable in the Christian faith, it is the teaching about forgiveness. Even non-Christians hold avowed followers of Christ to a high standard on this point. We know this truth intellectually, but instinctively we limit it to what seems reasonable. In other words, "I can forgive many things, but you can't expect me to forgive him/her for doing ___________!" (fill in the blank). We each know what it is to come to a point beyond which, humanly speaking, we cannot forgive.

Peter was not so much concerned with the severity of an offense as he was with the frequency of offenses, which can turn any sin into a severe pattern of destructive or abusive behavior. He asked, "How often should I forgive a person who sins against me?" then immediately offered what he thought was a magnanimous answer (seven times). To forgive once seemed generous. But Jesus moved the disciples not just to a higher plane but to a different dimension altogether. Jesus' hyperbole of forgiving someone 70 x 7 times—His standard—must have seemed an impossible yardstick. No one could even remotely come close to forgiving someone 490 times!

And that was Jesus' point: it *is* impossible. We can infer a few things here: (1) Jesus calls His disciples to accomplish something utterly impossible by mere human ability. (2) Jesus wants His disciples to get into the mode of forgiving people and not keeping score. (3) There is no limit to extending forgiveness to others. (4) Jesus wouldn't call His disciples to something He Himself did not embrace. This last point encourages us because His forgiveness has no limit, and we can be sure that when we repent, God will always forgive us: "If we confess our sins, He is faithful and righteous to forgive us our sins and to cleanse us from all unrighteousness" (1 John 1:9).

Lord, help me be a forgiving kind of person rather than the sort who keeps score and rations out forgiveness as seems "reasonable."

Week 30
Day 4

Forgiveness Illustrated

Matthew 18:23-27

[23] "For this reason the kingdom of heaven may be compared to a king who wished to settle accounts with his slaves. [24] When he had begun to settle them, one who owed him ten thousand talents was brought to him. [25] But since he did not have the means to repay, his lord commanded him to be sold, along with his wife and children and all that he had, and repayment to be made. [26] So the slave fell to the ground and prostrated himself before him, saying, 'Have patience with me and I will repay you everything.' [27] And the lord of that slave felt compassion and released him and forgave him the debt."

Being the Master Teacher that He was, Jesus not only used hyperbole and attention-grabbing phrases such as 70 x 7 forgiveness; He also drilled home His teaching about forgiveness with a story. We must not divorce this parable from His discussion of confronting the sinning brother, the one who has offended. We do well to use the biblical words carefully here and call sin "sin," so that we can call forgiveness "forgiveness" in the most profound sense of the word. Christendom today has watered down the seriousness of sin and its devastating effect on relationships. In so doing it has undermined what true forgiveness is—and its restorative power as well. Forgiveness, one of the most misunderstood concepts among Christians, exists precisely because sin exists. Furthermore, it has to do with restoring relationship broken by sin and the consequences of not releasing the sin. Where repeated sin separates relationships, grace—through forgiveness—restores.

In the first part of Jesus' illustration of the importance of forgiveness, the primary character is a slave who owes a king 10,000 talents. A talent in Roman currency was worth about 6000 days' wages for an average laborer. So the man owed about 60,000 days' worth of wages—an impossible sum to ever repay in a lifetime. The king, wanting to recoup at least some of his losses, goes to sell off the man and his family into further slavery. The slave humbles himself, pleading for patience and time to get his payment in order. It's a desperate plea from a desperate man. The king has compassion on the man, changes his mind; he releases him from his obligation, forgiving his debt.

When Jesus said the king "felt compassion," Matthew uses the same word he used to describe Jesus' response to the multitude (see 9:36). When the king "forgave him the debt," it is the same word Jesus used moments earlier about forgiving 70 x 7 times. So it is not difficult to conclude that this story illustrates the forgiveness of our Lord for the enormous debt we owe Him!

Father, I praise Your Son for the great price He paid to clear my great debt of sin–a debt I could never fully pay. I will never cease to sing of my redemption.

Unforgiveness Illustrated

Matthew 18:28-35

*28 "But that slave went out and found one of his fellow slaves who owed him a
hundred denarii; and he seized him and began to choke him, saying, 'Pay back
what you owe.' 29 So his fellow slave fell to the ground and began to plead with him,
saying, 'Have patience with me and I will repay you.' 30 But he was unwilling and
went and threw him in prison until he should pay back what was owed. 31 So when
his fellow slaves saw what had happened, they were deeply grieved and came and
reported to their lord all that had happened. 32 Then summoning him, his lord said
to him, 'You wicked slave, I forgave you all that debt because you pleaded with me.
33 'Should you not also have had mercy on your fellow slave, in the same way that
I had mercy on you?' 34 And his lord, moved with anger, handed him over to the
torturers until he should repay all that was owed him. 35 My heavenly Father will
also do the same to you, if each of you does not forgive his brother from your heart."*

The parable, to this point, could have stood alone as an illustration of God's forgiveness, building on the story of the shepherd who left the ninety-nine to find the one (18:12-14) and the teaching about forgiving 70 x 7 times (18:23). But this sets up an illustration of the requirement to extend forgiveness.

The audacity of the forgiven slave is obvious to the point of incredulity. He had been forgiven a debt far greater than he could ever pay back in his lifetime. Then finding a fellow slave who owed him 1/600th the amount of his own forgiven debt, he rejected the identical plea for mercy that he had himself made to the king.

That reminds me of a present-day story of a local man who trespassed into a home under construction to look around. While using a ladder to descend into the unfinished basement, he fell and broke his leg. The owners graciously decided not to charge him with trespassing, but the intruder subsequently sued the owners for negligence in having an unsafe house! Such is the impudent depth to which selfishness descends.

In Jesus' parable, word got back to the king. He became furious with the slave, blasting him with the obvious: forgiveness ought to beget forgiveness; mercy ought to beget mercy. God calls those of us who have been shown grace to "pay it forward." Note the inherent compulsion in this truth. God's grace sent Jesus on a mission to save us from the eternal weight of our sin debt. No sacrifice could pay for our offenses against God except one, the one which Christ would soon pay. His sacrifice on the cross would cancel our debt of sin. Jesus teaches His followers, therefore, to have a forgiving spirit—period.

*Lord, thank you so much for Your forgiveness. Help
me forgive others as You have forgiven me!*

Weekend Reading

Saturday – Proverbs 4
Sunday – Psalms 137–140

Personal Reflections

Culmination and *Commission*

Game Changer

Matthew 19:1-2

[1] When Jesus had finished these words, He departed from Galilee and came into the region of Judea beyond the Jordan; [2] and large crowds followed Him, and He healed them there.

Everything now changes in the movement of Jesus' ministry. Since the time of His baptism at the Jordan River near Jerusalem, He had spent relatively little time in the province of Judea. At that time, Israel was under Roman control and composed of two main areas, Galilee and Judea. Originally (hundreds of years earlier) the land was divided among the descendants of Jacob's twelve sons (called *tribes*). In time the nation split and the northern populace, the larger one (named Israel, or Ephraim, after the dominant tribe) was the first to stray from God by worshiping idols. They were eventually overrun by foreign powers, and these captives were forced into relocation. The people left in the land of Samaria intermarried with other people groups forced to relocate there. This mixed people group came to be known as *Samaritans.*

The southern populace coalesced around the tribe of Judah, carrying on the dynasty of King David. For the most part, they too strayed from God. But there were always a few who remained faithful to the true God of Abraham, Isaac, and Jacob. In time, this southern nation (called Judah, after the dominate tribe) were taken into captivity also. God orchestrated this discipline because of their idolatry and rebellion. Unlike the northern kingdom, the people of Judah retained their identity as the people of God, and eventually returned to their land.

In time, some of the people spread north into what became known as Galilee. The southern portion, the location of Jerusalem, was called Judea. The land in between was occupied by the despised Samaritans.

Apart from being born in Judea (in Bethlehem) and baptized there (in the Jordan River thirty miles from Jerusalem), Jesus spent most of His life and ministry in Galilee. In today's reading we witness a crescendo which led to the culmination of His mission. This juncture in the story is pivotal, for it signals the beginning of the end. There would be no "withdrawing" this time, and He would not be returning to Galilee until after His death (28:16).

Jesus' self-fulfilling prediction in Matthew 16:21 was about to prove true. Note His resolute determination prophesied in Isaiah: "I gave My back to those who strike Me, and My cheeks to those who pluck out the beard; I did not cover My face from humiliation and spitting. For the Lord God helps Me, therefore, I am not disgraced; therefore, I have set My face like flint ..." (Isa. 50:6-7).

Lord, thank you that You were not deterred in the slightest from Your purpose, which was to offer Yourself as the only and perfect sacrifice for our sins.

Week 31
Day 2

"Taking On" Marriage

Matthew 19:3-6

[3] Some Pharisees came to Jesus, testing Him and asking, "Is it lawful for a man to divorce his wife for any reason at all?" [4] And He answered and said, "Have you not read that He who created them from the beginning MADE THEM MALE AND FEMALE, *[5] and said,* 'FOR THIS REASON A MAN SHALL LEAVE HIS FATHER AND MOTHER AND BE JOINED TO HIS WIFE, AND THE TWO SHALL BECOME ONE FLESH'? *[6] So they are no longer two, but one flesh. What therefore God has joined together, let no man separate."*

Divorce proceedings supply ongoing business for lawyers today. Some research indicates about 50 percent of all first-time marriages end in divorce. In Jesus' time, divorce provided lucrative currency for the one-upmanship in ongoing debates over the Mosaic law. Some held to a lenient view—a man could divorce his wife for just about any reason. Others held a more restricted view. Some Pharisees wanted to embroil Jesus in that debate, testing Him for their own purposes.

Rather than give an opinion from a human standpoint, Jesus rebuked them for not understanding the simple description of marriage in the early chapters of Genesis. (He did a similar thing with Nicodemus in John 3:10: "Are you a teacher of the law and don't understand these things?") These "things" were foundational, so why was there a debate about them? God designed marriage; He is the One who joins a man and woman together. His directive? Marriage is permanent. Therefore any separation violates His intention for it. Case closed!

In the following verses, the Pharisees press for clarification. But we note a few points Jesus emphasizes. This union we call marriage dates to the beginning, the creation of human beings, and is fundamental to humanity. Sexuality is at the core of who we are as either men or women. Sex distinctions are not simply incidental to life. So marriage (and the proper relating of the two genders) is not incidental either. Nor is this something to be altered by the customs and caprice of human desires.

In addition, Jesus emphasizes that when a man and woman come together, they become united as one flesh. Obviously this does not refer to loss of individual identity. It conveys the strongest possible uniting of two individuals. God sees them as one, and any separation will naturally produce irreparable harm, like the damage caused when separating two pieces of glued paper. His command to "let no man separate [them]" anticipated that this union would be assaulted in succeeding generations. And history has proven that true.

Lord, the whole world system works against the permanence of marriage. Help me to honor and uphold my marriage and the marriages of others.

Uncommonly Hard Teaching

Matthew 19:7-12

[7] They said to Him, "Why then did Moses command to GIVE HER A CERTIFICATE OF DIVORCE AND SEND *her* AWAY?" *[8] He said to them, "Because of your hardness of heart Moses permitted you to divorce your wives; but from the beginning it has not been this way. [9] And I say to you, whoever divorces his wife, except for immorality, and marries another woman commits adultery." [10] The disciples said to Him, "If the relationship of the man with his wife is like this, it is better not to marry." [11] But He said to them, "Not all men can accept this statement, but only those to whom it has been given. [12] For there are eunuchs who were born that way from their mother's womb; and there are eunuchs who were made eunuchs by men; and there are also eunuchs who made themselves eunuchs for the sake of the kingdom of heaven. He who is able to accept this, let him accept it."*

Some biblical teachings are difficult, and Jesus seemed to be sympathetic to that. First, He acknowledged that God had *allowed for* divorce (through the teachings of Moses) even though it was not part of the original design. Following His teaching on divorce, He said, "He who is able to accept this, let him accept it," thus acknowledging that His teaching may be difficult to embrace.

Yes, God *did* allow for divorce according to Deuteronomy 24:1-4. It was given as a concession to people with hardened hearts as a means to regulate certain abuses in marriage. But if a person wanted to take advantage of that leniency, he would have acknowledge the reason, namely his own hardness of heart. God promised a time, however, when Messiah would come, according to Jeremiah 31:33, and He would give the people a new heart, and the hardness would be gone.

Many of the Jews had turned this "allowance" into a liberal privilege, clear evidence of the endemic hardness of their hearts. Jesus confronted this problem directly. In fact one of the remedies He taught was this: "Blessed are the pure in heart, for they shall see God" (5:8). Yet the heart resistance continued: "The heart of this people has become dull" (13:4). Solve the heart problem and you solve the divorce problem. That was essentially Jesus's teaching on all concerns.

He brought definition to the issue: divorce and remarriage is tantamount to committing adultery. The exception? Where the marriage bond has already been broken through infidelity.

Lord, help me accept those teachings in Scripture which are difficult to embrace and not just the things that fit my preference, lifestyle, or culture.

Week 31
Day 4

Let the Children Reign

Matthew 19:13-15

[13] *Then some children were brought to Him so that He might lay His hands on them and pray; and the disciples rebuked them.* [14] *But Jesus said, "Let the children alone, and do not hinder them from coming to Me; for the kingdom of heaven belongs to such as these."* [15] *After laying His hands on them, He departed from there.*

Tenderness characterized Jesus' way of relating to the most vulnerable of society—children. That could not be said of His disciples, however—at least not at this point in their training. So one more thing they had to learn by watching and listening to their Master was that the message of the kingdom was for all, even children.

Jesus emphasized this when someone presented a group of young ones to Christ. This apparently seemed natural—an appropriate thing to do. And it speaks of the faith of those who brought them. What a tremendous thing that in a world when children are introduced to many different influences, someone would dare to lead them to the Lord Jesus Christ, to introduce their young, formative minds and hearts to the One who came to establish righteousness and holiness, to expose them to the riches of His grace.

The ceremonial act of laying hands on someone conveyed a blessing. We see this in Jewish heritage when Jacob, for example, laid hands on Joseph's sons (Gen. 48:14). In Jesus' day, the people were seeking a blessing for these children, and who better to pray for a child than a godly man known to be close to God? He was recognized as that at least. Yet He was actually far greater, and therefore answers to *His* prayers would be assured.

We have no record of what Jesus actually prayed as He blessed the children. But we do know what He prayed for us. We would do well to listen in on what He prayed for us in that wonderful precrucifixion intercessory prayer (John 17:20).

Before Jesus blessed the children, Jesus rebuked His disciples (see also 16:22). Being a disciple requires a critiquing of our behavior. Some abandon ship due to pride. But true disciples heed admonitions and make corrections. Disciples must never forget that leading children to Christ is highly valued in the kingdom. Indeed, as the Lord instructed previously (18:3), the standard for coming to Christ is childlikeness. We can see that the disciples learned this truth because John even adopted this terminology in referring to believers as children (see 1 John 2:1).

Lord, help me not strive for sophistication, complexity, or status. Rather, I want to continually come to You and live in You with childlike faith.

Working Your Way Up?

Matthew 19:16-19

[16] And someone came to Him and said, "Teacher, what good thing shall I do that I may obtain eternal life?" [17] And He said to him, "Why are you asking Me about what is good? There is only One who is good; but if you wish to enter into life, keep the commandments." [18] Then he said to Him, "Which ones?" And Jesus said, "YOU SHALL NOT COMMIT MURDER; YOU SHALL NOT COMMIT ADULTERY; YOU SHALL NOT STEAL; YOU SHALL NOT BEAR FALSE WITNESS; [19] HONOR YOUR FATHER AND MOTHER; and YOU SHALL LOVE YOUR NEIGHBOR AS YOURSELF."

The final trip to Jerusalem had been set in motion. A wealthy young man (vv. 20, 22) approached him with a question which afforded Jesus the opportunity to point out the real purpose of the Law. The young man was ostensibly interested in how to be good enough to obtain eternal life. Jesus responded with two comments. First, He challenged the man's sense of "good." Only a perfectly good person would be able to answer what is good enough to qualify a person for eternal life. That one person would be God, who alone is good and therefore qualified to declare what is good. Logically, then, the natural thing would be to refer the man to the Scriptures; it is they that reflect God's thinking.

The backstory to this interview was a debate among the rabbis about their various systems for ranking the commandments. Essentially, if a person could not keep all the commandments, then which should he focus his efforts on most? Jesus listed the latter portion of the Ten Commandments, numbers five through nine, leaving out the tenth about coveting. He summarized with, "Love your neighbor as yourself," His teaching referring to all the commands regarding human relationships. (In 22:30, Jesus calls this "the second-greatest commandment.")

On the surface, this response of Jesus seems to go against later inspired teachings, particularly those in the writings of the apostle Paul, such as these: "The Law brings about wrath" (Rom. 4:15). "The Law came in that the transgression would increase" (Rom. 5:20). And "[we] are not under law but under grace" (Rom. 6:14). No one except the sinless Son of God in the flesh has ever, or will ever, be good enough to keep God's perfect standard encompassed in the Ten Commandments. All others fall short (Rom. 3:23).

This interview was designed to show the young man that "the Law is holy" (Rom. 7:12) and that he was not! Paul would later explain that Jesus came "so that the requirement of the Law might be fulfilled in us, who do not walk according to the flesh but according to the Spirit" (Rom. 8:4).

Lord, You are good and I am not. Thank you for graciously showing me that I need your goodness. Enable me to love others as myself.

Weekend Reading

Saturday – Proverbs 31
Sunday – Psalms 141–145

Personal Reflections

"Going for the Jugular"

Matthew 19:20-22

[20] The young man said to Him, "All these things I have kept; what am I still lacking?"
[21] Jesus said to him, "If you wish to be complete, go and sell your possessions and give to the poor, and you will have treasure in heaven; and come, follow Me."
[22] But when the young man heard this statement, he went away grieving; for he was one who owned much property.

Youthfulness is characterized by a certain naiveté. Ignorance is bliss, as the saying goes. In some regards this young man may have been simply idealistic, zealous with his checklist of do's and don'ts. However, his self-deception is true of multitudes of religious people in the world. They work hard trying to achieve spiritual rewards, even eternal life itself. In this case, the young man apparently knew he had come up short even though he had, to the best of his ability, kept the commandments Jesus mentioned.

The young man obviously was not just testing the Lord, as the Pharisees often did, because we see that "he went away grieving." Maybe he had been looking for assurance that his efforts counted for something and were, he hoped, sufficient to gain eternal life. But he was sadly disappointed.

What was missing? Despite all the young man's good efforts, he had no assurance that *all* his bases were covered. Believing that salvation comes by works will never give anyone assurance, for one question will always plague the person: Have I done enough?

So Jesus showed the man that he fell hopelessly short of finding any assurance through keeping the Law. The futility of that is clear, as Deuteronomy 27:26 states: "Cursed is the one who does not confirm the words of this law by doing them." James gives full expression to this truth, "For whoever keeps the whole law and yet stumbles in one point, he has become guilty of all" (James 2:10). Who could ever find assurance in keeping the Law?

Jesus went for the proverbial jugular, showing the fellow that he, contrary to his view of himself as a law-abiding Jew, was a failure. Jesus tells him, if you really want eternal life, then fulfill the law of love and give all your possessions to the poor. The young man was unwilling, however, to "love [his] neighbor as [himself]." In another place, Jesus used an interplay on the words to say, "This is the work of God, that you believe in Him whom He has sent" (John 6:29). The only way to ensure entry to eternal life was to come and follow Him.

Lord, help me to let go of things I hold tightly in order that I might follow You more closely.

Needling the Wealthy

Matthew 19:23-26

[23] And Jesus said to His disciples, "Truly I say to you, it is hard for a rich man to enter the kingdom of heaven. [24] Again I say to you, it is easier for a camel to go through the eye of a needle, than for a rich man to enter the kingdom of God." [25] When the disciples heard this, they were very astonished and said, "Then who can be saved?" [26] And looking at them Jesus said to them, "With people this is impossible, but with God all things are possible."

Sad as this story ends, it serves a good purpose; we do well to learn from the struggles and failures of others. Jesus confronted the wealthy young man with the stranglehold of his own wealth. Those possessions of his actually possessed *him!* And they choked out his desire for eternal life. The dark recesses of the soul are easily enticed, as Judas found also out when he betrayed his Master, the One who had words of eternal life, for a mere bribe.

The lesson is obvious: discipleship and wealth do not easily mix. Jesus said it straight out and then used a now-common proverbial expression: it is easier for a camel to go through the eye of a needle than for a rich man to enter the kingdom of God. The idea that this referred to a small city gate through which a camel could barely squeeze through is historically questionable. But the point of this expression is clear.

The disciples realized the lesson was not just about the wealthy. Reflecting the common notion that wealth was a sign of God's blessing, and poverty a sign of God's displeasure, they respond with an incredulous, "How then could anyone be saved?" Jesus affirmed their conclusion—with men this is impossible, but with God it is very much possible. Salvation is not just for the wealthy, but for all people.

We can learn a few lessons here. The less worldly wealth a person has, clearly the less hindrance there will be to following Christ. Matthew Henry puts it this way: "It should be a satisfaction to them who are in a low condition, that they are not exposed to the temptations of a high and prosperous condition." Even if it is harder for some, it is *impossible* for all, *apart from God.* As John states clearly at the beginning of his gospel, a person is born spiritually and gains eternal life, "not of blood, nor of the will of the flesh, nor of the will of man, but of God" (John 1:13).

Finally, note that Jesus described the life of those who follow Him using four different terms: eternal life (v. 16), kingdom of heaven (v. 23), kingdom of God (v. 24), and salvation (v. 25). What a tremendously wealthy life!

Father, thank you that You made the way of salvation possible though my efforts were a total failure. I trust You and follow Your Son, the Lord Jesus.

Reward of Glory

Matthew 19:27-30

[27] Then Peter said to Him, "Behold, we have left everything and followed You; what then will there be for us?" [28] And Jesus said to them, "Truly I say to you, that you who have followed Me, in the regeneration when the Son of Man will sit on His glorious throne, you also shall sit upon twelve thrones, judging the twelve tribes of Israel. [29] And everyone who has left houses or brothers or sisters or father or mother or children or farms for My name's sake, will receive many times as much, and will inherit eternal life. [30] But many who are first will be last; and the last, first."

Discipleship often brings to the surface a person's insecurities. The Twelve had just concluded that eternal life is not only difficult for the wealthy to attain, it is impossible for anyone apart from God's doing. *Where does that leave us?* they thought. Their lack of wealth was, at least in part, the result of walking away from earthly financial security to follow Christ. Their concern was natural. Peter, once again, was the spokesperson.

All who sacrifice for Christ wonder at times if it is worth it. The obvious comfort and pleasure seen in the wealthy reminds the disciple of his lack of wealth and can engender doubts. We can learn from the psalmist's struggle: "My feet came close to stumbling, my steps had almost slipped. For I was envious of the arrogant as I saw the prosperity of the wicked" (Ps. 73:2-3)—that is, "until I came into the sanctuary of God; then I perceived their end" (Ps. 73:17).

Jesus didn't rebuke His disciples, as He had at other times. Instead He acknowledged their great personal sacrifice and encouraged them with the promise of their coming reward. Clearly, rewards were not their motivation for following Christ. That would be self-serving, to say the least. Peter expressed their motive this way: "Lord, to whom shall we go? You have words of eternal life" (John 6:68). Rewards are meant to encouragement those already following the Lord to help them carry on in their sacrifice.

Awaiting the disciples was a privileged place in the kingdom, sitting on twelve thrones with Christ in authority over Israel. As disciples their earthly place was low, but their reward will be great. Our sacrifice now is nothing compared to the eternal glory coming (cf. 2 Cor. 4:17). Whatever a disciple gives up to follow Christ will be replaced with something far better, even here on earth. Flesh and blood may reject him, but the spiritual family he gains is far greater. God's order of things is counterintuitive to man.

Lord, thank you for the prospect of eternal rewards with You in eternity.
That encourages me when I think of what I have given up here.

Week 32
Day 4

Fair Is Fair

Matthew 20:1-7

1 "For the kingdom of heaven is like a landowner who went out early in the morning
to hire laborers for his vineyard. 2 When he had agreed with the laborers for a
denarius for the day, he sent them into his vineyard. 3 And he went out about the
third hour and saw others standing idle in the market place; 4 and to those he said,
'You also go into the vineyard, and whatever is right I will give you.' And so they
went. 5 Again he went out about the sixth and the ninth hour, and did the same thing.
6 And about the eleventh hour he went out and found others standing around; and
he said to them, 'Why have you been standing here idle all day long?' 7 They said
to him, 'Because no one hired us.' He said to them, 'You go into the vineyard too.' "

Jesus sometimes used parables to hide the truth from His antagonists (13:13) while revealing it to His followers. At other times, as in our story today, He used the parable form of teaching to convey the truth in a way that everyone could readily understand.

The Lord had just finished speaking to the disciples about sacrifice and rewards, saying that God's spiritual economy runs counter to our limited, human sensibilities. The big picture, however, from God's perspective, makes perfect sense. Jesus summarized with this statement: "Many who are first will be last; and the last, first" (19:30). He then illustrated this truth with a story of a vineyard owner and workers hired at various times during the day.

The first workers hired in the morning agreed to work for one denarius (a typical day's wage). Three hours later the owner hired more men (who had been idle) and sent them to work in the vineyard, agreeing to pay them "what is right." They apparently trusted their new employer to make good on his promise (possibly assuming that work for any pay was better than no work at all). This happened three more times. The last group of men worked in the vineyard for eleven fewer hours than the first group of men.

Human logic dictates that each man, doing the same work, ought to be paid according to the time he spent doing the work. Those who work more ought to receive more than those who work less. What's fair is fair, right? However, notice carefully that when the vineyard owner provided terms of employment, each group of men accepted the terms. The first group *agreed* to one denarius for a day's labor. The subsequent groups all implicitly agreed to work for the undefined terms of "what is right," apparently trusting the owner would fulfill that appropriately. The employer was being magnanimous in giving any of them work.

Lord, I believe that in my service for You I will not be shortchanged.

One Big Shovel

Matthew 20:8-16

8 "When evening came, the owner of the vineyard said to his foreman, 'Call the laborers and pay them their wages, beginning with the last group to the first.'
9 When those hired about the eleventh hour came, each one received a denarius.
10 When those hired first came, they thought that they would receive more; but each of them also received a denarius. 11 When they received it, they grumbled at the landowner, 12 saying, 'These last men have worked only one hour, and you have made them equal to us who have borne the burden and the scorching heat of the day.' 13 But he answered and said to one of them, 'Friend, I am doing you no wrong; did you not agree with me for a denarius? 14 'Take what is yours and go, but I wish to give to this last man the same as to you. 15 'Is it not lawful for me to do what I wish with what is my own? Or is your eye envious because I am generous?'
16 So the last shall be first, and the first last."

Like bookends around this parable come these words: "Many who are first will be last; and the last, first" (19:30) and "So the last shall be first, and the first last." Clearly Jesus was illustrating the promise that the disciples would be more than adequately compensated for the sacrifices they were making to follow Him.

As the story went, a farmer sent men out to work in his vineyard at various times of the day and each agreed to the terms of his employment. The first group of men agreed to work for one denarius for the day's work, which was the fair wage at that time. But at the time of agreement they did not know that at the end of the work day, those who started later in the day would receive the same compensation. When this was discovered, the men hired first no longer thought their employer was acting fairly. Yet everyone received *at least* what they deserved. Some received more than they deserved despite working fewer hours in the day. The owner could do as he pleased with what he owned and be generous with whom he desired. Generosity does not negate fairness.

Although this story certainly may have something to say about economics and employment, the primary application is to disciples who have given up "everything" to follow Christ (19:27). The world sees them as "last." But Paul writes the following concerning the apostles in particular: "We have become the scum of the world" (1 Cor. 4:9-13, esp. 13). What keeps followers of Christ going when they have given up so much? We have a generous God whose rewards far exceed what we deserve. An old saying goes like this: "God is no man's debtor. We shove from our pile into God's pile, and He in return shovels from His pile into ours—shovel for shovel. He, however, has a bigger shovel!"

Lord, I don't have to worry because I know that You are the kind of God who compensates with rewards that far outweigh my puny sacrifices.

Weekend Reading

Saturday – Job 1
Sunday – Psalms 146–150

Personal Reflections

Suffering Predicted

Matthew 20:17-19

[17] As Jesus was about to go up to Jerusalem, He took the twelve disciples aside by themselves, and on the way He said to them, [18] "Behold, we are going up to Jerusalem; and the Son of Man will be delivered to the chief priests and scribes, and they will condemn Him to death, [19] and will hand Him over to the Gentiles to mock and scourge and crucify Him, and on the third day He will be raised up."

The crescendo rises like an ominous dirge, building toward the dire climax. Jesus was now ready to go up to Jerusalem. (The Jews always considered Jerusalem "up" from anywhere in Israel, not only because it was the highest mountain in the area but also because it was considered the place of God's special presence.) Jesus prepped His disciples by repeating what He had already told them (see 16:21).

Four things, all in sequence, would happen to "the Son of Man," as Jesus often referred to Himself. First, He would be betrayed to the ruling authorities. The writer has already identified for us the agent of this impending treachery, namely Judas, one of the Twelve (10:25).

Second, the rulers were going to "condemn Him to death." The disciples knew about the conflicting attitudes toward Jesus, but they never thought it would come to that. Jesus was the promised Messiah who would reestablish the Jewish kingdom to the prominence and glory it had under King David. To the disciples, death could only mean utter failure. That was not an option! They had gone out on a spiritual limb, declaring Jesus to be the Christ, the Son of the living God.

Third, Jesus would be mocked and crucified at the hands of the Gentiles. This would be the worst kind of death. The Law said, "He who is hanged is accursed of God" (Deut. 21:23). Though the word *cross* is not mentioned in that OT passage, Luke, the author of the book of Acts, connected this to the crucifixion. He wrote that Jesus was killed by "*hanging* Him on a cross" (Acts 5:30, italics mine). Paul also applied this to the Lord's death: "Christ redeemed us from the curse of the Law, having become a curse for us—for it is written, 'Cursed is everyone who hangs on a tree'" (Gal. 3:13). Death by crucifixion was a sure sign of judgment from God.

Finally, His death would be at the hands of Gentiles. As it turned out, the Jews convinced their Roman overlords to crucify Him. The disciples must have been completely overwhelmed by the nightmare scenario Jesus painted for them.

Lord, like the disciples, I sometimes can't comprehend how Your glory will be made known, especially when things around me seem such a mess. Help my unbelief.

Week 33
Day 2

An Attempted Coup

Matthew 20:20-22

[20] Then the mother of the sons of Zebedee came to Jesus with her sons, bowing down and making a request of Him. [21] And He said to her, "What do you wish?" She said to Him, "Command that in Your kingdom these two sons of mine may sit one on Your right and one on Your left."

The attempted coup to gain the second- and third-most powerful positions in the kingdom reveals the disciples' frame of mind. Did this woman catch the significance of what Jesus said about being raised on the third day (v. 19)? Or was she simply blinded by motherly desires? The real movers behind the request, however, were the brothers, James and John (the sons of Zebedee); they were the ones whom Jesus addressed in the next verses.

The right hand and left hand are pictured here as the highest positions of authority next to the King Himself. Rivalry among the disciples was not unknown (cf. 18:1), despite efforts to hide their competitiveness from the Master (cf. Mark 9:34). While Peter desperately wanted to prove his loyalty, James and John were nonetheless the boldest of the bunch. What right or qualification did they have for such a prerogative? Possibly they thought they had achieved prominence because they were among the first disciples selected by Jesus (4:21). The gospel writer, in fact, list them as second and third in the list of the Twelve (10:2), and they were part of the "inner three" along with Peter (for example, on the Mount of Transfiguration, 17:1-2). Most likely, in their minds, Peter had disqualified himself because he had verbally rebuked the Lord (16:23), so maybe they thought they were the logical choice.

Had they demonstrated loyalty that deserved more honor than the others? Nothing in the story so far would suggest that. One of the supreme deceptions in the human experience is that of self-exaltation—thinking of ourselves more highly than others. After all, we spend copious amounts of time thinking about ourselves. Our own self-view and self-talk magnifies our imagined sense of self-importance to the point that it seems quite natural that we should receive favorable treatment from and above others. Self-justification prompts us to think it quite reasonable and appropriate for us to assume the position of prominence. How often we justify our own self-importance! How often this is the root of conflict in life!

The clandestine way James and John approached Jesus tells us they qualified for a place of honor. So they sought out an unjustified personal favor.

Lord, I confess my biased, subjective, arrogant sense of self-importance. Help me see my veiled attempts at sinful self-promotion for what they really are.

Misplaced Confidence

Matthew 20:22-24

[22] But Jesus answered, "You do not know what you are asking. Are you able to drink the cup that I am about to drink?" They said to Him, "We are able." [23] He said to them, "My cup you shall drink; but to sit on My right and on My left, this is not Mine to give, but it is for those for whom it has been prepared by My Father." [24] And hearing this, the ten became indignant with the two brothers.

The brothers James and John had clearly put their mother up to this request, thinking her petition on their behalf would disguise their power grab. Their mother voiced the question, but Jesus responded to her sons. Despite their self-serving motives, this move did reflect that they truly believed Jesus was the Messiah; the question showed they anticipated participating in His kingdom restoration. However, they had yet to learn that life in the kingdom was going to be quite different from what they were expecting; Christ's kingdom was "not of this world" (John 8:36).

Jesus had earlier surprised them with the teaching that entrance into the kingdom of heaven required becoming like a child, and that the greatest in the kingdom is the one who humbles himself like a child (18:3-4). Not yet understanding that, the brothers still felt attaining prominence would only come through their conniving behind the others' backs, positioning themselves for preferential treatment when the kingdom did arrive.

The prospect of reigning with Christ in the kingdom was still fresh in their minds (19:28). Little did they understand what Jesus meant when He spoke of the cup He was about to drink (see John 18:11). When they said that they, too, were able to "drink" of it, they talked, as Matthew Henry puts it, "as blind men do of colors."

The Lord replied that they would, indeed, "drink the cup." Later this must have provided a bitter memory during the dark days between the crucifixion and resurrection, and also during the still darker days of persecution they would all experience after the resurrection. As for positions of prominence in the kingdom, those appointments belonged to the Father alone. The disciples would have done better to concern themselves with weightier matters.

This personal competitiveness was not unique to James and John. That is clear from the reaction of the rest when they heard about it. They were "indignant," probably because they wanted the chief positions as well!

Lord, pride seems to always be present in me. Help me become more like a child in humility. I accept the struggles of faith that You allow.

Greatness in Serving

Matthew 20:25-28

[25] *But Jesus called them to Himself and said, "You know that the rulers of the Gentiles lord it over them, and their great men exercise authority over them.* [26] *It is not this way among you, but whoever wishes to become great among you shall be your servant,* [27] *and whoever wishes to be first among you shall be your slave;* [28] *just as the Son of Man did not come to be served, but to serve, and to give His life a ransom for many."*

Rivalry among the disciples for prominence in the kingdom set the stage for Jesus' summary teaching on greatness. Lest we be too hard on the disciples, sober reflection reveals this struggle in all of us. Even in our churches, the quest for prominence frequently lurks in both the pew and pulpit. The desire for recognition often reveals a servant heart mixed with much pride. To some degree, that will always be with us this side of the grave; however, we need to root it out when it first appears.

Nowhere does this show up more than in church leadership when men or women strive for titles. In most churches, the spiritual *gift* of being a pastor has been replaced with the *title* of pastor. This unfortunate dividing of believers into classes (laity v. clergy) began surprisingly soon after the death of the apostles. Distinctions have become even more parsed, with a present emphasis now on the *senior pastor* as opposed to just *pastor*, not to mention other common titles such as *reverend, right reverend, and most reverend.* We find none of these as titles anywhere in Scripture. Such titles separate rather than unite, and they reflect the ambitions and yearnings for recognition among men. The roles of leadership in the church were never identified by titles but simply by function or spiritual gift (e.g. elder, deacon, evangelist, and teacher). These were simply descriptions.

Jesus presented a revolutionary idea of greatness not found in the worldly aspirations for prominence—what is called *servant leadership.* Yes, we need authority in life's relationships, as seen in biblical teachings concerning family, church, and government (see Ephesians 5:22-24; Hebrews 13:17; and Romans 13:1-7). But those things that are a means for self-promotion—to gain personal prominence and control over others—resemble Gentile ways more than Christ's ways.

Building on His teaching that the first shall be last (19:30, 20:16), the Lord Jesus defined greatness by using Himself as the example: He rendered the ultimate servant act by substituting Himself for us on the cross.

Lord, I confess any aspiration lurking in my heart trying to make a name for myself, to be great and prominent. Help me, instead, to serve others as You did.

Walls Fall Down

Matthew 20:29-34

[29] As they were leaving Jericho, a large crowd followed Him. [30] And two blind men sitting by the road, hearing that Jesus was passing by, cried out, "Lord, have mercy on us, Son of David!" [31] The crowd sternly told them to be quiet, but they cried out all the more, "Lord, Son of David, have mercy on us!" [32] And Jesus stopped and called them, and said, "What do you want Me to do for you?" [33] They said to Him, "Lord, we want our eyes to be opened." [34] Moved with compassion, Jesus touched their eyes; and immediately they regained their sight and followed Him.

Jericho was situated on the Jordan River along the path Jesus took from Galilee to Jerusalem on this "final" journey. Historically, it was the first city the people of Israel invaded in their quest for the Promised Land after their exodus from Egypt more than 1400 years earlier. When Jesus entered Jericho, the barriers of physical blindness crumbled—a sign that walls of spiritual blindness would soon fall just as the physical walls fell when the Israelites invaded under Joshua's leadership.

Two blind men accosted Him with their desperate need, correctly calling Him "Son of David." The Lord honored them by inviting them to make their request. They simply wanted to be able to see. As Matthew records it, "Lord, we want our eyes to be opened." There are more straightforward ways to express the desire to see, but their words seems to reflect a desire for deeper perception. Indeed, the Lord is concerned with more than a social gospel that only deals with people's felt needs. If that were the objective, then He would have spent far more time healing everyone and avoiding at all cost His supposedly premature death. However, His goal was to restore spiritual sight, bringing people to repentance and turning them back to God. And that required His suffering and death.

Jesus responded to the blind men with compassion. Simply touching His hand to their eyes, He healed them completely. The beggars immediately joined the crowd and followed Him. Jesus cared for both people's physical needs *and* their greater spiritual ones—so they followed Him.

Note: Mark 10:46 and Luke 18:35 record accounts of an event identical to this one except that it speaks of only one beggar. This is not a contradiction, for we often use language like that today. For example, "I saw John at church this week," and also, "I saw John and Mary at church this week." Just as those statements are not contradictory, neither are the gospel accounts.

Lord, thank you for curing my spiritual blindness. Help me to see clearly and not be blinded by a preoccupation with my physical needs.

Weekend Reading

Saturday – Job 2
Sunday – Job 3

Personal Reflections

A Donkey Fit for the King

Matthew 21:1-3

[1] When they had approached Jerusalem and had come to Bethphage, at the Mount of Olives, then Jesus sent two disciples, [2] saying to them, "Go into the village opposite you, and immediately you will find a donkey tied there and a colt with her; untie them and bring them to Me. [3] If anyone says anything to you, you shall say, 'The Lord has need of them,' and immediately he will send them."

This incident takes place a mere five days before Jesus was crucified. The main event leading up to the crucifixion is what is commonly called the triumphal entry, and the town of Bethphage is its staging area. This small, nondescript community is near the better known Bethany (home of Mary, Martha, and Lazarus. Bethphage was situated two miles from Jerusalem (John 11:18), on the Mount of Olives.

Indicating advanced planning, Jesus sent two of His followers to retrieve a donkey and its colt in preparation for His formal presentation in Jerusalem as King of the Jews. Jesus told the disciples that if anyone was suspicious when they took two animals that clearly did not belong to them, they could respond with the apparently prearranged code phrase, "The Lord has need of them." That would secure immediate permission and passage back to Jesus with the animals in tow.

Having just healed the two Jericho beggars of their physical blindness, the Lord was heading into Jerusalem, where He would face the spiritual blindness of the Jewish nation. While the blind men received *their* sight, tragically, the nation as a whole would reject Christ, and thus their opportunity for spiritual enlightenment.

All four gospel accounts include this event in detail. Here we find Jesus soliciting a borrowed animal to ride on in what should be His glorious presentation as King. On this earth the Lord and Creator of all things possessed little, humbling Himself as nothing more than a servant. While great men rode fine horses, Jesus chose a common form of transport used by peasant folk. "For you know the grace of our Lord Jesus Christ, that though He was rich, yet for your sake He became poor, so that you through His poverty might become rich" (2 Cor. 8:9). This verse speaks clearly of Christ's meekness.

One personal lesson we might learn from this is: whatever Christ directs us to do, He will provide the means for us to accomplish. The disciples would be successful in their mission to bring the animals back as long as they followed the Lord's instruction regarding what to say. So, we, too, can only accomplish the Lord's desires in our lives if we follow the Lord's instruction at every step, humbling as it might be.

Lord, Your ways at times seem insignificant to the human eye.
Help me to walk faithfully in Your Word and in Your ways.

Triumphal Entry

Matthew 21:4-7

[4] This took place to fulfill what was spoken through the prophet: [5] "Say to the daughter of Zion, 'Behold your King is coming to you, Gentle, and mounted on a donkey, Even on a colt, the foal of a beast of burden.' " [6] The disciples went and did just as Jesus had instructed them, [7] and brought the donkey and the colt, and laid their coats on them; and He sat on the coats.

Once again Matthew reveals ways Jesus' actions fulfilled prophecy—in this case, Zechariah 9:9. The prophet foresaw a return to the land in full blessing, with victory over the nations completed—something that had not yet happened even though God's people were physically in the land.

The symbolism of this triumphal entry into Jerusalem would have certainly electrified the crowds on two accounts. First, they would unmistakably see in Jesus' grand entrance at that time after the pattern of Zechariah's prophecy—tacit evidence that He was consciously coming in the image of the Messiah. This would have irked the Jewish leaders. If true, the long awaited prophetic fulfillment was unfolding. The people were excited.

Second, the imagery of someone entering the city with great pomp, riding on a donkey, was significant. In the ancient world, when a new king entered a city on a *horse,* it meant he was coming in military conquest. But to ride in on a *donkey,* a common beast of burden, would indicate a benevolent king coming in peace, having previously settled the matter of war and conquest. Now was the time for rejoicing. A new order of peace had arrived. So Christ's mode of transportation was intended to bring in peace and a new order.

Notice, the disciples made no objection nor did they raise any questions for clarification. In their minds, this was far more palatable than talk of His suffering and death (see 20:18-19). This was the big day. Jesus was making His big move! While the disciples and Jesus were perfectly aligned in this grand event, their joining together was limited to surface details. Human perceptions are so faulty, so limited, so superficial. Little did the disciples realize what Jesus had been warning them about all along. This great entrance would not precipitate the restoration of the kingdom at this time. Rather, He was about to be rejected as the King of Israel, the Messiah. The prophetic time clock of Zechariah would be put on hold. The events demonstrated that even when Messiah was present, the hearts of the people were stone cold, rejecting their God. Sin had to be exposed for what it was: not just a misunderstanding or mistake, but a rejection of God Himself.

Lord, as I see increasingly that sinfulness is rooted in rejection of Your kingship, I also see Your grace more and more as greater than all my sin.

Joy Unbridled

Matthew 21:8-11

[8] Most of the crowd spread their coats in the road, and others were cutting branches from the trees and spreading them in the road. [9] The crowds going ahead of Him, and those who followed, were shouting, "Hosanna to the Son of David; BLESSED IS HE WHO COMES IN THE NAME OF THE LORD; *Hosanna in the highest!" [10] When He had entered Jerusalem, all the city was stirred, saying, "Who is this?" [11] And the crowds were saying, "This is the prophet Jesus, from Nazareth in Galilee."*

Word had gotten out that something big was about to happen! Prophetic hopes were stoked to a near fever pitch in the reception Jesus received. Although the NASB translation renders verse 8 as "Most of the crowd...," it has been better translated "a very large crowd" in other English versions. The emphasis is on the overwhelming size of those meeting Christ. Once before, a crowd had abandoned Jesus because of His hard sayings (see John 6:66). Now a different crowd came out in force, supporting Him—at least for the moment.

The people apparently saw this as the beginning of the consummation of long-standing prophecies that Israel would be restored to full prominence in the world. Soon, they thought, all the nations would go up to Jerusalem to celebrate the Feast of Booths in worship of the "King, the LORD of Hosts" (Zech. 14:16). So, the people, in celebration and preparation, put branches down in the road and laid their coats across the path that Jesus was taking.

The Feast of Booths was a Jewish celebration remembering the time when their ancestors set up temporary shelters—after leaving Egypt and before entering the Promised Land. For forty years God provided for them. And He commanded them to celebrate that occasion while in the land of promise as a reminder of their wilderness wanderings. Zechariah's prophecy foretold that the Feast of Booths would also be celebrated in the restored kingdom. No wonder the people brought branches and laid them down before the Lord. They were expecting wonderful things, things they had hoped for and dreamed about all their lives.

Their exclamation was taken from Psalm 118:25-26. The term *hosanna* is transliterated from a Hebrew word and means, "O Lord, save!" This psalm, probably a regular part of the Jewish liturgy by that time, connoted messianic expectations. Further, the crowd called Jesus the "Son of David," another messianic term.

Every messianic expectation now hovered at the point of realization.

Lord, as I consider that You will one day return again as King, help me to live in anticipation with faithfulness and loyalty to You.

Week 34
Day 4

Cleansing the Prayer House

Matthew 21:12-17

12 *And Jesus entered the temple and drove out all those who were buying and*
selling in the temple, and overturned the tables of the money changers and the
seats of those who were selling doves. 13 *And He said to them, "It is written, 'MY*
HOUSE SHALL BE CALLED A HOUSE OF PRAYER'; but you are making it a ROBBERS' DEN."
14 *And the blind and the lame came to Him in the temple, and He healed them.*
15 *But when the chief priests and the scribes saw the wonderful things that He had*
done, and the children who were shouting in the temple, "Hosanna to the Son
of David," they became indignant 16 *and said to Him, "Do You hear what these*
children are saying?" And Jesus said to them, "Yes; have you never read, 'OUT OF
THE MOUTH OF INFANTS AND NURSING BABIES YOU HAVE PREPARED PRAISE FOR YOURSELF'?"
17 *And He left them and went out of the city to Bethany, and spent the night there.*

King Jesus, after His "triumphal entry" went immediately to the temple, the center of Jewish religious life. It is not difficult to imagine Him angrily kicking out the merchandisers of religious paraphernalia. He created quite the ruckus, disrupting the status quo, as perverse and blatant as it had become.

There will always be a legitimate need for some commercial activity related to teachings on the spiritual life of the Christian. Books written for the edification of believers, for example, cost money to publish. Buildings for congregational worship need purchasing and maintenance. Mission organizations provide a useful function in exchanging donor's funds into a currency useful on the mission field. In Jesus' time, moneychangers ostensibly performed a useful service—currency exchange for Jews coming from various locales to donate their temple tax and other offerings.

However, the ones Jesus kicked out of the temple area were apparently skimming extra off the top for themselves. They conducted business solely for their own benefit. It was the same with those selling doves; poor people could bring money and purchase doves for sacrificing, but again, the dealers inflated their prices.

Jesus acted on two prerogatives. First, as King, He rebuked the merchants for their extortion, calling the place where this took place "a robber's den." Second, as the Son, He quoted Isaiah 56:7, asserting that the temple was "[His] house," and its purpose was for prayer and not for making money (see Luke 2:49, where as a child He spoke of the temple as "My Father's house"; see also John 2:16). The simple folk, including the blind and the lame, accepted all this. The religious leaders were indignant. What a contrast to Jesus' indignance at the treatment of the temple of God!

Lord, help me not to be blinded by greed for money or to feel indignant when my religious status quo is disrupted, rather than seeing my need for genuine prayer.

Fulfillment at the Doorstep

Matthew 21:18-22

[18] Now in the morning, when He was returning to the city, He became hungry.
[19] Seeing a lone fig tree by the road, He came to it and found nothing on it except leaves only; and He said to it, "No longer shall there ever be any fruit from you." And at once the fig tree withered. [20] Seeing this, the disciples were amazed and asked, "How did the fig tree wither all at once?" [21] And Jesus answered and said to them, "Truly I say to you, if you have faith and do not doubt, you will not only do what was done to the fig tree, but even if you say to this mountain, 'Be taken up and cast into the sea,' it will happen. [22] And all things you ask in prayer, believing, you will receive."

Did Jesus fly off the handle in frustration before His morning cup of coffee simply because of an inconvenience? That would seem rather petty. How then do we explain this enigmatic behavior?

Jesus, as God, is the Creator over all that exists. He is the One who designed fruit trees to do what they were created to do, namely, to give fruit. And here was a fig tree that was not doing what it was created to do. How insolent!

On another level, this incident may be an illustration of God's assessment of Israel, particularly after Jesus had, the day before, cleaned up the temple from its racketeering. It is not hard to imagine Hosea's railing against Israel, "I found Israel like grapes in the wilderness; I saw your forefathers as the earliest fruit on the fig tree in its first season. But they came to Baal-peor and devoted themselves to shame, and they became as detestable as that which they loved" (Hos. 9:10). Yet now, with messianic fulfillment at their doorstep, Israel was completely without spiritual fruit—barren, as it were, like that fig tree. Jesus said later in Matthew 24:32 that there was a lesson to learn from the parable of the fig tree. When leaves are present, summer is near. However, the lack of fruit indicated that something very serious was wrong. Israel needed to repent because of their fruitlessness due to unbelief.

The disciples, dull in understanding all this, as usual, focused on the mechanics of what happened rather than its meaning. Jesus condescended with an explanation that has become a prime teaching point on prayer—that God expects those who make requests of Him to have faith in Him to fulfill those requests. Miraculous possibilities open to those who believe He can do what they ask of Him. This is not a matter of whether we believe hard enough, but whether we simply believe God can do what we ask. He may choose to answer no, but faith means we believe He *can* do it, and we trust Him.

Lord, I believe You can do anything I ask of You. However, help me overcome the issues of unbelief that produce fruitlessness.

Weekend Reading

Saturday – Job 4
Sunday – Job 5

Personal Reflections

A Commanding Situation

Matthew 21:23-24

[23] When He entered the temple, the chief priests and the elders of the people came to Him while He was teaching, and said, "By what authority are You doing these things, and who gave You this authority?" [24] Jesus said to them, "I will also ask you one thing, which if you tell Me, I will also tell you by what authority I do these things."

The Lord had entered Jerusalem with messianic flourish. Then He forced His will on the temple moneychangers who, if truth be told, were under the protection of the ruling religious parties. It should be no surprise that the authorities were incensed by Christ's action. Such is the reaction of those who spurn God's authority. The chief priests and elders were to be the people's representatives to God. Yet pride and arrogance prevented them from seeing or acknowledging that God was there in their presence in the person of Jesus Christ.

These who were the highest religious authorities of the Jews demanded to know by what authority Jesus would dare take such liberties in the temple. The temple was their domain, and His actions were an affront to their authority. We can't help but hear the echo from the garden of Eden long prior to this event, when another dared to question God's spoken word over the issue of authority: "Indeed, has God said, 'You shall not eat from any tree of the garden'?" The serpent did not ask Eve this question to gain information! The devil engaged in a power struggle over who had the right to command the allegiance of God's image-bearing creation. The chief priests, likewise!

Their questioning was not like the gut-wrenching pleas of Job, who cried out, "Why is God causing me to suffer?" Neither was theirs the ignorant questioning of the prophet Habakkuk: "How long, O Lord, will I cry for help and You will not hear?" (Hab. 1:2). Nor was this anywhere near the confused inquiry of Zacharias, the prospective father of the Messiah's forerunner, asking how he could be sure God was speaking through the angel (Luke 1:18). Asking God questions is not wrong in itself; He welcomes the honesty of searching hearts. But arrogant questioning that challenges His authority is never acceptable. With that kind of leadership, is it any wonder that the nation was about to reject her Messiah? The prophet Zechariah foretold this, "Therefore the people wander like sheep, they are afflicted, because there is no shepherd. My anger is kindled against the shepherds" (Zech.10:2-3).

Jesus' response? He will ask them a question, and if they can answer it, He will answer theirs. Once again, the Lord takes command of the situation.

Lord, help me to honestly bring my questions to You, humbly seeking to understand, not, in arrogance, challenging You.

Week 35
Day 2

Playing Hardball

Matthew 21:25-27

[25] *"The baptism of John was from what source, from heaven or from men?" And they began reasoning among themselves, saying, "If we say, 'From heaven,' He will say to us, 'Then why did you not believe him?'* [26] *But if we say, 'From men,' we fear the people; for they all regard John as a prophet."* [27] *And answering Jesus, they said, "We do not know." He also said to them, "Neither will I tell you by what authority I do these things."*

A debate with God never turns out in man's favor. Even the most learned scholars are no match for the One who is the originator of all wisdom and who embodies it perfectly. Jesus met the religious leaders' challenge to His authority with His masterful counterchallenge: He would answer their question if—and only if—they would answer His first. So the Lord Jesus interrogated them, essentially asking by what authority John the Baptist called people to repentance and baptism.

He knew the dilemma this would cause those cloistered clerics. They stood to lose, no matter how they answered Him. Either they would be in trouble with the people for countering their popular belief that John was heaven-sent, or else Jesus would lambast them for not submitting to John's message. Either way, their moral leadership would be compromised. Such is the dilemma of insecure individuals who seek power over God's people.

Now, the Lord was never reluctant to speak the truth, but it was always on His terms. He understood the manipulative power of human words and reasoning, how even the framing of a question can control the outcome of a debate. This was the One who spoke the universe into existence, who confounded human speech at the tower of Babel, and who enables humans to miraculously speak other human languages not previously learned (i.e. the spiritual gift of tongues). The religious leaders could not box this One into a corner by the same verbal gymnastics they used to gain power over the masses.

Though they answered, "We do not know," in reality they were caught in their own game. They had hoped to snare Jesus in a transgression of insubordination against the chief priests and elders. They were playing hardball but were up against the One who invented human reasoning.

Lord, I don't want to play around with what You have said, twisting it to justify my own power grab over others. Forgive me for times I have done that, and help me avoid it in the future.

Duplicity Condemned

Matthew 21:28-32

28 "But what do you think? A man had two sons, and he came to the first and said,
'Son, go work today in the vineyard.' 29 And he answered, 'I will not'; but afterward
he regretted it and went. 30 The man came to the second and said the same thing;
and he answered, 'I will, sir'; but he did not go. 31 Which of the two did the will of
his father?" They said, "The first." Jesus said to them, "Truly I say to you that the
tax collectors and prostitutes will get into the kingdom of God before you. 32 For
John came to you in the way of righteousness and you did not believe him; but the
tax collectors and prostitutes did believe him; and you, seeing this, did not even
feel remorse afterward so as to believe him."

Poignantly, Jesus told this story as a judgment on the attitude of His critics. The chief priests and elders, who had for so long put on a show of submitting to God's authority, were now being exposed for not being obedient at all. They had looked down their noses at those who outwardly did not keep the Law. Remember the attitude of the Pharisee (Luke 18:11) who essentially prayed to himself: "God, I thank You that I am not like other people: swindlers, unjust, adulterers, or even like this tax collector." Remember the obvious distaste for common people when the scribes saw Jesus eating with the sinners and tax collectors. They asked His disciples, "Why is He eating and drinking with tax collectors and sinners?" (Mark 2:16). The religious elite viewed themselves as righteous and gave the outward appearance of obedience to God.

Jesus made it absolutely clear that such superficiality would not protect them from the authority of God preached through John the Baptist. In other words, from the beginning of John's and Jesus' preaching about the kingdom of God, they feigned interest but had no intention of obeying it. That is Jesus' point!

Jesus contrasts the Pharisees with the tax collectors and prostitutes (to name a couple examples)—those who came repenting and believing, those considered obedient. What a slam against the duplicity of the religious leaders—and all who pretend religiosity outwardly, but inwardly are gripped with pride and rebellion. The Lord Jesus pulls no punches here. The down-and-outers who repent and believe will find favor with God long before the hypocritical religious leaders with hearts of stone. What's more, even after the Pharisees saw the restoration and reformation of such obvious sinners, they refused to acknowledge their cold-heartedness. It would have been a loss of pride to consider themselves in need of the same repentance as prostitutes and crooked tax collectors. Oh, the tragic yet rich irony of grace!

Lord, forgive me for arrogantly thinking I don't need Your grace as much as other more "obvious" sinners need it.

Week 35
Day 4

Spiritual Insubordination

Matthew 21:33-39

33 "Listen to another parable. There was a landowner who PLANTED A VINEYARD AND PUT A WALL AROUND IT AND DUG A WINE PRESS IN IT, AND BUILT A TOWER, *and rented it out to vine-growers and went on a journey. 34 When the harvest time approached, he sent his slaves to the vine-growers to receive his produce. 35 The vine-growers took his slaves and beat one, and killed another, and stoned a third. 36 Again he sent another group of slaves larger than the first; and they did the same thing to them. 37 But afterward he sent his son to them, saying, 'They will respect my son.' 38 But when the vine-growers saw the son, they said among themselves, 'This is the heir; come, let us kill him and seize his inheritance.' 39 They took him, and threw him out of the vineyard and killed him."*

Following one parable with another, Jesus drove home the point of the religious leaders' spiritual insubordination. This story captured the core problem of Israel. Jesus likened Israel to a carefully planned and developed vineyard. The "produce" was to be an effective witness in the world and to bring God's blessing to all people of the world. God had said to Abraham, "I will bless those who bless you, and the one who curses you I will curse. And in you all the families of the earth will be blessed" (Gen. 12:3).

God had built the descendants of Abraham into a great nation, entrusting it to leaders who were to guide them in following His commandments for life and community. He gave them the sacrificial systems to constantly remind them of their sinfulness and their need of His grace. He showed His favor to them, giving them military victory and material prosperity.

Despite all this, the people continually strayed. Yet God "spoke long ago to the fathers in the prophets in many portions and in many ways" (Heb. 1:2) to bring them to repentance. The people would not listen, just as the vine growers wouldn't listen to the messengers sent by the vineyard owner. They persecuted those messengers, thinking the vineyard was theirs for the taking.

Finally, though, "in these last days [He] has spoken to us in His Son, whom He appointed heir of all things, through whom also He made the world" (Heb. 1:2). And Israel was about to reject the vineyard owner's Son, Jesus.

In this parable, Jesus reveals that the religious leaders knew what they were doing! They knew He had come from God. As early as Nicodemus's interview with Jesus in John 3, the Pharisees had recognized that Jesus had been sent from God. And His miracles proved it. Their resistance did not indicate a lack of understanding it. They simply refused the truth of who He was and is.

Lord, the horror of seeing others so knowingly and blatantly reject You strikes fear in me. Help me see areas where I am rejecting Your lordship in my life.

Week 35
Day 5

Kingdom Hiatus Foretold

Matthew 21:40-46

40 "Therefore when the owner of the vineyard comes, what will he do to those
vine-growers?" 41 They said to Him, "He will bring those wretches to a wretched
end, and will rent out the vineyard to other vine-growers who will pay him the
proceeds at the proper seasons." 42 Jesus said to them, "Did you never read in the
Scriptures, 'The stone which the builders rejected, this became the chief corner
stone; this came about from the Lord, and it is marvelous in our eyes'? 43 Therefore
I say to you, the kingdom of God will be taken away from you and given to a people,
producing the fruit of it. 44 And he who falls on this stone will be broken to pieces; but
on whomever it falls, it will scatter him like dust." 45 When the chief priests and the
Pharisees heard His parables, they understood that He was speaking about them.
46 When they sought to seize Him, they feared the people, because they considered
Him to be a prophet.

At this point the chief priests and Pharisees understood clearly that the parable of the vineyard was a judgment against them. In the dexterity of masterful deduction, Jesus led them to their own denunciation of themselves. The moral conclusion was obvious. The owner of the vineyard would, expressed in their own words, justly "bring those wretches to a wretched end."

Jesus turned their own verdict back on them by referring them to the passage in the Psalms about the stone which the builders rejected (Ps. 118:22-23). That psalm anticipated the day when God's blessing in the kingdom would be fulfilled. Yet what the Jews anticipated would be taken from them and given to others because they rejected Christ. As events unfolded, God's plan would shift—at least temporarily—from the Jews to the Gentiles. Israel would be "broken to pieces" and God would "scatter him like dust." That was what Jesus had warned earlier: "The first shall be last, and the last first" (20:16).

God would bypass the Jews as He moved to fulfill the promises to Abraham, blessing the world in a new way. Instead of using the Jews as a whole, He would use one Jewish descendant of Abraham, the "seed" that Galatians 3:16 speaks about, that is, Jesus, to reach the world—and do that using the Gentiles! Later, in Romans 10 and 11, Paul explains this hiatus in God's plan for Israel (what we call *the church age*) was temporary—until Israel is fully restored.

The Jewish leaders' response to the parable indicates their dilemma: in their rage they wanted to seize Jesus to kill Him, but their fear of the people hindered them—at least for the moment.

Lord, thank you that the message reached me, despite the rebellion of Your chosen people. I will be forever grateful that You found another way!

Weekend Reading

Saturday – Job 6
Sunday – Job 7

Personal Reflections

The Greatest Storyteller

Matthew 22:1-2

[1] Jesus spoke to them again in parables, saying, [2] "The kingdom of heaven may be compared to a king who gave a wedding feast for his son."

The time of Jesus' crucifixion was coming fast, but He stayed focused on teaching the people in stories meant to warn them. In particular these stories pointed to the religious leaders, who were "blind guides of the blind" (15:14). Jesus' teaching method continued to invoke the power of story. Socrates, the ancient Greek philosopher, taught by means of questions (what has been called the Socratic method). Aristotle taught didactically, but Jesus taught primarily through parables. In fact, God's message to all of humanity comes in the grandest "story" of all, the story of Jesus Christ. The One who came telling stories *is* the story!

One reason we relate to the stories in the Bible is that they show us that God does, in fact, understand us. Stories are effective because they take us from the known to the unknown. In the stories Jesus told He always began with something people could relate to. They draw us in, so that we inevitably find ourselves participating mentally in the developing plot without realizing it. In the parable of the prodigal son, some people identify with the son who strayed, readily seeing themselves as ones who have also strayed from their heavenly Father. Others see themselves, as the Pharisees surely did, in the older brother who was quite annoyed at the father's forgiveness of the wayward son. Those religious leaders were annoyed that Jesus welcomed and forgave crooked tax collectors and prostitutes. Jesus' stories always drew people in, so they could readily see and comprehend the truth.

Parables are best understood as elaborate innuendoes, where people went away thinking, "Was He saying that against me?" A kind of "If the shoe fits, wear it" lesson. The genius of this is that if someone were to take offense, it would be tacit admission that the shoe did indeed fit!

In our passage for today, Jesus set the stage for a message against the Jewish leaders who were rejecting the kingdom of God, yet He did not come right out and say that. However, the story lined up well with the events transpiring—that Christ's arrival had been announced with pomp and celebration a few days earlier, and that Israel, a few days later, would reject Him. One can hardly deny the parallel. Through the final days of Christ's trial and crucifixion, this parable must have nagged the memory of each of His rejecters.

Lord, help me to listen carefully to Your stories so that my heart will not be so dull that I miss Your message for me.

Week 36
Day 2

God's Limitation

Matthew 22:3-7

---

[3] "And he sent out his slaves to call those who had been invited to the wedding feast, and they were unwilling to come. [4] Again he sent out other slaves saying, 'Tell those who have been invited, "Behold, I have prepared my dinner; my oxen and my fattened livestock are all butchered and everything is ready; come to the wedding feast." ' [5] But they paid no attention and went their way, one to his own farm, another to his business, [6] and the rest seized his slaves and mistreated them and killed them. [7] But the king was enraged, and he sent his armies and destroyed those murderers and set their city on fire."

Those who say Jesus was only about love and kindness either haven't read the actual gospel accounts at all or have read them selectively. Modern purveyors of politically correct truth pick and choose what they want to believe about Jesus, trying to tame Him to their own sensitivities and sentiments. But on what basis do they make their choices? We must take Jesus as He actually was. The only way we can objectively and historically know anything about Him is through what was written by the NT writers. The real Jesus was, to be sure, the epitome of love. Ultimately, however, those who reject Him would suffer terrible consequences. That is the point of this parable.

The Lord spoke this parable just a few days before His final rejection by the Jews. It was clearly an indictment against them; the parallels are fairly obvious. The king in the story portrays God. He has invited many to the celebration of His son's wedding. From later revelation we see the analogy of Christ and His bride, the church (cf. Eph. 5:23-27; John 3:29; Rev. 19:7). The guests unwilling to come clearly referred to the religious leaders and ultimately to all who resisted Jesus. Historically, God's chosen people had continually rejected the messengers (prophets) God had sent. Despite a few intervals of revival, for the most part they rejected God's message and the prophets. The king (God) invited the people repeatedly, reasoning that there would be great blessings and celebration. But the response was still the same—the people were consumed with self-interest.

God is extremely patient (Ps. 103:8; Isa. 57:16), to be sure. But as Jesus recounts this parable, we see there is a limit to God's patience. This is not new information, for many events of the OT testify to this: the flood, the Babylonian captivity, and (in Jesus' day) Israel's suffering under Roman domination. Jesus spoke frequently of those who will be cast into "outer darkness," where there will be "weeping and gnashing of teeth" (8:12).

Father, help me to not take Your patience as a sign of slackness (2 Pet. 3:3-9), but to recognize You are withholding judgment for a time, not wanting any to perish.

A Broad Invitation

Matthew 22:8-10

[9] "'Go therefore to the main highways, and as many as you find there, invite to the wedding feast.' [10] Those slaves went out into the streets and gathered together all they found, both evil and good; and the wedding hall was filled with dinner guests."

As Jesus continued His story of the king who invited people to his son's wedding feast, the plot took an interesting turn. The first and second set of invitees, those who made up the "A" and "B" list, refused to attend; they couldn't be bothered. They even abused and killed the king's messengers. After destroying them, He extended the invitation to anyone willing to come. A mixed bag of people responded and accepted the invitation, some described as "evil" and some "good." The celebration could now begin.

The parallel with the Jews' present situation was clear. They were God's "prime list" of invitees, and the first ones to receive God's message of salvation. When Jesus sent out His disciples. He instructed them, "Do not go in the way of the Gentiles, and do not enter any city of the Samaritans; but rather go to the lost sheep of the house of Israel" (10:5-6). He clarified this way: "I was sent only to the lost sheep of the house of Israel" (15:24). Paul affirmed this when he wrote that the gospel was being proclaimed "to the Jew first and also to the Greek" (Rom. 1:16).

This Jews-first invitation fulfilled God's promise to Abraham, "in you all the families of the earth will be blessed" (Gen. 12:3). God planned to bless the descendants of Israel and, through them, bless the world. So in sending the Messiah, God would give Israel the first opportunity to receive God's message. (In the words of the parable, they were the first ones invited to the wedding celebration.) But Israel's rejection brought about their judgment and as a result, being bypassed. God would then reach the Gentiles directly—not via the Jews. Though the parable described this situation figuratively, the message is clear. God would now judge the Jews because of their insolence and bless the Gentiles despite their absence from the prime list.

This should be nothing new for the readers of this gospel account, for Jesus previously emphasized, "The last shall be first and the first last" (19:30; 20:16). The status of "first invited" did not exempt Israel from God's judgment. However, their rejection meant the wonderful message would now come to the rest of us.

Father, thank you that although I had no privileged standing with You, You graciously invited me to an intimate relationship with You and Your Son.

Not Dressed for Success

Matthew 22:11-13

11 *"But when the king came in to look over the dinner guests, he saw a man there who was not dressed in wedding clothes,* 12 *and he said to him, 'Friend, how did you come in here without wedding clothes?' And the man was speechless.* 13 *Then the king said to the servants, 'Bind him hand and foot, and throw him into the outer darkness; in that place there will be weeping and gnashing of teeth.' "*

The second thrust of Jesus' parable of the wedding feast for the king's son has to do with those who finally did attend. These were not the A listers or even the B listers who rejected the king's request, but rather those found in the "highways"—anyone willing to come. One man who did accept the invitation drew attention to himself for not having come dressed properly. He had no legitimate excuse for this *faux pas*, this disregard for accepted custom and an affront to the king and his son. As a result, he provoked the monarch's anger.

A number of lessons may be learned at this point. First, Jesus expected that those invited to the kingdom of heaven must come on God's terms, not in their own cavalier way. Just coming as you are is not enough. There must be proper attire. The OT speaks of being "clothed with salvation" (2 Chron. 6:41; Isa. 61:10). Paul expands on this when he describes himself as "not having a righteousness of my own derived from the Law, but that which is through faith in Christ, the righteousness which comes from God on the basis of faith" (Phil. 3:9). Jesus' parable also points to the need of faith when coming to Christ. God will accept no one who attempts to enter presumptuously.

Second, God will respond in righteous anger when people presume upon Him. Some have trouble with the idea that God can get mad at people; but Jesus, who is Love Incarnate, taught that His loving Father is also by nature a God of anger. Arrogance, in the face of His love, rejects that love, deeming it unneeded. The one who does not respond to God's love, which He demonstrated in sending His Son, "will not see life, but the wrath of God abides on him" (John 3:36).

Third, there is a literal hell. The parable, though not using the word *hell*, depicts a place of confinement (binding) and suffering (weeping and gnashing of teeth), bereft of truth (outer darkness). Some today teach that Jesus only spoke in exaggerated terms to make a point. How could a loving God send someone to a literal, eternal place like hell? We would rebut by asking why Jesus would picture Him in such an extreme way if it were not so. The all-knowing Son of God did not use "scare tactics" but justifiably warned His detractors of the serious consequences of refusing God's invitation.

Father, help me never to take a minimalistic view of the consequences of people rejecting Christ. The stakes are too great to be wrong on these things.

The Chooser Choosing

Matthew 22:14

[14] *"For many are called, but few are chosen."*

This short verse carries huge questions and implications. Who are the chosen? How does one become chosen? How does one influence the chooser? What does it mean to be called but not chosen?

To attempt to answer these questions it is essential to understand the context of the statment. Jesus was summarizing the message of the parable He had just given—the king inviting his subjects to the wedding celebration of his son. Clearly, many were called—from the select group of first- and second-round invitees and then everyone else in the kingdom. The "chosen ones" are those who came and were properly attired. Out of the many invited, only a small number were welcomed into the celebration by the king. What are the spiritual implications? First, the invitation to repent and believe was for all people, the "whoever" of John 3:16. The Lord instructed His disciples to take the message into the whole world (28:18-20). The pervasiveness of the invitation is clear. But the limited nature of "being chosen" is a bit more difficult to understand.

Some have said that God has predestined only a few for salvation, and that the payment for sin (Christ's atoning death) was limited to only those who were predetermined to believe. A better way to understand this enigmatic statement is to see that the *criteria* of repentance and faith were predetermined by God, and that among the "called" ones, only those who, in the end, meet the criteria, are actually received into the God's kingdom. So in that sense, they are chosen. Theologians have debated these things for centuries. But Jesus' death for all (see 1 John 2:2) made the invitation to all people *possible*.

The point of Jesus' statement must not be lost in theological debate. The vast majority will not be found in the kingdom of God because they refuse to believe. This is tragic because God is "not wishing for any to perish but for all to come to repentance" (2 Pet. 3:9). Unfortunately, "the gate is wide and the way is broad that leads to destruction, and there are many who enter through it. For the gate is small and the way is narrow that leads to life, and there are few who find it" (7:13-14). In His grace, though, "as many as received Him, to them He gave the right to become children of God, even to those who believe in His name" (John 1:12).

Lord, help me to not get so bogged down in debating "predestination versus the free will of man" that I miss Your heart for the lost souls of this world.

Weekend Reading

Saturday – Job 8
Sunday – Job 9

Personal Reflections

Hypocrisy Nailed

Matthew 22:15-18

[15] Then the Pharisees went and plotted together how they might trap Him in what He said. [16] And they sent their disciples to Him, along with the Herodians, saying, "Teacher, we know that You are truthful and teach the way of God in truth, and defer to no one; for You are not partial to any. [17] Tell us then, what do You think? Is it lawful to give a poll-tax to Caesar, or not?" [18] But Jesus perceived their malice, and said, "Why are you testing Me, you hypocrites?"

The Pharisees knew perfectly well that Jesus was targeting them with this parable. The gloves came off! They laid plans to frame their Messiah, trapping Him with a trick question. They cleverly enlisted the Herodian party. The Herodians were theologically similar to the Sadducees and, thus, opposed the Pharisees in religious matters. More importantly here, they were politically affiliated with the Herodian dynasty, whose power depended upon their loyalty to Rome. The Pharisees' alliance with the Herodians, therefore, made for strange bedfellows. Such is the nature of vengeance.

The setup would have been a stroke of political genius if their opponent had not been the King of the Universe! First came the insincere compliments, which, unbeknown to them, dripped with an ironic admission that Jesus spoke truthfully. If that were really the case, then why did they not accept His teachings? According to what Nicodemus said in John 3:2, in the early days of Jesus' public ministry, they apparently accepted in principle that God was with Him.

Second, they recognized that Jesus showed no partiality, deferring to no one. This was the setup for their trap. They were encouraging Him to show no deference to Caesar or the Roman taxing system. That stance would fit right in with Christ's coming into Jerusalem presenting Himself as the King of Israel.

So the question followed: should Jews give a poll-tax to Caesar? (This tax was a levy imposed on every Jew simply because they were under the domination of Rome.) If Jesus said yes, then He could hardly be the Jewish King, the long expected Messiah. Nothing would change, and the people's hope for political freedom from Rome would dissipate. If He said no, then the Herodians would have their pretext for arresting Him. However, Jesus saw through their duplicity and called them out on their hypocrisy.

Lord, You will not be manipulated, so help me not to manipulate others with ridiculous theological arguments.

Week 37
Day 2

Whose Image?

Matthew 22:19-22

[19] *"Show Me the coin used for the poll-tax." And they brought Him a denarius.*
[20] *And He said to them, "Whose likeness and inscription is this?"* [21] *They said to Him, "Caesar's." Then He said to them, "Then render to Caesar the things that are Caesar's; and to God the things that are God's."* [22] *And hearing this, they were amazed, and leaving Him, they went away.*

The Herodians' trick question about whether to give tax to Rome would have won the day against anyone else, but they were up against the One who created the very minds they were using to try to thwart Him. Jesus' answer was at once deft and simple. Even a child could answer easily. Requesting a coin for His object lesson, the Lord asked whose image was on the coin. One can almost picture a teacher condescending to instruct his immature charges, who should know better!

He asked one simple question: "Whose image is on the coin?" The answer was obvious. Jesus then replied that they should give to Caesar the things that belong to him, and to God the things that belong to Him. On one level, Jesus expertly sidestepped their question. But the implications ran deeper than appeared at first glance. Clearly, the coin belonged to Caesar in the political sense, but the thrust of the question had to do more with whether Jews should submit to Roman authority. And that was precisely the rub—the issue of submitting to authority!

The Jews did not like being ruled by Rome. At the same time, they were refusing to submit to *God's* authority. The coin bore the image of Caesar, but where was the image of God to be found? Every Jew knew well that they had been created in the image of God and bore His likeness, as Genesis 1:26-27 and Genesis 5:1 made clear. They were taught this from childhood. Furthermore, they were the chosen people of God, and bound to Him in the covenant relationship as spelled out in the law of Moses. So when Jesus said, "Render to God the things that are God's" He meant those "things" which are stamped with His likeness—not mere coins, but something far greater, namely themselves.

The Jews had not "rendered to God, the things that are God's," but were living in rebellion. The message of both John the Baptist and Jesus had all along been, "Repent, for the kingdom of heaven is at hand." This, in Jesus' estimation, was of far greater concern than whether or not they should submit to Rome. Submission to God was paramount! The Herodians left speechless and unbowed, but they knew they had been outwitted!

Lord, You created me in Your image and likeness and redeemed me by Your blood, so I belong to You twice over. I resubmit my life to Your purposes.

False Premise

Matthew 22:23-28

[23] On that day some Sadducees (who say there is no resurrection) came to Jesus and questioned Him, [24] asking, "Teacher, Moses said, 'If a man dies having no children, his brother as next of kin shall marry his wife, and raise up children for his brother.' [25] Now there were seven brothers with us; and the first married and died, and having no children left his wife to his brother; [26] so also the second, and the third, down to the seventh. [27] Last of all, the woman died. [28] In the resurrection, therefore, whose wife of the seven will she be? For they all had married her."

The Sadducees spoke up next after the Pharisees and the Herodians had their shots at Jesus. The various religious and political opponents in Israel all joined in their efforts to undercut Jesus' influence with the people. Each of these groups had the same fear: loss of their own following to Jesus. The Sadducees' unique role in the religious debates of the day concerned their denial of a bodily resurrection. They tried to trap Jesus in this debate with a cleverly concocted argument they believed would undermine the belief in resurrection.

Their question was straightforward. If there were a resurrection, the implications would be untenable, they asserted. They presented a simple illustration to "validate" their case. The logic of it would, under normal circumstances, be compelling. But they, like other groups, were going after the One who knows all and understands all.

The argument ultimately proved faulty because it was built on the wrong premise. They built their case by supposing a woman had a series of husbands. To justify the elements of the scenario, the Sadducees even tossed in support from the Torah (Deut. 25:5-6) that a man should marry his brother's widow if she were childless. In their case study the woman had seven husbands and each one died. All this had the markings of a refined religious dispute, with careful wording and scriptural support. The Sadducees then posed their question with an air of certain victory: which of the seven men would be her husband in the resurrection (if there were such a thing)?

Building an argument on a false premise is nothing new in religious circles. Skilled rhetoricians, slick pulpiteers, and suave homiliticians can weave cultured words and esoteric ideas into convincing arguments with biblical support. One "proves" that ____________ (fill in the doctrine) is correct, while another "proves" that the same thing is not correct. And the common use of strategic questions can often form the wedge of false teaching. Again, we hear the voice of Satan, "Indeed, has God said…?" (Gen. 3:1).

Lord, help me not to be duped by the clever arguments of false teachers who mount up with persuasive arguments that contradict Your Word.

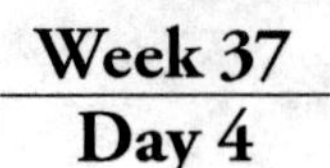

God of the Living

Matthew 22:29-33

[29] But Jesus answered and said to them, "You are mistaken, not understanding
the Scriptures nor the power of God. [30] For in the resurrection they neither marry
nor are given in marriage, but are like angels in heaven. [31] But regarding the
resurrection of the dead, have you not read what was spoken to you by God: [32] 'I
AM THE GOD OF ABRAHAM, AND THE GOD OF ISAAC, AND THE GOD OF JACOB'? He is not
the God of the dead but of the living." [33] When the crowds heard this, they were
astonished at His teaching.

A preacher once spoke at a funeral about how the departed elderly woman was having a joyous reunion in heaven with her predeceased husband. Unfortunately the minister didn't know the woman had been married twice, the first husband having died after just a few years of marriage. So which husband was she enjoying the reunion with?! This was the same basic scenario the Sadducees presented to Jesus. They assumed the same faulty premise concerning the resurrected state.

The Lord made clear that marriage is a union for this life *only* (see Romans 7:1-3). While we often like to say marriages are "made in heaven," the resurrected state is like that of the angels: there is no marriage between humans in heaven. There will be a different kind of marriage—that of Christ and His bride, the church (see Eph. 5:26-27; Rev. 19:7-9). The completeness and intimacy that believers will experience in this union with Him will supersede and nullify any need for union with another human being. So the Lord easily turned aside the Sadducees' trick question as a false premise.

Jesus then directly challenged their denial of the resurrection by quoting Exodus 3:6, where God spoke to Moses from the burning bush: "I am the God of Abraham" This conversation took place in the context of God revealing His divine, name, *Yahweh,* a poignant wordplay (see Exodus 3:14-16). *Yahweh* and *I am* come from the same root word. God is the eternal Present One, always acting on behalf of His people. In particular, Jesus asserted that Yahweh is still the God of the Patriarchs. Jesus spoke of being (present tense) their God when He spoke to Moses and in Jesus' day as He spoke to the Sadducees. This could not be the case if the Patriarchs were gone, never to be raised from the dead. If they ceased to exist, God could only be thought of as *having been* their God, not as *being* their God. If God is still, in fact, God of the Patriarchs, however, resurrection logically follows!

Father, You are the God of Abraham, Isaac, and Jacob—and of me, both now and for eternity. I look forward to being with You forever, fulfilled in every way.

The Greatest Commandments

Matthew 22:34-40

34 But when the Pharisees heard that Jesus had silenced the Sadducees, they gathered themselves together. 35 One of them, a lawyer, asked Him a question, testing Him, 36 "Teacher, which is the great commandment in the Law?" 37 And He said to him, "'You shall love the Lord your God with all your heart, and with all your soul, and with all your mind.' 38 This is the great and foremost commandment. 39 The second is like it, 'You shall love your neighbor as yourself.' 40 On these two commandments depend the whole Law and the Prophets."

Next, a lawyer from among the Pharisees took his turn at Jesus. Lawyers were the experts at interpreting the Law; they had incisive minds and were well-versed in the rabbinical debates over the relative importance of God's many commandments. Then, as now, many spent copious amounts of time and energy arguing the "finer" points of Scripture, the relative merits of the plethora of Scripture teachings. It seems that each group in Christendom has its defining doctrine or characteristic, supposing that they themselves have the corner on a specific truth or doctrine which no one else appreciates as much, or emphasizes enough.

Pride of doctrine is detestable in God's sight. If God has revealed to you clarity in the truth, it is only by His grace. As such it should be held with humility, not as a means of exalting oneself above other Christians. The lawyer, as one example of this, came in his arrogance to test Jesus with his disingenuous question about which are the greatest commandments.

In response, Jesus gave a straightforward answer: Love God completely and unreservedly (quoting Deuteronomy 6:5), and then love your neighbor as yourself (quoting Leviticus 19:18). All other teachings in Scripture depend upon these two commandments. Pretty simple. Modern liberal Christianity (which rose in the early twentieth century) got this backward, setting the salt and light ministries of the social gospel (loving your neighbor) as the pinnacle of the Christian faith, rather than a right relationship with God (loving God).

There is a move in the early part of the twenty-first century among some evangelicals to revisit this liberal position, swinging the pendulum to balance dry evangelicalism that has confused fidelity to the letter of Scripture with the love of God, the spirit of Scripture. The apostle Paul described biblical teaching this way: "The goal of our instruction is love from a pure heart and a good conscience and a sincere faith" (1 Tim 1:5).

Lord, because You first loved us, we can love You in response. Only then can we truly love others (1 John 4:19). Help me keep that order straight.

Weekend Reading

Saturday – Job 10
Sunday – Job 11

Personal Reflections

Derailing the Darers

Matthew 22:41-46

41 Now while the Pharisees were gathered together, Jesus asked them a question:
42 "What do you think about the Christ, whose son is He?" They said to Him, "The
son of David." 43 He said to them, "Then how does David in the Spirit call Him
'Lord,' saying, 44 'THE LORD SAID TO MY LORD, "SIT AT MY RIGHT HAND, UNTIL I PUT
YOUR ENEMIES BENEATH YOUR FEET" '? 45 If David then calls Him 'Lord,' how is He his
son?" 46 No one was able to answer Him a word, nor did anyone dare from that
day on to ask Him another question.

Turning the tables, Jesus took the initiative in the interrogations. In so doing He brought the debate to a close. He focused on the core issue of His mission, the identity of the Messiah (*Christos,* you will remember, is the Greek form of the Hebrew term *Messiah.* English translators transliterate the Greek term into *Christ*). The issue of heritage was important to the Jews. It established one's right to ancestral lands and to privileges among God's people. In particular, the issue of the Messiah's heritage was crucial, so Jesus quizzed them about who the father of the Christ was.

The Pharisees responded with the standard answer: Christ would be the son of David. Every child in Israel knew that. He then quoted from Psalm 110:1, a messianic psalm. From this well-known passage He added a penetrating question that baffled them completely. The essence of Jesus' point was, how could the Jews reject Him as the Messiah when they were so ignorant about such a fundamental truth from a well-known prophecy?

The Jews believed Psalm 110:1 represented the Messiah as the one referred to as *the Lord*, the one before whom all God's enemies would bow. It was all about the Messiah. Jesus zeroed in on verse 1 ("The LORD said to my Lord"), where the original Hebrew reads, literally, "Yahweh said to my Adonai..." *Yahweh* refers to "the covenant God of Israel," and *Adonai* means "Lord" in the sense of "master." So this verse means "The covenant God of Israel said to my Master..." Therefore if Psalm 110:1 refers to the Messiah, the crux of Jesus' argument was this: how could Messiah be both the son of David and, at the same time, David's Master?

The Pharisees were stumped. His question ended their jousting, trying to trip Him up. They abandoned their attempts to trap Jesus in self-condemning words. From there Jesus continued on the offensive, launching into a blistering condemnation of those hypocritical leaders with a series of "woes."

Lord, I don't want to be like those religious leaders of Jesus' day. Help me not to be so stubborn and proud that I turn a blind eye to what You want to teach me.

Week 38
Day 2

Do as They Say, Not as They Do

Matthew 23:1-7

[1] Then Jesus spoke to the crowds and to His disciples, [2] saying: "The scribes and the Pharisees have seated themselves in the chair of Moses; [3] therefore all that they tell you, do and observe, but do not do according to their deeds; for they say things and do not do them. [4] They tie up heavy burdens and lay them on men's shoulders, but they themselves are unwilling to move them with so much as a finger. [5] But they do all their deeds to be noticed by men; for they broaden their phylacteries and lengthen the tassels of their garments. [6] They love the place of honor at banquets and the chief seats in the synagogues, [7] and respectful greetings in the market places, and being called Rabbi by men."

Following the intense debate, Jesus began to speak with open disdain for the scribes and the Pharisees with the force of a judge passing definitive judgment on them. This must have echoed in the memory of Jesus' half-brother James, years later, when he wrote, "Let not many of you become teachers, my brethren, knowing that as such we will incur a stricter judgment" (James 3:1).

The problem with the Pharisees was not only the impossibility of doing everything they taught but also the fact that they themselves did not do what they demanded of others. They presumed to add to the law of Moses as though they carried the same authority. All this multiplied the burden on the people. What were these burdens? They were the kind that religious leaders throughout history have always tended to lay on people: religious deeds meant to control the people rather than help them live. This was not God's intention. Through Moses God said, "This commandment which I command you today is not too difficult for you, nor is it out of reach" (Deut. 30:11). Even if sin makes God's commandments challenging, the additional manmade elements can cause the burden to be big enough to crush us. Even religious leaders can't handle that burden.

The Pharisees found it far easier to enact things that had the appearance of piety yet lacked reality, such as phylacteries and tassels. Phylacteries were leather containers strapped to the forehead or arm. Tassels were related to prayers—and the Pharisees made sure they had the largest! Pharisees took the best seats at banquets and synagogues, demanding to be addressed with utmost respect and titles. Those were the things that were important to them—not genuine piety.

Jesus' monologue here is depressing, but let's not fail to heed the warning: Don't be like this!

Father, show me when my words and actions are out of sync with You and I prove to be hypocritical. Illuminate me and convict me, so that I might live with integrity.

The Greatest Among You

Matthew 23:8-12

[8] "But do not be called Rabbi; for One is your Teacher, and you are all brothers. [9] Do not call anyone on earth your father; for One is your Father, He who is in heaven. [10] Do not be called leaders; for One is your Leader, that is, Christ. [11] But the greatest among you shall be your servant. [12] Whoever exalts himself shall be humbled; and whoever humbles himself shall be exalted."

Using the Pharisees as an illustration, Jesus warned the people of the pride of title and position. These things are not wrong in themselves. Jesus accepted such terms as *Rabbi* (Mark 9:5; John 11:8). However, the Pharisees showed how easily exalted titles can lead to self-exaltation.

The terms Jesus spoke of were the common epithets of the day for religious authorities. But this problem was not limited to the leaders of Jesus' time. The apostle John encountered this desire for prominence at the end of the first century. He described a man called Diotrephes, "who loves to be first among them, [and who] does not accept what we say" (3 John 9). Certainly, some do rise in prominence to become "first among equals" (as some have termed it), leaders among leaders. However, lusting for that for the sake of personal prominence can bring about one's downfall.

Unfortunately, worldly passions creep into the church. Even believers often try to distinguish themselves with titles. It is a heady thing to be in a position of authority or influence over people.

Jesus simply and essentially said not to seek greatness through titles or positions of prominence. He brought to their attention two great truths. First, only God is truly the Rabbi, Teacher, Father, and Leader. These terms may describe the ministry God calls a Christian to, but as titles describing the essence of a person, they apply only to God. We all fall short. For example, God calls some to "shepherd the church of God" (Acts 20:28), but only Christ is "the Chief Shepherd" (1 Pet. 5:4).

The second truth, and more to the heart of the matter, concerns the real path to greatness. Why settle for superficial greatness, which lasts only as long as the praise of men?

True greatness comes through humbling oneself. The irony is that we cannot embrace with pride the greatness resulting from humbling ourselves. If it could, then it would not have come through humility!

Father, I want to have the attitude that Jesus had when He took on the form of a bond-servant, living His life for the benefit of others.

"Woe to You"

Matthew 23:13-15

[13] *"But woe to you, scribes and Pharisees, hypocrites, because you shut off the kingdom of heaven from people; for you do not enter in yourselves, nor do you allow those who are entering to go in.* [14] *Woe to you, scribes and Pharisees, hypocrites, because you devour widows' houses, and for a pretense you make long prayers; therefore you will receive greater condemnation.* [15] *Woe to you, scribes and Pharisees, hypocrites, because you travel around on sea and land to make one proselyte; and when he becomes one, you make him twice as much a son of hell as yourselves."*

Jesus now turned to the most prominent religious leaders, the scribes and Pharisees, calling them hypocrites! He spoke openly to these who justified themselves, and, in so doing, actually condemned themselves. Enough time had passed to make obvious who were the ones who had hardened their hearts and rejected Jesus and His message.

He lays out a series of seven or eight woes to indicate the dire consequences of their actions. (Bible scholars debate whether verse 14 was original or was added by later copyists.) This was not a message calling them to repent anymore, but rather a message of judgment! What was coming for them would be overwhelmingly horrible! They not only failed to enter the kingdom themselves, but they kept others from entering in as well. They oppressed the disadvantaged while pretending to be religious. They went to great lengths to bring individuals under their power and then made them "twice as much a son of hell" as themselves. An acid comment indeed! Jesus proved their manmade religious system was a complete failure.

Many people today criticize church leaders, even using Jesus' actions here as precedence. True, there is much hypocrisy in church leadership, as evidenced by such things as media reports of pastors who commit immorality. However, which of us can so glibly level that accusation against Christian leaders, or anyone else for that matter, without making ourselves hypocrites in the process? The fact of the matter is that, as Christians, we have subscribed to a standard of living that none of us has yet reached (Phil 3:12). Anyone who attempts to lead or teach Scripture has an inherent difficulty: how can he teach what he himself has not mastered? The answer is that a teacher's job is to call others to *mutually* reach toward a higher standard. The hypocrisy comes when the leader acts like he has arrived. Nowhere is that more evident than when we judge others of hypocrisy! Only Jesus can make that judgment without being stained with the same sin.

Lord, I know that I fall short of the righteous standard to which I aspire. Help me live a life that inspires others to join me in reaching forward.

More Woes

Matthew 23:16-22

[16] "Woe to you, blind guides, who say, 'Whoever swears by the temple, that is nothing; but whoever swears by the gold of the temple is obligated.' [17] You fools and blind men! Which is more important, the gold or the temple that sanctified the gold? [18] And, 'Whoever swears by the altar, that is nothing, but whoever swears by the offering on it, he is obligated.' [19] You blind men, which is more important, the offering, or the altar that sanctifies the offering? [20] Therefore, whoever swears by the altar, swears both by the altar and by everything on it. [21] And whoever swears by the temple, swears both by the temple and by Him who dwells within it. [22] And whoever swears by heaven, swears both by the throne of God and by Him who sits upon it."

The scribes and Pharisees were blind guides, according to Jesus—and fools. (See Matthew 5:22; only Jesus can justly call someone a fool!) This third woe increased the intensity of His judgment on the scribes and Pharisees. By using hyperbole (exaggerated symbolisms), Jesus was conveying the severity of their callous offenses against God. By cataloguing these "woes" He was saying, in effect, "If you knew what was coming, you would avoid it at all costs!"

The temple in Jesus' day was not the original one that had been built by King Solomon in accordance with God's instructions and design. That one was destroyed during the Babylonian invasions of 605 BC and in the years following. The temple the Jews reconstructed after the exile did not achieve the glory of the first temple (see Haggai 2). However, the one of Jesus' day was a renovation, and it resulted in one of the larger constructions of the first century. The Jews gloried in their temple with great pride; it was central to life and religion for them.

Yet we see the greed, characteristic of our own times, evident then as well, even in the motivation for taking an oath. In earlier times, a person took an oath by saying, "As surely as the Lord lives…" to indicate the unquestioned certainty of his promise (cf. Num. 14:21; 1 Sam. 14:39). To break that oath would be tantamount to blasphemy; it meant the oath maker had little regard for God's existence. To the Jews of Jesus' day, that oath had morphed into swearing by the temple; they had put the temple in place of God. And Jesus accused them of replacing even the temple with what they saw as the ultimate reality—money! In effect, the acquisition of wealth was more important to them than the existence of God! The money people brought to support the religious leaders—not God, not even His earthly dwelling place—was what they prized most. The bottom line for them was money, not God.

Lord, in a world of greed, help me resist the lure of what satisfies my sinful heart. I want to fix my eyes only on You, the author and finisher of faith.

Weekend Reading

Saturday – Job 12
Sunday – Job 13

Personal Reflections

Hypocrisies Five and Six

Matthew 23:23-26

[23] "Woe to you, scribes and Pharisees, hypocrites! For you tithe mint and dill and cummin, and have neglected the weightier provisions of the law: justice and mercy and faithfulness; but these are the things you should have done without neglecting the others. [24] You blind guides, who strain out a gnat and swallow a camel! [25] Woe to you, scribes and Pharisees, hypocrites! For you clean the outside of the cup and of the dish, but inside they are full of robbery and self-indulgence. [26] You blind Pharisee, first clean the inside of the cup and of the dish, so that the outside of it may become clean also."

Continuing His attack on the scribes and Pharisees, relentlessly calling them hypocrites, Jesus turned to their incessant pickiness over the minutiae of law. This had become a fine art for these lovers of religious law. The Pharisees as a group may have originally felt God was withholding blessing until Israel sufficiently came in line with His righteousness. They hoped the Lord would see their attention to details as a sincere effort to bring blessing to Israel again. But in time they felt the need to make a public show of their extreme devotedness and also to coerce others to follow their example, lest God continue to hold out on them. Certainly, there was some precedent for this thinking. In the OT record, after the Israelites initially arrived in Canaan, Achan's individual sin led to the whole nation's defeat at Ai (Joshua 7). It is unlikely that the Pharisees were being motivated by that course of events, however.

Jesus Himself did not allow them that courtesy. In fact, He blasted them for their arrogance, the fallacy of their thinking they could coerce God and, in the process, make a good showing of themselves by their very public actions. God was, and continues to be, more interested in the *heart,* which was their real problem. They demonstrated a lopsided attention to the small things and neglected the large things like justice, mercy, and faithfulness. Jesus' graphic statement captures this well in His fifth woe to them: "You blind guides, who strain out a gnat and swallow a camel!" His sixth woe builds on the fifth with another memorable image, "You clean the outside of the cup and of the dish, but inside they are full of robbery and self-indulgence." This was not new teaching. In the Sermon on the Mount, Jesus made this case already, beginning with "Blessed are the pure in heart …" (5:8).

Jesus pulled no punches. Notice the repeated use of the words *hypocrites*, *blind*, and *woe*. The gloves were off. Parables set aside. Gentle persuasion shelved. Arrogant disregard for heart issues invoked Jesus' strongest wrath!

Lord, I don't want to be like the Pharisees! Grant me the insight and humility to accept Your rebuke when I am guilty of blind hypocrisy.

Week 39
Day 2

Hypocrisies Seven and Eight

Matthew 23:27-30

27 "Woe to you, scribes and Pharisees, hypocrites! For you are like whitewashed tombs which on the outside appear beautiful, but inside they are full of dead men's bones and all uncleanness. 28 So you, too, outwardly appear righteous to men, but inwardly you are full of hypocrisy and lawlessness. 29 Woe to you, scribes and Pharisees, hypocrites! For you build the tombs of the prophets and adorn the monuments of the righteous, 30 and say, 'If we had been living in the days of our fathers, we would not have been partners with them in shedding the blood of the prophets.'"

Hypocrisy knows no limit. For the seventh and eighth time, Jesus calls out a woe against the scribes and Pharisees, again calling them hypocrites. This popular word is used today to identify those whose lives do not match their talk. Yet who of us can use that term to describe others without condemning ourselves also? Jesus, however, used the term freely, letting loose a torrent of criticism against—and disdain for—those religious leaders. What a terrible thing to come under the ominous cloud of judgment.

It is important at this point to recognize that "God did not send the Son into the world to judge the world, but that the world might be saved through Him" (John 3:17). His woes here must be construed as the harshest possible warning to a group of people who refused to listen to the more gentle approach. This is the shock treatment. (See 1 Corinthians 5 for an example of this in the church.)

The seventh woe likens their blatant attitudes to a tomb. It may look nice on the outside, but the inside is rotten. It stinks, and it's full of decay. That describes well the inner lives of the scribes and Pharisees. None of us has the unique insight to judge another man's heart. But Jesus, being perfectly man and perfectly God, does, in fact, know the inner thoughts of humans (John 2:24). So His assessment of the religious leaders was right on.

The eighth and final woe focuses on the disingenuous honor they paid to the prophets. The Pharisees and scribes boasted of their own courage and loyalty, and even made a parade of their exalting righteous men. All the religious talk, speaking well of godly people, and honoring others, does not take the place of an inner life that is built on character and a loving response to the Lord. The evil of their forefathers was well established—and the Pharisees and scribes made sure to let everyone know that they themselves would never have allowed such evil to take place. Yet they were already scheming to kill Jesus! Even on the supposition that Jesus was only a prophet, their own actions and words condemned them.

Lord, since You warn people so strongly against hypocrisy, help me avoid that attitude and occupy myself with living for Christ and for others.

Somber Warning

Matthew 23:31-36

[31]*"So you testify against yourselves, that you are sons of those who murdered the prophets.* [32]*Fill up, then, the measure of the guilt of your fathers.* [33] *You serpents, you brood of vipers, how will you escape the sentence of hell?* [34] *Therefore, behold, I am sending you prophets and wise men and scribes; some of them you will kill and crucify, and some of them you will scourge in your synagogues, and persecute from city to city,* [35] *so that upon you may fall the guilt of all the righteous blood shed on earth, from the blood of righteous Abel to the blood of Zechariah, the son of Berechiah, whom you murdered between the temple and the altar.* [36] *Truly I say to you, all these things will come upon this generation."*

In His final diatribe, Jesus pulled out all the stops and unleashed His stinging judgment of the scribes and Pharisees. They had incriminated their ancestors who murdered the prophets; and they were about to follow suit. Judgment would be severe. Jesus called them serpents and vipers, recalling John the Baptist's denunciation of them three years earlier (3:7).

Despite all their rejection, God would not stop sending His messengers. First it would be the apostles, then those who believed through their testimony. The religious leaders of the Jews would continue to show their colors, persecuting, even killing, those sent with the message of warning, just as they were about to do to Jesus. Ultimately their rebellion in killing Christ and His followers would bring the weight of judgment deserved by all who killed the prophets before them. Hypocrites take on themselves the judgments they heap on others! That principle is no more true than for those who kill the Messiah, the Son sent by God the Father. The parable of the vineyard would be fulfilled.

Is this judgment on the scribes and Pharisees final? No, I don't think so. The judgment of Nineveh bears a remarkable resemblance here. The message Jonah finally (though reluctantly) preached sounded just as definitive. But when the Ninevites repented, "God saw their deeds, that they turned from their wicked way, then God relented concerning the calamity which He had declared He would bring upon them. And He did not do it" (Jonah 3:10).

So the definitive message of Jesus should have struck fear in the hearts the Pharisees, with the goal of bringing repentance. The message of warning is ultimately a gracious message. Jonah finally had to admit, "I knew that You are a gracious and compassionate God, slow to anger and abundant in lovingkindness, and one who relents concerning calamity" (Jonah 4:2).

Lord, help me see that, for some people, the most gracious thing I can do is to warn them of judgment.

Week 39
Day 4

Compassionate Anger

Matthew 23:37-39

[37] *"Jerusalem, Jerusalem, who kills the prophets and stones those who are sent to her! How often I wanted to gather your children together, the way a hen gathers her chicks under her wings, and you were unwilling.* [38] *Behold, your house is being left to you desolate!* [39] *For I say to you, from now on you will not see Me until you say, 'Blessed is He who comes in the name of the Lord!'"*

Wrath from God is not without balance. The judgment of God is always accompanied by the message of repentance—whether implied in God's character or stated overtly, as in this passage. Following the Lord's most condemning warning regarding their impending rejection of their Messiah, He revealed that His anger for them was borne out of compassion, and He longed to show mercy. He therefore provided a way of escape from divine judgment.

The tone is that of a grieving mother who mourns for her erring chicks. God's anger is not capricious or without just cause. Some people today view God as a frustrated deity who reacts in knee-jerk impulses, and when he doesn't get his way with humans, he uses force. But that is not the God of the Bible. Others, trying to tame God, selectively choose only those biblical passages that fit their image of a peace-loving, moralistic preacher of love. True, "God is love," as John wrote in 1 John 4:8. But, as we have seen, He is not to be trifled with. Rejecting God invokes His terrible anger.

Because only God can comprehend the full import of His anger on sinners (and the justifiable consequences), how awesome it is that He "is patient toward you, not wishing for any to perish but for all to come to repentance" (2 Pet. 3:9). And in the case of God's chosen people themselves, "… if the word spoken through angels proved unalterable, and every transgression and disobedience received a just penalty, how will we [Jews] escape if we neglect so great a salvation?" (Heb. 2:2-3).

For the Jewish nation, that salvation will come only when they are ready to say, "Blessed is He who comes in the name of the Lord." In quoting from Psalm 118:26, Jesus showed that Israel has a future. God did not dismiss them and replace the nation forever with the church, as taught by some today. Paul explained it this way: "I say then, they [i.e., Israel] did not stumble so as to fall, did they? May it never be! But by their transgression salvation has come to the Gentiles, to make them jealous" (Rom. 11:11). God will once again restore the nation, but not until they are willing to accept their Messiah.

Father, thank you for Your faithfulness. Even in Your wrath, You still remember Your promises to your chosen people, and I believe You will fulfill them.

When Will Christ Return?

Matthew 24:1-3

[1] Jesus came out from the temple and was going away when His disciples came up to point out the temple buildings to Him. [2] And He said to them, "Do you not see all these things? Truly I say to you, not one stone here will be left upon another, which will not be torn down." [3] As He was sitting on the Mount of Olives, the disciples came to Him privately, saying, "Tell us, when will these things happen, and what will be the sign of Your coming, and of the end of the age?"

Knowledge of the future gives hope to the suffering faithful. So Jesus embarked upon what is often called the Olivet Discourse, giving the disciples an outline of what would happen in the future. He left Jerusalem and traveled across the Kidron Valley to the Mount of Olives, the elevated area where Bethany and Bethphage were located. This was where He would spend His last hours before being apprehended for execution. Dark times were coming, and His faithful followers were going to need hope, not just for the next few days, but for the persecution that would be their lot for the rest of their lives.

Eschatology is the study of the end-time events, when God consummates His plan for the ages. These verses begin one of the key NT teachings on the subject. The first thing Jesus predicts, as He leaves Jerusalem with the disciples, is that the temple itself would be torn down! The temple was the center of spiritual life for the Jewish people. Without it there would be no place to bring sacrifices and offerings to God. In previous days God meted out judgment on Israel by using the Babylonians to invade the land, destroy the temple, and take the nation away into exile. So again, in the end times, God would pour out His anger because of their rejection of their Messiah. The destruction of the temple would demonstrate God's extreme displeasure. Every Jew would understand that! In AD 70, some forty years later, the Romans, in fact, ransacked Jerusalem, tearing down the temple—stone by stone. And today, some twenty centuries later, it remains unbuilt.

The disciples picked up His drift and inquired about two things: the timing of these events, and the confirmatory signs signaling His coming and the end of the age. He revealed much here that would keep His disciples, both then and now, anticipating the end—but without hard-and-fast timing data. Just before He ascended to heaven His disciples asked Him again, and then He answered, "It is not for you to know times or epochs which the Father has fixed by His own authority" (Acts 1:7). Each generation is left with the hope that theirs could be the one in which God brings everything to an end.

Lord, help me keep alive the anticipation that You will settle all accounts in the end. I can trust in You; that gives me hope.

Weekend Reading

Saturday – Job 14
Sunday – Job 15

Personal Reflections

The Beginning of the End

Matthew 24:4-8

[4]*And Jesus answered and said to them, "See to it that no one misleads you.* [5]*For many will come in My name, saying, 'I am the Christ,' and will mislead many.* [6]*You will be hearing of wars and rumors of wars. See that you are not frightened, for those things must take place, but that is not yet the end.* [7]*For nation will rise against nation, and kingdom against kingdom, and in various places there will be famines and earthquakes.* [8]*But all these things are merely the beginning of birth pangs."*

Prophecy over the years has been the subject of much speculation as well as much sensationalism. Many teachers claim highly detailed and imaginative interpretations that supposedly line up with current world events. Some even claim to be *the* manifestation of Christ. Jesus warned that these things would happen and counseled His followers not to be fearful.

In our family, when our children were preteens, we began preparing them for the teen years—with all the accompanying emotional upheaval and peer pressures. When those years arrived, our children were better prepared because of their foreknowledge. By analogy, that is what Jesus was doing in this discourse on the Mount of Olives.

Jesus, of course, was right. In the past one hundred years things have gotten worse: two world wars, then the Korean War, the Vietnam War, and continuing conflicts across the Middle East today, not to mention the innumerable reports of many nations' internal wars. We see increasing numbers of natural disasters: earthquakes and tsunamis in Indonesia, Haiti, Peru, and Japan; hurricanes and tornadoes wreaking havoc in various places. Paul put it this way: "The whole creation groans and suffers the pains of childbirth together until now" (Rom. 8:22). Jesus said all these things are only the "beginning of birth pangs" that will lead to the advent of God's consummation of all things. Yet events like these have been going on for more than 2000 years—ever since Christ predicted them. How then are they warning signs when the return of Christ has obviously been so far off? What reasonable expectation can we have that Christ is returning soon?

Some are skeptical, just as Scripture predicted: "In the last days mockers will come with their mocking … saying, 'Where is the promise of His coming? For ever since the fathers fell asleep, all continues just as it was from the beginning of creation'" (2 Pet. 3:3-4). Jesus' point was that being aware ahead of time should encourage us during times of suffering. We don't rejoice in the judgment itself, but we worship and praise our Lord who is just and will make all things right. His coming judgment is inevitable! Let us follow Him more closely.

Lord, when difficult times come, even times of hardship, help me not to be surprised or to be knocked off the path of following You.

Week 40
Day 2

Endurance to the End

Matthew 24:9-14

9 "Then they will deliver you to tribulation, and will kill you, and you will be hated
by all nations because of My name. 10 At that time many will fall away and will
betray one another and hate one another. 11 Many false prophets will arise and will
mislead many. 12 Because lawlessness is increased, most people's love will grow
cold. 13 But the one who endures to the end, he will be saved. 14 This gospel of the
kingdom shall be preached in the whole world as a testimony to all the nations,
and then the end will come."

Christians through the years have found a strange comfort in these prophecies of Jesus. Since Christ knew ahead of time about their persecutions, His knowledge of their ultimate deliverance has been equally certain.

From Jesus' day forward, persecution would increase. Christians would be hated, not just by the Jews but by all nations. History bears this out. First came harassment and martyrdom at the hands of the Romans through the first and second centuries AD. After Christianity became the "official" religion of the Roman Empire in the fourth century, it grew into a monolithic manmade religion, which eventually persecuted those who recaptured the doctrine of faith in Christ alone by grace alone. The Reformation unfolded with the martyrdom of men like John Huss and John Wycliffe, and the harassment of men like Martin Luther and Ulrich Zwingli. Even now, Christians around the world who believe in Jesus Christ as their sole and sufficient Savior are martyred for their faith.

The disconcerting part of this persecution is the complete turmoil within the community of believers. Many so-called Christians will fall away, betraying true believers to the authorities. In the early centuries, while many Christians died for their faith, many others recanted. Only the Lord knows if they were true believers.

Jesus pointed out that persecution would bring out false teachers. Many of these over the years would teach that persecution is a sign of God's judgment for disobedience. People then fall prey to such teachers who promise a "better way of truth" that will lead them out of persecution. As a result, disobedience to the truth (lawlessness) will actually grow. And one of the most distressing results of false teaching is that, ultimately, genuine Christian love will "grow cold," replaced by a superficial imitation of love.

Despite all this, some will persevere and will be "saved"—that is, saved from a false way of living. God's true message will march ahead despite persecution! And today there is an increased effort to preach the gospel to every nation, tribe, and tongue.

Lord, help me never to be sidetracked from the mission You left me here to do. Despite personal hardships, help me to convey the good news to others.

Abomination of Desolation

Matthew 24:15-16

15 "Therefore when you see the ABOMINATION OF DESOLATION which was spoken of through Daniel the prophet, standing in the holy place (let the reader understand), 16 then those who are in Judea must flee to the mountains."

Persecution would continue unabated during the predicted time of tribulation (v. 9). Jesus indicated the predictions of Daniel the prophet were pivotal. The "abomination of desolation" (Dan. 9:27, 11:31) referred to an idol that would be set up in the Jewish temple, the absolute worst-case scenario for the Jews. According to Daniel's cryptic statement, this would take place during the middle of the "70th week."

Much ink has been spent trying to understand Daniel's prophecy in some historical context. Some feel the abomination of desolation happened when Antiochus Epiphanes, a Greek overlord, invaded Israel in 167 BC and set up idol worship in the Jewish temple—sacrificing pigs and other creatures that defiled God's holy presence. While this did happen in history (it's recorded in the books of the Maccabees in the Apocrypha), the timing does not match the timing of Daniel.

Modern Bible scholarship has proved helpful here. In the context of the passage in Daniel, a "week" represents seven years, so "70 weeks" refers to a time frame of 490 years. Given all the historical markers in Daniel's prophecy, the end of the 69th "week" of years coincides with the entry of Christ into Jerusalem, just days before His crucifixion. The prophet wrote that after the 69th week, the Messiah would be "cut off," that is, killed (see Daniel 9:25-26). Then, during the middle of that final week of years, the 70th "week," the abomination of desolation would be set up.

How then do we reconcile the fact that in the seven years following Christ's death, there is no historical record of any such desecration of the Jewish temple? This dilemma can be resolved by understanding that Daniel's prophetic time clock was put on hold with the Jews' rejection of Christ.

The clock will start up again, as it were, when God's people are prepared to say, "Blessed is He who comes in the name of the Lord" (23:39). Therefore, the abomination of desolation, along with the rest of the events of the 70th week (that seven-year period of tribulation) remains future. But the warning stands: rebellion against God will increase.

Lord, being aware that You know the future gives me assurance that I have nothing to fear. I praise You that in the end Your justice wins.

Week 40
Day 4

A Time of Tribulation

Matthew 24:17-22

[17]*"Whoever is on the housetop must not go down to get the things out that are in his house.* [18]*Whoever is in the field must not turn back to get his cloak.* [19]*But woe to those who are pregnant and to those who are nursing babies in those days!* [20]*But pray that your flight will not be in the winter, or on a Sabbath.* [21]*For then there will be a great tribulation, such as has not occurred since the beginning of the world until now, nor ever will.* [22]*Unless those days had been cut short, no life would have been saved; but for the sake of the elect those days will be cut short."*

The coming time of tribulation will be severe, Jesus warned. The difficulty will be unprecedented in the history of the world. The horror will be so extreme that God will cut the trajectory short lest all human life be lost.

In the minds of Jesus' hearers these words must have evoked the images of God's wrath that ancient prophets had foretold. During the time of King Josiah, for example, Zephaniah spoke God's word, "'I will completely remove all things from the face of the earth,' declares the LORD. 'I will remove man and beast; I will remove the birds of the sky, and the fish of the sea, and the ruins along with the wicked; And I will cut off man from the face of the earth,' declares the LORD" (Zeph. 1:2-3). But in tribulation, there is mercy: "Seek the LORD, all you humble of the earth who have carried out His ordinances; seek righteousness, seek humility. Perhaps you will be hidden in the day of the LORD's anger" (Zeph. 2:3).

God's message of warning reflected His mercy. If God were uncaring, He would not have warned of the coming wrath; judgment would come unannounced. God is not willing that any should perish (2 Pet. 3:9), and He shows mercy by warning of His anger.

Who was Jesus speaking about? Who would experience this tribulation (the seven-year tribulation period, Daniel's 70th week)? Jesus' immediate audience would not go through that experience, as it turns out. It could be, as seen in our previous meditation, that the 70th week of Daniel was delayed, and another generation of believers would experience it. However, Scripture passages like 1 Thessalonians 4 seem to indicate that believers will be removed from the earth *before* the tribulation period. Jesus could be referring to people who would come to faith in Him during that seven-year period.

These things are debated among Christians today. But what we can count on is God's judgment. He will vindicate His holiness and righteousness.

Father, when I think about Your terrible judgment and anger against sinners, I thank You that You have already rescued me from that awful fate.

An Obvious Christ

Matthew 24:23-28

[23]"Then if anyone says to you, 'Behold, here is the Christ,' or 'There He is,' do not believe him. [24] For false Christs and false prophets will arise and will show great signs and wonders, so as to mislead, if possible, even the elect. [25]Behold, I have told you in advance. [26]So if they say to you, 'Behold, He is in the wilderness,' do not go out, or, 'Behold, He is in the inner rooms,' do not believe them. [27]For just as the lightning comes from the east and flashes even to the west, so will the coming of the Son of Man be. [28]Wherever the corpse is, there the vultures will gather."

History has no lack of men claiming to be the Christ. We shouldn't be surprised; Jesus clearly prophesied that would happen. Those false Christs, however, will sound quite convincing—so much so that even true believers (which Jesus referred to as "the elect") will be tempted to follow them. These false prophets will even be able to do great signs and wonders, which at other places in Scripture indicated who were true apostles (see Romans 15:19; 2 Corinthians 12:12; Hebrews 2:4). These false Christs will proliferate, as the apostle John writes about in his epistles. It seems that Satan, the Serpent from Eden, is still trying to coerce people to worship him instead of the true Christ. In fact, he tipped his hand when attempting to manipulate Jesus into worshiping him (see 4:9). It makes sense that as the end times approach, there will be an increasing effort to deflect worship from the true God toward a substitute. The devil is the ultimate Antichrist!

So how do we avoid being deceived, since these false Christs and false prophets are so convincing? Well, they will be mere humans who will have to assert themselves, trying to prove who they are. The coming of the true Christ, however, will be without debate or discussion. There will be no question about who He is. Jesus said that the "Son of Man" (His favorite description of Himself), will come like a flash of lightning. It will be obvious to everyone on the planet, from one horizon to the next. His presence will be overwhelming. No question! It will be as certain as vultures gathering wherever there is a corpse.

Many people have gone running off to follow some cult leader, usually a charismatic personality who mesmerizes his followers, leading them to unmitigated devotion. However, if anyone *says* he is the Christ, we can be sure he is not. When Christ does come back, everyone will instinctively *know* it! As the false Christs increase, we can take courage that the end times are drawing nearer—and so is the return of our Lord.

Lord, thank you that Your return will be so obvious that we don't need to worry about being deceived. Help me trust in You and Your Word only.

Weekend Reading

Saturday – Job 16
Sunday – Job 17

Personal Reflections

The Trumpet Sound

Matthew 24:29-31

29 "But immediately after the tribulation of those days THE SUN WILL BE DARKENED, AND THE MOON WILL NOT GIVE ITS LIGHT, AND THE STARS WILL FALL *from the sky, and the powers of the heavens will be shaken. 30 And then the sign of the Son of Man will appear in the sky, and then all the tribes of the earth will mourn, and they will see the* SON OF MAN COMING ON THE CLOUDS OF THE SKY *with power and great glory. 31 And He will send forth His angels with* A GREAT TRUMPET *and* THEY WILL GATHER TOGETHER *His elect from the four winds, from one end of the sky to the other."*

Skeptics and liberal scholars scoff at the literal interpretation of Christ's return. They say the "apocalyptic" genre of literature (such as the books of Daniel and the Revelation) is to be taken figuratively. To be sure, prophecy can be difficult to interpret. However, from our perspective today, with nuclear power in human hands and video footage of natural disasters regularly shown on the evening news, the image Jesus presented in verse 29 is not so farfetched. Jesus said the intensity of these things would increase to unprecedented levels. Finally, creation will convulse at the reentry of its Creator into the physical universe—the return of the Lord Jesus Christ.

A few observations are in order. First, His return will be literally in the clouds. After His resurrection, when Jesus, in the presence of His disciples, ascended into the clouds two men in white told the disciples Jesus would return in the same way (Acts 1:9-11)—that is, in the clouds. This is exactly what Daniel prophesied (Dan. 7:13).

Second, people who have rejected Christ will be overwhelmed with their loss ("all the tribes of the earth will mourn"). The stark truth of their complete loss of relationship with their Creator will fully sink in. Third, Christ will still be identified as the Son of Man and therefore closely associate with humans forever as an incarnated being.

Fourth, His second coming will be "with power and great glory." The first time around, Jesus veiled His glory and limited His power. This will not be the case the second time around. He will act decisively, in plain view of everyone.

Fifth, His second coming will be announced with a "great trumpet," a common instrument used throughout the ancient world to announce the start of a battle or the entrance of a regal character. Jesus Christ will be heralded in no uncertain terms. Finally, there will be a great gathering of all the people of God from the entire earth. God's plan of redemption will find its ultimate fulfillment when the Lord returns for His own!

Lord, I so look forward to the trumpet sound, announcing Your return to bring everything to a fitting conclusion. Help me to remain faithful until then.

Week 41
Day 2

The Signs of His Return

Matthew 24:32-36

[32] *"Now learn the parable from the fig tree: when its branch has already become tender and puts forth its leaves, you know that summer is near;* [33] *so, you too, when you see all these things, recognize that He is near, right at the door.* [34] *Truly I say to you, this generation will not pass away until all these things take place.* [35] *Heaven and earth will pass away, but My words will not pass away.* [36] *But of that day and hour no one knows, not even the angels of heaven, nor the Son, but the Father alone."*

The question of when Christ will return hovers over life, whether one believes in it or not. If there is no Christ, we stand before an absolutely holy God, and we come up short. If there is no God, then either fate or blind chance controls our future (over which we don't have ultimate control anyway). In an atheistic belief system, the question is purely academic.

For the Christian, the future has meaning and purpose because Christ said He would return. The question of when Christ will return is therefore legitimate as well as intriguing. The future is better than the present; Christ gives us this hope and it motivates us.

The Lord fanned the flames inherent in following Him. For just as His life and His teachings about this present world gave hope, His words about the future give a new kind of hope—the confident assurance that He will one day return. It's a hope that will continue in His absence. But when will it occur?

Jesus resorted again to a parable, not to hide the truth from unbelievers but to illustrate the truth in a way that would continually inspire hope. There will be certain indicators of His return. (He again speaks of Himself in the third person as the Son of Man, v. 30.) Just as the fig tree sprouting leaves is a sure sign that summer is near, the "generation" that observes the specified sign-events will be the generation that sees His return.

The return of Christ, as described in the preceding verses, is of such magnitude that we humans naturally want to put a date on it. Many efforts to do so have come and gone. One example was the book titled *88 Reasons Why Christ Will Return In 1988*. While human writings about the end times fail, Jesus made it very clear that His words will not fail or ever pass away. We can count on that! However, as for specific dating (day and hour) no one knows or can know it. That is privileged information, which even Jesus, in His role as the incarnate Son of God, did not know. It is the Father's prerogative only. In the incarnation, the knowledge of His return date was one of the aspects of deity Jesus laid aside.

Lord, I look forward to Your return because I can count on Your promises. Help me recognize the potential signs and be spurred on to holiness.

The Suddenness of the Rapture

Matthew 24:37-41

[37] *"For the coming of the Son of Man will be just like the days of Noah.* [38] *For as in those days before the flood they were eating and drinking, marrying and giving in marriage, until the day that Noah entered the ark,* [39] *and they did not understand until the flood came and took them all away; so will the coming of the Son of Man be.* [40] *Then there will be two men in the field; one will be taken and one will be left.* [41] *Two women will be grinding at the mill; one will be taken and one will be left."*

Suddenness will be an apt characteristic of the rapture event. For a while now Jesus had been telling the disciples that He would be coming back—despite the fact that they had not yet fully comprehended that He was leaving! He had just said there would be indicators of His return, giving His followers ample warning. But for unbelievers the event will seem abrupt.

The Lord conveyed this in two ways. First, He reminded them of the well-known story of the days before the flood. Scoffers and cynics ignored Noah's warnings and carried on with life's merriment—even up to the moment Noah and his family entered the ark and were taken up on the floodwaters. Second, Jesus pictures for them a couple of scenarios in which two individuals are together; one is taken, the other left behind. Christ's return will, by analogy, be so sudden that most people will experience it as an immediate interruption of the normal happenings of life.

Traditionally this teaching has been understood as referring to the rapture of believers from earth before the second coming of Christ, and the ones "taken" are believers. Some, more recently, have suggested that this refers rather to judgment, where those "taken" are non-believers like the people of Noah's day who were destroyed by the flood. Yet, the more natural interpretation would be to see Noah and his family being "taken" away from the rest who were left for the judgment flood. So, this passage probably does refer to the rapture of believers who will be taken away while unbelievers are left behind. (See 1 Thessalonians 4:13-18 for more on the rapture.)

Scripture tells us that in the last days, "mockers will come …saying, 'Where is the promise of His coming? For ever since the fathers fell asleep, all continues just as it was from the beginning of creation'" (2 Pet. 3:3-4). Nothing is more pathetic than people carrying on with life in willful ignorance of impending disaster. Christians, walking by faith, are neither oblivious nor scared; we are motivated to live in a constant state of anticipation of His return!

Lord, keep reminding me, when I am feeling down, that Your return could come at any time. Let my daily focus not be on the things of the world, but on You!

Week 41
Day 4

An Alert Readiness

Matthew 24:42-44

42 "Therefore be on the alert, for you do not know which day your Lord is coming.
43 But be sure of this, that if the head of the house had known at what time of the night the thief was coming, he would have been on the alert and would not have allowed his house to be broken into.
44 For this reason you also must be ready; for the Son of Man is coming at an hour when you do not think He will."

Alertness is one of the catchwords of discipleship. Following Christ is not for those who desire to meander through life in carefree leisure. Yes, there is rest, as Jesus promised in Matthew 11:28-30. That restfulness of inner spirit and freedom from the endless striving under the weight of sin gives us a solid foundation for carrying on the work of the Lord—and helps us remain alert. Our task as Christians is the same as Jesus' task: "... to do the will of Him who sent Me and to accomplish His work" (John 4:34). Alertness is a prime prerequisite.

The first order of alertness is to be ready for the Lord's return. He is coming back at any time with the suddenness of a thief in the night breaking into your home. This story resonates with us because if someone knew the exact time a thief would come, he could relax the rest of the time and carry on without fear of surprise or loss. By application, if we knew the exact timetable for the return of Christ, we could simply live our lives selfishly, indulging the flesh for our own self-aggrandizement, and then clean up our lives just before He returns. However, that would be a mockery!

The only reasonable alternative is to live as though Christ were returning today! Thirty years ago there was much anticipation of Christ's return. Many churches, conferences, and books focused so much on end-times prophecy that some evangelical circles today shy away from prophetic teaching. For many, the thinking now goes, "Why focus on the future? We need instead to concern ourselves, rather, with social justice issues and living missionally."

While there is some truth to this, the pendulum can swing to the extreme in either direction. We need both—to live with the anticipation that Christ could be returning at any time, and also to be about our Father's business. That awareness provides motivation. We need to be ready for His return by letting Him live His life through us now!

Lord, I affirm that "I have been crucified with Christ; and it is no longer I who live, but Christ lives in me; and the life which I now live in the flesh I live by faith in the Son of God, who loved me and gave Himself up for me" (Gal. 2:20).

Week 41
Day 5

Faithfulness Wanted

Matthew 24:45-51

45 "Who then is the faithful and sensible slave whom his master put in charge of
his household to give them their food at the proper time? 46 Blessed is that slave
whom his master finds so doing when he comes. 47 Truly I say to you that he will
put him in charge of all his possessions. 48 But if that evil slave says in his heart,
'My master is not coming for a long time,' 49 and begins to beat his fellow slaves
and eat and drink with drunkards; 50 the master of that slave will come on a day
when he does not expect him and at an hour which he does not know, 51 and will
cut him in pieces and assign him a place with the hypocrites; in that place there
will be weeping and gnashing of teeth."

Jesus now brought this parable to its moral and spiritual conclusion. There are, in the end, only two responses. Either we are "good" stewards of God's assignment for us or we are "evil" ones, not faithful to our assignment from God.

A steward is someone given the responsibility of looking after his master's property. In this story, Jesus used the first-century practice of slavery to drive home His point. He was not condoning slavery but simply using it for illustration purposes. Elsewhere in Scripture we find teaching that transforms the practice of slavery by applying Christian principles to relationships. (See the episitle to Philemon, for example.)

The slave in today's passage was given a stewardship, the responsibility of looking after his master's possessions. By analogy, God is the master. But who do the stewards in the story represent? One obvious answer would be the Jewish religious leaders, who were clearly not being faithful in their stewardship because they were rejecting Jesus and His teachings. Faithfulness to God should have led them to belief in Christ. In contrast, the apostles were faithful to the message, and God ultimately would appoint them to greater things. Jesus had said earlier, "Truly I say to you, that you who have followed Me, in the regeneration when the Son of Man will sit on His glorious throne, you also shall sit upon twelve thrones, judging the twelve tribes of Israel" (19:28; see also Revelation 21:14). Jesus pulled no punches in His graphic depiction. For the believer, the suddenness of Christ's return will be a joyous surprise. The unbeliever, however, will be horrorstruck.

God is still looking for faithfulness: "It is required of stewards that one be found trustworthy" (1 Cor. 4:2). What is needed today, more than ever, is trustworthy Christians, who make Jesus Christ the central focus of their life and who see themselves simply as ambassadors for His kingdom!

Lord, I confess to You that much of my life is spent in self-advancing, self-comfort efforts. Thank you for reminding me that I am to be simply Your steward to faithfully carry out Your will.

Weekend Reading

Saturday – Job 18
Sunday – Job 19

Personal Reflections

Be Alert!

Matthew 25:1-13

[1] "Then the kingdom of heaven will be comparable to ten virgins, who took their lamps and went out to meet the bridegroom. [2] Five of them were foolish, and five were prudent. [3] For when the foolish took their lamps, they took no oil with them, [4] but the prudent took oil in flasks along with their lamps. [5] Now while the bridegroom was delaying, they all got drowsy and began to sleep. [6] But at midnight there was a shout, 'Behold, the bridegroom! Come out to meet him.' [7] Then all those virgins rose and trimmed their lamps. [8] The foolish said to the prudent, 'Give us some of your oil, for our lamps are going out.' [9] But the prudent answered, 'No, there will not be enough for us and you too; go instead to the dealers and buy some for yourselves.' [10] And while they were going away to make the purchase, the bridegroom came, and those who were ready went in with him to the wedding feast; and the door was shut. [11] Later the other virgins also came, saying, 'Lord, lord, open up for us.' [12] But he answered, 'Truly I say to you, I do not know you.' [13] Be on the alert then, for you do not know the day nor the hour."

Alertness is a vital part of being a true follower of Christ, according to His teaching on the Mount of Olives. Having already stressed this in the previous chapter (v. 42), our Lord presented another illustration to drive His point home. His coming again, a primary theme of this sermon, is pictured as a bridegroom coming for the bridesmaids (called virgins) so they could enter the wedding feast. Some of them did not adequately prepare. Each brought her own oil lamp, but some did not bring enough oil. When the bridegroom finally came, five of the women were gone, looking for oil, and thus missed out on the feast. Jesus finished the story by warning His listeners to be alert because the exact timing of His return would not be revealed. We need not get hung up on the parable's details. The point is that some were not alert when they should have been!

We conclude from this parable a number of things. First, Christ's coming again will be sudden. Second, the exact time of His return is not known to anyone but the Father (24:36). Third, not being prepared is tantamount to not being known by Christ (v. 12). Jesus characterized eternal life as a relationship founded on "knowing" Him and the Father (John 17:3). Fourth, there comes a point after which no further recourse for salvation will be offered. If this teaching refers to the second coming of Christ, then all that can be expected after this is judgment. If, on the other hand, this refers to the rapture, we know from later teaching that there will be a minority who will come to Christ during the tribulation period—but at great cost! Either way, people must be alert to Jesus' return—at any time.

Lord, You have warned us that Your return will be sudden. It could be today, even before I finish this prayer. "Even so, come, Lord Jesus" (Rev 22:20 KJV).

Week 42
Day 2

Entrusted by God

Matthew 25:14-18

[14] *"For it is just like a man about to go on a journey, who called his own slaves and entrusted his possessions to them.* [15] *To one he gave five talents, to another, two, and to another, one, each according to his own ability; and he went on his journey.* [16] *Immediately the one who had received the five talents went and traded with them, and gained five more talents.* [17] *In the same manner the one who had received the two talents gained two more.* [18] *But he who received the one talent went away, and dug a hole in the ground and hid his master's money."*

Our story today conveys a clear message in light of what Jesus had been teaching so far in His Olivet Discourse. Remember, He is only a few days away from being betrayed by Judas and turned over to the authorities for crucifixion (26:2). Preparing His disciples for His departure and ultimate return is foremost in His teaching.

Jesus talked frequently about money. He spoke about various kinds of money (e.g., denarii and talents) at least thirty-nine times in the gospel writings. This common commodity consumed much of the focus in the culture of that day just as it does today. So it was a frequent point of connection in His teachings.

A talent was equivalent to fifteen years' wages for a common worker—a considerable sum of money. Obviously, the master trusted all three servants in the story. He gave the amounts of five, two, and one talent(s), measuring them out according to each one's ability. We might assume that the one given five talents had previously demonstrated ability to responsibly handle larger sums of money for his master. The servant given one talent may have been new to this kind of responsibility and therefore given a smaller sum to begin with.

As the story unfolds, the first two servants sprang into action, putting their master's funds to work immediately, an ongoing endeavor, while the master was away. They labored hard at increasing their master's investment, and in time both doubled the money. The third servant went away and buried the master's money and did nothing more with it.

While Jesus did not explicitly interpret the parable for His disciples, the message is obvious: God is the master and we are the servants. He entrusts us with His resources. Whatever we have of value belongs to Him. This would include our lives, our money, our time, our relationships—everything. For the time being, we have sole freedom to do with these things as we like. But we need to remember they are His, not ours!

Lord, help me to remember that everything that I am and have belongs to You. I want to multiply Your possessions faithfully.

The Secret

Matthew 25:19-23

[19] "Now after a long time the master of those slaves came and settled accounts with them. [20] The one who had received the five talents came up and brought five more talents, saying, 'Master, you entrusted five talents to me. See, I have gained five more talents.' [21] His master said to him, 'Well done, good and faithful slave. You were faithful with a few things, I will put you in charge of many things; enter into the joy of your master.' [22] Also the one who had received the two talents came up and said, 'Master, you entrusted two talents to me. See, I have gained two more talents.' [23] His master said to him, 'Well done, good and faithful slave. You were faithful with a few things, I will put you in charge of many things; enter into the joy of your master.'"

The actions of the first two servants in this parable demonstrate the virtue of faithfully carrying out a master's instructions. They had been given five and two talents respectively, and while their master was away, they put the money to work and doubled it. Upon his return the master praised them for their actions.

The story begs a deeper understanding than just that the master was happy to get more money. First, the servants understood their master's desires without being explicitly told what to do with the money. Second, they were wise in the ways they invested the money. Third, they acted consistent with the ability the master recognized in them (v. 15). Fourth, they genuinely kept in mind their master's best interest. They didn't fear him in a negative sense. Fifth, they understood clearly that it was all about their master, not about them.

The result is the most telling of all. First, the master affirms them as "good and faithful." The Christian is driven by the accolades of his heavenly Master. Second, their faithfulness is rewarded. Notice that the reward is not ease and comfort or financial blessings, but rather added responsibility. While to some this may seem a poor reward, to the Christian there truly is joy in serving Jesus. More opportunity translates into more joy. Both the servant and the master implicitly know that the greatest result is sharing the joy that comes from working together for the master's purposes. The faithful servant is the one who catches onto the heart of the master, and therefore the faithful servant's reward is the opportunity to share more of what the master does. As Christians, we become good and faithful servants as we increasingly share in the work of our heavenly Father.

Unfortunately, people often waste time seeking happiness and fulfillment in everything else (and never finding it) when the answer is simply to live our lives in service to our heavenly Master. That is the secret to real joy!

Father, thank you that the Lord Jesus Christ came not to be served but to serve. Help me know the joy that comes from being fully committed to Your work.

Warning Against Laziness

Matthew 25:24-30

[24] "And the one also who had received the one talent came up and said, 'Master, I knew you to be a hard man, reaping where you did not sow and gathering where you scattered no seed. [25] 'And I was afraid, and went away and hid your talent in the ground. See, you have what is yours.' [26] But his master answered and said to him, 'You wicked, lazy slave, you knew that I reap where I did not sow and gather where I scattered no seed. [27] 'Then you ought to have put my money in the bank, and on my arrival I would have received my money back with interest. [28] 'Therefore take away the talent from him, and give it to the one who has the ten talents.'
[29] For to everyone who has, more shall be given, and he will have an abundance; but from the one who does not have, even what he does have shall be taken away.
[30] Throw out the worthless slave into the outer darkness; in that place there will be weeping and gnashing of teeth."

The third servant's problem was his view of his master—seeing him as "a hard man," stiff, unyielding, and austere. The other two servants understood the master's desires and worked hard to fulfill them. But this servant had little interest in advancing the master's goals. He operated on the basis of fear.

His view of the master became self-fulfilling because, in the end, the master responded to his actions quite severely. This servant's laziness was evident because investing the money in a bank wouldn't have taken any more effort than burying it. His refusal to do that proved he had no interest in the master's desires. His own words incriminated him! Judgment was twofold: loss of any future responsibility, and being cast out "into outer darkness"—an image of absolute destitution and agony.

The fact that Jesus went on to speak of His return in judgment puts this parable in context. The criterion for determining a person's eternal fate at Christ's return is his faithfulness in serving God's purpose on the earth. Those of us who do His will and work to further His goals will enter into the life God has designed for us. Jesus called it "abundant life" (John 10:10) and "eternal life" (John 17:3).

Jesus was not contradicting the idea of what might be called "forensic justification." That is a concept the apostle Paul taught in Romans 3:28—that a man is justified apart from the works of the Law. Jesus here was emphasizing that God created us in this life to be His servants, carrying out His will. Paul said that because we fail at doing this, we need to be made right with God. But Jesus' point still stands: we are to be faithful servants; that is the means for experiencing life the way God intended.

Lord, I don't want to be a lazy believer. I want to serve You more, working to advance Your purposes here on earth.

The Great Divide

Matthew 25:31-33

[31] "But when the Son of Man comes in His glory, and all the angels with Him, then He will sit on His glorious throne. [32] All the nations will be gathered before Him; and He will separate them from one another, as the shepherd separates the sheep from the goats; [33] and He will put the sheep on His right, and the goats on the left."

The Great Divide—the final judgment—is coming. The event will be binary in nature—that is, there will be, at the most fundamental level, two outcomes. If there is one thing Christianity teaches absolutely, it is the final judgment of every person who has ever lived. Jesus here depicted it in metaphorical, agricultural terms. The apostle John, inspired by the Spirit of God, later described it as the great white throne judgment (see Revelation 20:11).

The picture is magnificent: Christ, the Son of Man, is seated on a throne described as glorious. The *kenosis*, or "emptying Himself" of glory (to which Philippians 2:7 refers), will have come to an end. All will see the answer to Jesus' prayer of John 17:5: "Now, Father, glorify Me together with Yourself, with the glory which I had with You before the world was." In His first coming, Jesus' ministry was not one of judgment but of grace for salvation. "For God did not send the Son into the world to judge the world, but that the world might be saved through Him" (John 3:17). At His second coming, He will sit with His Father on the throne of judgment. It will be a glorious time, for true justice (the catchword of *our* times) will be evident in all its glory. God will be seen as the one true and just Judge.

Furthermore, "all the nations" will stand before God. This means every single individual within every nation. No one will escape, for He is, " able to judge the thoughts and intentions of the heart. And there is no creature hidden from His sight, but all things are open and laid bare to the eyes of Him with whom we have to do" (Heb. 4:12-13). All religions, all faith systems, everything human—we will all be judged by the same objective standard: the living Word, Jesus Christ Himself.

The division will be simple, like a shepherd separating out the sheep from the goats, the sheep going on the right and the goats on the left. All that matters to us humans is on which side we will find ourselves. It is one or the other—no in-between. No purgatory, no limbo, no halfway. Jesus often reduced things to a binary perspective. You are either for Him or against Him, He would say. The criterion remains to this day. Which side are you on?

Lord, out of genuine "fear" of You, I have cast my eternal destiny into Your nail-pierced hands. Thank you for already taking the judgment I deserved.

Weekend Reading

Saturday – Job 20
Sunday – Job 21

Personal Reflections

Week 43
Day 1

Reward for the Sheep

Matthew 25:34-40

34 "Then the King will say to those on His right, 'Come, you who are blessed of
My Father, inherit the kingdom prepared for you from the foundation of the world.
35 For I was hungry, and you gave Me something to eat; I was thirsty, and you gave
Me something to drink; I was a stranger, and you invited Me in; 36 naked, and you
clothed Me; I was sick, and you visited Me; I was in prison, and you came to Me.'
37 Then the righteous will answer Him, 'Lord, when did we see You hungry, and
feed You, or thirsty, and give You something to drink? 38 And when did we see You
a stranger, and invite You in, or naked, and clothe You? 39 When did we see You
sick, or in prison, and come to You?' 40 The King will answer and say to them,
'Truly I say to you, to the extent that you did it to one of these brothers of Mine,
even the least of them, you did it to Me.'"

Well known to most Christians, this passage lays the foundation for Christian social responsibility. Adherents of the so-called social gospel find much here to support the thinking that meeting humanitarian needs is more important than securing eternal salvation for the future. In fact, they say that the criterion for determining our ultimate disposition before God above is our good works toward the disadvantaged here below. However, that teaching represents a superficial view of Jesus' teaching here. A few observations are in order.

Jesus continued His teaching about the final judgment, illustrating it with the separating of sheep from goats. First, He addressed the sheep, who represent the good. They will be blessed and will inherit the kingdom of God, which was prepared from the beginning. We are told in Ephesians 2:10 that "we are His workmanship, created in Christ Jesus for good works, which God prepared beforehand so that we would walk in them."

To serve in God's kingdom is to do His will, so He taught His disciples to pray, "Your kingdom come. Your will be done, on earth as it is in heaven" (6:10). Ultimately, He expects us, who are created in His image, not only to tend to His creation (Gen. 1:29, 2:15) but also to look out for our fellow human beings. The answer to Cain's question is that yes, we are our brother's keeper (Gen. 4:9)!

Why is this so pivotal in the great judgment? Humans, as opposed to animals and plants, are created in God's image. When we show care for others, we show care for Christ Himself. This is particularly so when we care for other followers of Christ because He calls us His "brothers" (12:50; Heb. 2:11-12; Gal. 6:10).

Father, though I have failed to love the least of my neighbors as myself, I thank You that Your Son perfectly loved His "neighbors," including me.

Week 43
Day 2

The Punishment of the Goats

Matthew 25:41-46

41 "Then He will also say to those on His left, 'Depart from Me, accursed ones, into the eternal fire which has been prepared for the devil and his angels; 42 for I was hungry, and you gave Me nothing to eat; I was thirsty, and you gave Me nothing to drink; 43 I was a stranger, and you did not invite Me in; naked, and you did not clothe Me; sick, and in prison, and you did not visit Me.' 44 Then they themselves also will answer, 'Lord, when did we see You hungry, or thirsty, or a stranger, or naked, or sick, or in prison, and did not take care of You?' 45 Then He will answer them, 'Truly I say to you, to the extent that you did not do it to one of the least of these, you did not do it to Me.' 46 These will go away into eternal punishment, but the righteous into eternal life."

Those pictured as goats are bad news. Their destiny is put plainly: eternal fire (v. 41) and eternal punishment (v. 46). We observe a number of facts. Their punishment will be painful. It is said that burning is the most painful way to die; how much worse, burning for eternity! Yet this painful consequence of a life selfishly lived will be eternal. Cessation of existence will never come. The idea of a painful punishment without end is repugnant to many today, as though retribution for eternity far exceeds the sins committed in a relatively short time span on earth. However, the Sovereign Lord of creation sets the standard of what is appropriate punishment. In fact, He finds the sin of the "goats" to be repugnant. In this context, the goats exhibited a total disregard for their fellow human beings—made in the image of God. In essence, the goats were disregarding God. What a tragedy that something created by God would treat God's image in that way.

The duration of the punishment for the goats is comparable to the duration of the reward for the sheep—eternal. Both are judged on how they treated the needy of society. That is where the similarity ends. On the surface of it, Christians need to look after the hungry, the outcast, the sick, the imprisoned. Smugness and self-righteousness have no place here.

Is this not what James referred to in his letter? "What use is it, my brethren, if someone says he has faith but he has no works? Can that faith save him? If a brother or sister is without clothing and in need of daily food, and one of you says to them, 'Go in peace, be warmed and be filled,' and yet you do not give them what is necessary for their body, what use is that? Even so faith, if it has no works, is dead, being by itself" (James 2:14-17).

This does not mean that good deeds bring about salvation. Paul teaches otherwise (Eph. 2:8-9). But it does mean that faith which does not result in caring for the needs of others may not be genuine faith at all.

Lord, help me to be a doer of Your word, not just a hearer (James 1:22).

The Die Is Cast

Matthew 26:1-5

[1] When Jesus had finished all these words, He said to His disciples, [2] "You know that after two days the Passover is coming, and the Son of Man is to be handed over for crucifixion." [3] Then the chief priests and the elders of the people were gathered together in the court of the high priest, named Caiaphas; [4] and they plotted together to seize Jesus by stealth and kill Him. [5] But they were saying, "Not during the festival, otherwise a riot might occur among the people."

The die has now been cast in Jesus' life, the inevitable has begun, the predetermined has commenced to unfold. Peter later understood what he couldn't see at that moment: "This Man, delivered over by the predetermined plan and foreknowledge of God, you nailed to a cross by the hands of godless men and put Him to death" (Acts 2:23). The religious leaders had been plotting for some time (12:14), and Jesus had been predicting it for just as long (12:40; 16:21; 7:9, 12, 22; 20:18). The disciples still could not believe it.

The chief priests and elders were simply the pawns in the diabolical, master-plan that began in the garden of Eden. Satan was determined to frustrate God's plan for His image and glory on the earth. Death and destruction has reigned ever since the devil led Adam and Eve—and subsequently the entire human race—into sin. The Son of God came as Messiah to establish the kingdom of God on earth, and redemption was central to that plan. The Messiah would die as a propitiation for sin—that is, He would completely satisfy God's anger over the sin problem. At once sin would finally be dealt with and God's eternal judgment would be absolutely and completely satisfied. The breach in His glory would not just be mended but woven gloriously into a much bigger and more beautiful tapestry than we ever could have imagined. God is in complete control.

So the leaders went through the motions of their little vignette, totally oblivious to the eternal ramifications of their bit part. What a tragic-glorious thing to happen. In their sinful rejection of Christ, they became the instruments to bring about the greatest sacrifice of all. Not just a covering of sins, like the OT sacrifices which could never take away sin, but a complete and exhaustive sacrifice—fully satisfying to God—that takes away sin forever. "By this will we have been sanctified through the offering of the body of Jesus Christ once for all.... For by one offering He has perfected for all time those who are sanctified" (Heb. 10:10, 14).

Lord, Your plan is amazing, using even the worst that man or Satan can do as a master stroke in the magnificent revelation of Your glory!

Lavish Worship

Matthew 26:6-9

[6] Now when Jesus was in Bethany, at the home of Simon the leper, [7] a woman came to Him with an alabaster vial of very costly perfume, and she poured it on His head as He reclined at the table. [8] But the disciples were indignant when they saw this, and said, "Why this waste? [9] For this perfume might have been sold for a high price and the money given to the poor."

Devotion breeds extravagance—nothing but the best for the Master. That is what this story is all about. Unaware of the deeper significance Jesus was about to give her actions, the woman simply used what she had to honor Him. The value of this sacrifice did not go unnoticed.

There were many better things that could have been done with the perfume. At the least, as the disciples thought, it could have been converted into something more useful—money. The disciples were not motivated by their own benefit but by how much that money could have been used to help the poor. To simply pour it out seemed an outrageous waste. They were indignant, just as ten of them were annoyed at James and John for trying to out-maneuver them into places of prominence (20:24).

Does this story justify the lavish embrace of ornate basilicas, temples, and cathedrals so evident in some areas of Christendom today? Indeed, many consider such things a waste. Is this the same thing as our story? I don't think so.

First, her sacrifice was an individual one, not an institutional one. Second, it was completely voluntary and under her control. Third, she gave the gift directly to the Lord Jesus, not to a religious organization. Fourth, as we shall see shortly, this action was interpreted by Jesus as being prophetic. Fifth, her actions did not result in anyone living in luxury, as is often the case of those who make their living by the basilicas, temples, and cathedrals of today.

At whom were the disciples indignant? If at the woman, then what right did they have to judge her for what she did with her own perfume? But Christians today often criticize the way others serve the Lord. Were the disciples indignant at Jesus? Certainly that would not be beyond them, considering Peter's attitude when he rebuked Jesus (16:22). Yet who are we to question His glad acceptance of gifts given liberally to Him? Paul later commended the Macedonians because "in a great ordeal of affliction their abundance of joy and their deep poverty overflowed in the wealth of their liberality" (2 Cor. 8:2). Yes, God accepts lavish sacrifice! When was the last time you or I gave abundantly to the Lord?

Lord, You gave abundantly for me, I want to do the same for You.
The value of my gifts to You reflects how precious You are to me.

Appreciated Worship

Matthew 26:10-13

[10] But Jesus, aware of this, said to them, "Why do you bother the woman? For she has done a good deed to Me. [11] For you always have the poor with you; but you do not always have Me. [12] For when she poured this perfume on My body, she did it to prepare Me for burial. [13] Truly I say to you, wherever this gospel is preached in the whole world, what this woman has done will also be spoken of in memory of her."

A number of women in the Gospels were commended for their devotion to God (see, for example, Mark 12:41-44, the woman who gave her two coins into the temple treasury). The woman in our story today went about her worship without the self-consciousness that usually accompanies more ostentatious shows of "spirituality." All that mattered was giving to God something of great worth.

The disciples were annoyed at her intrusion (v. 8) and at her extravagant "waste." Jesus cuts off this objection quickly, defending the woman as having "done a good deed to [Him]." To the disciples' complaint about giving the money to the poor, Jesus responded rather curtly, "You always have the poor with you." In one fell swoop He brought into balance the popular notion today that Jesus was all about helping the poor. That is true, He was about that, but He was about more than that. He taught that "an hour is coming, and now is, when the true worshipers will worship the Father in spirit and truth; for such people the Father seeks to be His worshipers" (John 4:23). He came to gather worshipers, of whom this woman was a supreme example. The disciples (and all followers of Christ ever after) should watch closely this woman's exemplary demonstration of how to worship Him.

She chose a good thing, just as Mary had done in setting aside her service to sit at the feet of Christ (Luke 10:42). The woman with the perfume had the privilege, by virtue of her sheer devotion to Him, of preparing Him for His burial. Let this sink in. The grand finale of God's solution to the sin problem that began in the garden of Eden was about to begin. The plan from eternity past (with enduring repercussions for eternity future) was about to teeter on the fulcrum of crucifixion. And this woman had the unparalleled privilege of being the one to prepare His body ahead of time.

From that moment until His death, He would carry the fragrance of her worship—through the cruel beatings, mockery, and indignity of public torture and death. No wonder her action will be remembered wherever the gospel is preached.

Lord, help me to see that even the seemingly small things of life are elevated in Your memory when they are done for Your honor and glory.

Weekend Reading

Saturday – Job 22
Sunday – Job 23

Personal Reflections

Christ Before the Poor

Matthew 26:11 (pt. 1)

11 "For you always have the poor with you; but you do not always have Me."

What an enigmatic statement—almost callous, it would seem. A woman had just used expensive perfume to anoint Jesus when it could have been sold and given to the poor. Would that not have been more like Jesus than to have accepted the expensive gift for Himself? Today's modern picture of Jesus would have us think that. So what do we make of this?

Some scholars question whether Jesus did, in fact, make this statement; they suggest it was added into the gospel story by later copyists. (And some say Jesus never would have made a statement like that.) This is a specious argument on a number of levels. First, the earliest copies of the gospel accounts include this statement. Jesus Himself said the woman would be remembered wherever the gospel would be preached. Further, how can we know what Jesus would have said, other than from the record of what is reported by eyewitnesses? And though Mark was not an eyewitness, Matthew and John certainly were. They were in a better position to tell us what Jesus would have said than modern scholars.

But then how do we mesh this statement with other places where Jesus *did* emphasize helping the disadvantaged? Even the statement itself alludes to Deuteronomy 15:11: "For the poor will never cease to be in the land; therefore I command you, saying, 'You shall freely open your hand to your brother, to your needy and poor in your land.'" That verse makes the case to help the poor. Certainly this season in Jesus' life would have been a great opportunity to help the poor in a significant way.

Jesus' point, though, was not to disregard the poor. Rather, it was a matter of priorities. This coincides with the priority of the two greatest commandments—to love God above all else, and then to love one's neighbor as oneself (22:36-40). To get this priority wrong will result in very little love for the poor! If we don't love God, we can never love our neighbor because we will end up loving ourselves. If we don't put God first, we won't put the poor first; we will put ourselves first. The order is inviolable!

Ultimately, any efforts we may make to help the poor—apart from centering our lives on God—will, in reality, be done for our own benefit. It's like the commercial one charity prominently displays: "Give, because you will feel good about yourself." Such a subtle, self-centered goal is far from genuine altruism.

Lord, let my love and worship of You move my heart to beat with Your compassion toward the disadvantaged around me.

Week 44
Day 2

Always the Poor

Matthew 26:11 (pt. 2)

11 *"For you always have the poor with you; but you do not always have Me."*

The ubiquitous presence of the poor is the subject of much church work today. The fact is, poor people are everywhere, and always have been. Jesus asserted this 2000 years ago, and things haven't changed much since then. So, where has the church been all these years? Why hasn't poverty been stamped out by now? Is it that the teachings of Christ have been inadequate, or the ability of His followers lacking?

The fact that poverty exists today testifies to the truth of Jesus' statement in this verse. Was this simply the wise observation of a Jewish prophet looking back on 1500 years of Jewish existence and seeing no measurable gain in relieving the hardships of the poor? No, Jesus was more than a social reformer, as the context shows. Feeding and clothing the poor is secondary to honoring Christ. Yet the poor continue to be with us.

Poverty comes in many different forms. The poor can include those who lack other things than finances. Some people are poor in social skills, intelligence, common sense, mental health, emotional balance, or life skills. For some, poverty is a lack of wholesome, healthy upbringing. Some have a poverty of health. For sure, the poor will always be with us because we live in a fallen, broken world. I once spent a year helping a poor couple with their finances, setting up a budget and teaching them financial principles on a monthly basis. But when their tax-refund check arrived, they disregarded everything they had learned and used the money to replace their TV with a bigger, newer one—despite the fact that their car was in poor repair. The poor you will always have. This doesn't mean we should not help people. But because poverty will never be completely eliminated, we need to temper our expectations. We continue to reach out and help, however, because Jesus bids us do that.

It is easy to become discouraged in our efforts to help the poor; our meager help gets lost in the vortex of unending, overwhelming needs. What's the use when our own poverty of *spirit* sets in and we lose the drive to serve others? Jesus said, "Blessed are the poor in spirit, for theirs is the kingdom of heaven." So, we buoy up our spirit as we put God and His kingdom first. We have to, for the poor will always be with us.

Lord, help me not succumb to spiritual poverty, exhausted by compassion, in helping meet the needs of the poor, who are always with us.

Checkmate

Matthew 26:14-16 (pt. 1)

[14] Then one of the twelve, named Judas Iscariot, went to the chief priests [15] and said, "What are you willing to give me to betray Him to you?" And they weighed out thirty pieces of silver to him. [16] From then on he began looking for a good opportunity to betray Jesus.

The name *Judas* has become infamous because of the incident before us today. Like *Benedict Arnold* during the American Revolution, the name of Judas is synonymous with betrayal. Even in Matthew's telling of the gospel story, he "spills the beans" about Judas' betrayal long before it actually happens in the historical sequence (see 10:4). The story obviously had been circulated before Matthew wrote his account, so this reference wasn't a "spoiler."

Various theories have been devised to explain Judas's behavior. Some think he was trying to protect Jesus, reasoning that if his master were to be taken into custody, the growing conflict would calm down and Jesus would eventually be released. Others think Judas was simply being enterprising. He saw an opportunity to make some money and, thinking Jesus could escape as He had done previously, Judas anticipated there'd be no real harm done. I suppose some could believe he had a moment of temporary insanity; others may frame the incident some other way. But Luke 22:3 indicates a demonic cause, in which Judas played into the hands of Satan, the archenemy of Jesus.

We know for sure that Judas recognized he was, in fact, betraying Jesus, and there was an exchange of money. The import of the story, though, regardless of his motivation, is the tragic nature of his behavior. One of Jesus' hand-chosen disciples turned a treacherous hand against his Master.

This turn of events was not a surprise to Christ, for He had previously said, "Did I Myself not choose you, the twelve, and yet one of you is a devil?" (John 6:70). Here, three wills intertwine in the same action—those of Satan, Judas, and God. Like a chess player playing into the hand of the Master, Satan used his pawn to check his opponent. In so doing he finds himself checkmated by that very move. God's sovereign will eclipses all others.

In the final judgment, every excuse will be stopped, and every tongue will confess that Jesus Christ is the sovereign Lord!

The rebellion Satan began in the garden of Eden continues on. And he enlists the Creator's image bearers to join the resistance movement.

Lord, I don't want to unwittingly join Satan's campaign to rebel against You. Give me the strength to resist personal advancement at Your expense.

The Irrationality of Betrayal

Matthew 26:14-16 (pt. 2)

[14] Then one of the twelve, named Judas Iscariot, went to the chief priests [15] and said, "What are you willing to give me to betray Him to you?" And they weighed out thirty pieces of silver to him. [16] From then on he began looking for a good opportunity to betray Jesus.

Thirty pieces of silver was all Jesus was worth to Judas. What was he thinking? He had been handpicked by Jesus and had spent some three years with the one who was the Messiah. Judas had a front-row seat to Jesus' profound teaching, personal tutoring, an insider's understanding of His teachings. He saw Jesus heal the sick, raise the dead, refute the best teachers and the greatest minds in the land. He had seen Jesus tenderly set children on His lap yet face down the most violent storms on the Sea of Galilee. Judas had witnessed Jesus rebuking demons and religious leaders alike. He saw Jesus walk through angry crowds untouched yet heal a woman who simply touched His garment. Judas helped pass out the bread miraculously provided through the prayer of Him who called Himself the Bread of Life. Judas even knew that Jesus knew he was going to betray Him. Despite all this, he went through with it. What was he thinking?

Which of us has not identified with Peter when he denied Christ, fearful for his own life? Who has not joined Thomas in doubting the reality of a Savior he cannot see? Do any of us criticize the disciples for their boat hugging in the midst of a violent storm, frightened by what appeared to be a water-walking ghost? But how can we understand the pitiful Judas, the turncoat, traitor, dealer in treachery? In what way could he have possibly thought Jesus was worth only thirty pieces of silver? Is greed that blinding, so laughably ridiculous that someone so close to Jesus could make such an assessment?

Contrary to the demoniac who, once healed, was found to be "clothed and in his right mind" (Mark 5:15), Judas was clearly not in his right mind. In Judas we see an absolute, irrational contradiction of all that would make sense.

Even more incomprehensible (and amazing) is to "consider Him who has endured such hostility by sinners against Himself" (Heb. 12:3). It doesn't get much worse than being betrayed by a close friend. Therefore, since Christ went through this, we are exhorted to "not grow weary and lose heart" in our walk of faith. For there is a great "cloud of witnesses" to encourage us, and Christ is the chief One, the One who Himself did not lose heart over Judas.

Lord, thank you that You have chosen me to be one of Your followers.
Let me not fail You because of irrational unbelief and self-centeredness.

All We Like Judas

Matthew 26:14-16 (pt. 3)

[14] Then one of the twelve, named Judas Iscariot, went to the chief priests [15] and said, "What are you willing to give me to betray Him to you?" And they weighed out thirty pieces of silver to him. [16] From then on he began looking for a good opportunity to betray Jesus.

We, as fallen individuals, live in a fallen world. Judas represents to us the worst of the fall. Yet at a very deep, core level, there is a Judas in every one of us. If the circumstances were right, each of us, but for the grace of God, would imitate the betrayer's actions.

Consider Adam and Eve, who lived in a perfect, well-provided-for environment, yet they wanted more than God's abundant supply. Consider Abraham, who had the promises of God for a multitude of descendants, yet he betrayed his wife by portraying her as his sister when he feared the king's threat on his own life. Consider King David, who brazenly violated God's commandments in his adultery with Bathsheba, his murdering of Uriah, and his feeble attempt at covering up his sin.

The Scriptures abound with examples of the hard cold truth of what Jeremiah wrote so long ago: "The heart is more deceitful than all else and is desperately sick; who can understand it?" (Jer. 17:9). David puts it this way: "God has looked down from heaven upon the sons of men to see if there is anyone who understands, who seeks after God. Every one of them has turned aside; together they have become corrupt; There is no one who does good, not even one" (Ps. 53:2-3). Paul applied it this way: "All have sinned and fall short of the glory of God" (Rom. 3:23).

The story of Judas strikes terror in our hearts because it could so easily be our story. Our expression of rebellion against God may not look the same as Judas's, but every time we deliberately sin, do what we know is wrong, or don't do the right thing we should do, we are, in a way, betraying God. We are willing to sacrifice the glory of God in us, as His image bearers, for the sake of some self-satisfying sin, some enjoyment of "spiritual endorphins." Do you doubt this? James says, "For whoever keeps the whole law and yet stumbles in one point, he has become guilty of all" (James 2:10). When we whom Christ has befriended commit sin, we cause Him to suffer disgrace before Satan, before the unseen world, and before other image bearers of God.

But praise God for His unmatched grace toward us in that "while we were [and still are] sinners, Christ died for us" (Rom. 5:8)!

Lord, thank you for saving me and keeping me despite my rebellious heart. Your love is so amazing.

Weekend Reading

Saturday – Job 24
Sunday – Job 25–26

Personal Reflections

Was There No Glimpse?

Matthew 26:16-19

[16] From then on he began looking for a good opportunity to betray Jesus. [17] Now on the first day of Unleavened Bread the disciples came to Jesus and asked, "Where do You want us to prepare for You to eat the Passover?" [18] And He said, "Go into the city to a certain man, and say to him, 'The Teacher says, "My time is near; I am to keep the Passover at your house with My disciples."'" [19] The disciples did as Jesus had directed them; and they prepared the Passover.

Judas's action was premeditated, his movements calculated. In one sense, he was in full possession of his faculties, but his mind had been twisted by sin, manipulated by the deceiver (see Luke 22:3 and John 13:27). The tempter was roaming around like a lion (1 Peter 5:8), picking off Jesus' disciples, using greed or impetuousness (Luke 22:31) to get at the big prey, Jesus Himself.

In the midst of this, Jesus arranged for a banquet, echoing Psalm 23:4-5, "Even though I walk through the valley of the shadow of death, I fear no evil ... You prepare a table before me in the presence of my enemies." The tempest was coming, but Jesus still had more to teach the Twelve (though only eleven would be listening) in the short time left. This was the calm before the storm.

The disciples, oblivious, concerned themselves with the Passover tradition. Jesus gave them instructions for preparing the venue. They were to go into Jerusalem, meet an unnamed man, and follow him. According to Matthew 14:13 and Luke 22:10, they would know him because he would be carrying a pitcher of water. Now whether this rendezvous was planned out ahead of time or not, the sovereignty of Christ is plainly evident. He who caused the fish to overflow the fishermen's nets and who miraculously fed the multitudes could also orchestrate the reservation of a room for His last evening with His closest disciples. And so the disciples went and found the room as He said, and they prepared the Passover, the last food He would have with them before His death.

The disciples, from childhood, had rehearsed the lesson of the Passover. Did they glimpse any hint from that of what was about to come? God had provided their ancestors redemption from bondage in Egypt through the blood of a sacrificial lamb. Did the disciples not suspect a connection with Jesus' predictions of His death? Hindsight after the resurrection must have been clear. Later they must have thought, *How could we have missed the obvious back then at the Passover Feast?* But, then again, as they had probably eaten at least one Passover meal with the Lord before, they blithely went on their way preparing for this one as usual.

Lord, help me to see that even in the seemingly mundane things of life You are ever present, orchestrating events and people for Your grand purposes. Help me not to miss the lessons hidden in the OT stories of Israel.

Dropping a Bombshell

Matthew 26:20-22

[20] *Now when evening came, Jesus was reclining at the table with the twelve disciples.*
[21] *As they were eating, He said, "Truly I say to you that one of you will betray Me."*
[22] *Being deeply grieved, they each one began to say to Him, "Surely not I, Lord?"*

Less than twenty-four hours until His crucifixion, and the day grows ominous. Dinner, the Passover, was supposed to be a happy time, remembering God's goodness and redemption of Israel. It was a celebration of their relationship with the covenant God of Abraham, Isaac, and Jacob—a relishing in their freedom from Egyptian slavery many years previous, and a fanning of the flame of hope that they would someday be freed from their current oppression under Rome. But the Master spoke that night of betrayal.

Despite the external opposition from the religious leaders, the disciples had been riding the wave of popularity. The sights and sounds of the triumphal entry of Jesus, riding humbly into Jerusalem on a donkey (as Zechariah prophesied). All these things must have reverberated in their minds, overwhelming the overtures of opposition against Him and them. Failure of Jesus' mission was simply not an option they considered.

In the middle of the meal, however, Jesus dropped a bombshell. As was His custom, for emphasis He began with the word *truly* (or as the KJV renders it, *verily*). Take special note, He says, "One of you will betray Me." He had mentioned before that He was going to suffer and die, and they had reacted the same way then: they were "deeply grieved" (17:22-23).

Their grief could have come from a number of sources. First, they could have been reacting to the thought that Jesus could even question their allegiance to Him: "How could He think that of us!" A second possibility is that they could have been grieving that one of their fellow disciples could be messing up the plan for liberation. Luke records their rivalry: "There arose also a dispute among them as to which one of them was regarded to be greatest" (Luke 22:24). The third and most probable explanation of their grieving is that there was genuine fear in each one of them that the duplicity of their hearts was about to be exposed. Every one of them had outwardly demonstrated sacrifice, having left their homes and families to follow Christ. But who does not have secret, hidden places of the heart where our loyalty is questionable? Which of us can say with absolute assurance that we would remain loyal even to death? Desperately, they cried out, "Surely you don't mean me, do you, Lord?"

O Lord, You search hearts and minds. Please forgive me for my doubts and weak loyalty. I want to love You with all my heart, soul, mind, and strength.

Sour Taste

Matthew 26:23-25

[23] And He answered, "He who dipped his hand with Me in the bowl is the one who will betray Me. [24] The Son of Man is to go, just as it is written of Him; but woe to that man by whom the Son of Man is betrayed! It would have been good for that man if he had not been born." [25] And Judas, who was betraying Him, said, "Surely it is not I, Rabbi?" Jesus said to him, "You have said it yourself."

Alluding to Psalm 41:9, Jesus identified His betrayer as one who "dipped his hand with Me in the bowl." During the Passover there were times when, like today, people sharing a meal would serve themselves food from the same containers, like dipping bread or a sprig into a some type of dip. Until now Jesus had directed His pronouncements of woe only toward the religious hypocrites who opposed Him. But now He leveled this against one of His intimates, one of His hand-chosen disciples—better if that one had never been born!

Judas was not just a volunteer; Jesus had selected him along with the others, as He said to them earlier, "Did I Myself not choose you, the twelve, and yet one of you is a devil?" (John 6:70). That's odd. Why would Jesus have chosen one He knew would betray Him, and then say, it would have been good if that person had never come into existence? This begs another question: why did God create people whom He knew would reject Christ? At this point we touch on a wild vortex of God's purposes for all of creation: His sovereign foreknowledge, predestination, election, and the free, responsible choices inherent in humanity. None of us (not even atheists) can escape difficult questions, nor can we fully comprehend the mystery of them. Our finite minds are simply too puny to figure it all out.

Though this may confound us, it should not cause us to worry. As believers in Christ, we rejoice that we are His. Those with hardened hearts have nothing to complain about, for they do only as they choose. They are not coerced against their wills. Objections to the contrary are unconvincing, for no one can legitimately use philosophical or theological reasoning to argue against his own choices. That would be self-defeating. In any case, atheists shouldn't care, because they don't believe in God!

Judas, like the others, said, "Surely it is not I?" But he added "Rabbi" instead of "Lord." Jesus was not his master at all! The Lord responded by simply pointing out the sourness of those words in the betrayer's mouth. And as we know from John 13, Judas did not wrestle with his conscience, but immediately left after being exposed by the all-seeing Christ.

Father, thank you for giving me the knowledge of the Lord Jesus Christ. Though I don't understand all Your mysteries, I know that You chose me and that You love me.

The Last Supper–part 1

Matthew 26:26-29

---

[26] *While they were eating, Jesus took some bread, and after a blessing, He broke it and gave it to the disciples, and said, "Take, eat; this is My body."* [27] *And when He had taken a cup and given thanks, He gave it to them, saying, "Drink from it, all of you;* [28] *for this is My blood of the covenant, which is poured out for many for forgiveness of sins.* [29] *But I say to you, I will not drink of this fruit of the vine from now on until that day when I drink it new with you in My Father's kingdom."*

Nothing in the history of Christianity is so well attested to as the Last Supper of our Lord. Probably the earliest record of it is about AD 55 when Paul wrote his first letter to the Corinthians (1 Cor. 11:18-34). This was about twenty years after the actual incident. Luke, the historian, besides recording it in his gospel account, also noted in the history of the Acts of the Apostles that the early church, after Pentecost, was highly committed to enacting the Lord's Supper, also called the "breaking of bread" (Acts 2:42). Later in the first century we find reference to it as a regular event in Acts 20:7 on Sundays.

First, Jesus gave a "blessing," which at that time, as today, was a reference to giving thanks for their meal. Then Jesus gave to His disciples the simple staples of life and designated them as memorial tokens. He took the bread and broke it, explaining that it symbolized His body. Breaking it had the obvious force of reminding them that His body was to be "broken" for them.

Much debate had taken place over the years about what goes on at the Lord's Supper. Some think Jesus empowered the disciples (and ultimately the clergy) to transform the bread into the actual body of Jesus. This doctrine, called *transubstantiation,* taught by Roman Catholics and others, relies on passages such as John 6:41-65.

Another view, called *consubstantiation,* taught by Lutherans and others, conveys the idea that Jesus meant the symbols would carry His spiritual, not physical, presence.

However, Jesus used common, figurative language that we are quite familiar with even today. If I take out my wallet and show you a picture of my wife, and say, "This is my wife," you instinctively know that I am just showing you a *symbol* of her, an image on photographic paper that represents her. So, when Christ said, "This is My body," He was using bread to *symbolize* His body.

Lord, as a genuine follower of Yours, I commit to celebrating the Lord's Supper just as You commanded—as often as my local church holds it.

The Last Supper–part 2

Matthew 26:26-29

[26] While they were eating, Jesus took some bread, and after a blessing, He broke it and gave it to the disciples, and said, "Take, eat; this is My body." [27] And when He had taken a cup and given thanks, He gave it to them, saying, "Drink from it, all of you; [28] for this is My blood of the covenant, which is poured out for many for forgiveness of sins. [29] But I say to you, I will not drink of this fruit of the vine from now on until that day when I drink it new with you in My Father's kingdom."

In this simple and poignant action, Jesus enshrined the practice of remembering Him. It was concise and simply stated. Yet I grieve today because so few Christians obey the Lord in this simple way. Some write it off as a stale ritual; others view it as boring. Today too many of our Bible-believing churches relegate this observance to once a month or once a quarter and then tack it on in the last fifteen minutes of a preaching service. They miss so much blessing that comes from remembering the Lord weekly in a focused way.

Some say that holding it too often renders it common and rote. But does that logic hold for Christians gathering for prayer, for teaching of the Word, or for fellowship? The early church was committed to all four practices: "They were continually devoting themselves to the apostles' teaching and to fellowship, to the breaking of bread and to prayer" (Acts 2:42). Why should the Lord's Supper be emphasized less than the other three?

There are three biblical reasons for observing the Lord's Supper today: (1) Jesus commanded it; (2) the early church practiced it; and (3) the apostles taught it (see 1 Corinthians 11:17-34). There are also three spiritual reasons: (1) it keeps our focus on what is absolutely central to the Christian walk, namely, Jesus' sacrificial death: (2) it reminds us that His death is as important to our spiritual life as basic food is to our physical life; and (3) it portrays the one thing that binds us together as Christians. "Is not the cup of blessing which we bless a sharing in the blood of Christ? Is not the bread which we break a sharing in the body of Christ? Since there is one bread, we who are many are one body; for we all partake of the one bread" (1 Cor. 10:16-17).

There are also three strategic reasons: (1) It is better to obey than sacrifice (1 Sam. 15:22); (2) it is better to worship than to serve (cf. Luke 10:41-43); and (3) the Lord's Supper helps keep our priorities in place by centering our lives on Christ's work on the cross. As we devote ourselves to worshiping the Lord through remembering Him in the way He appointed, we are placing ourselves on the solid footing that gives us traction in the Christian life.

Lord, as I take the bread and wine in remembrance of You, I worship You in the beauty of holiness. I want to be constantly reminded of Your sacrifice for me.

Weekend Reading

Saturday – Job 27
Sunday – Job 28

Personal Reflections

Week 46
Day 1

Undeniable Denial

Matthew 26:30-35

30 After singing a hymn, they went out to the Mount of Olives. 31 Then Jesus said
to them, "You will all fall away because of Me this night, for it is written, 'I WILL
STRIKE DOWN THE SHEPHERD, AND THE SHEEP OF THE FLOCK SHALL BE SCATTERED.' 32 But
after I have been raised, I will go ahead of you to Galilee." 33 But Peter said to
Him, "Even though all may fall away because of You, I will never fall away."
34 Jesus said to him, "Truly I say to you that this very night, before a rooster crows,
you will deny Me three times." 35 Peter said to Him, "Even if I have to die with You,
I will not deny You." All the disciples said the same thing too.

Following the dinner in the upper room, Jesus and His disciples retreated to one of His favorite places—the Mount of Olives, just east of Jerusalem. By quoting Zechariah 13:7, He warned the disciples of what was about to happen. He depicted Himself as the Shepherd who would be killed and the disciples as the scattered sheep. Pointedly He told them they would all abandon Him. But, not to worry—He would rise from the dead and precede them in returning to Galilee.

This did not go over well with the disciples, especially Peter. He adamantly rejected the notion. *Jesus may be right about the others, but not about me*, he thought. Peter saw himself as the most loyal of all Jesus' followers. He was not one to cower before difficult challenges; his impetuous actions demonstrated that he was fearless.

Without arguing, Jesus simply told Peter that he would deny his Master not once, but three times that very night. In other words, Peter's actions would not be a momentary lapse, which one might easily overlook. "Three times" meant that Peter would have opportunity after the first denial, and even the second, to come to his senses. But, no, Peter's denial would take place with full awareness of his situation and of himself. And it would happen soon, before the morning, when the rooster crowed—less than twelve hours away.

Peter insisted that he would never do that to Jesus. The other disciples all echoed his commitment. After three years, and having left all, they would never abandon Jesus, even if it meant they had to die. How tragic was their blindness! The fear of their own deaths would lead them to deny their Master during the events about to strike with lightning speed.

Yet the Lord predicted their failure ahead of time so they would experience His grace after it all happened.

Lord, even though You know ahead of time that I will at times deny You by my actions or lack of witness, I am encouraged that You still love me.

Week 46

Day 2

Grief Unshared–part 1

Matthew 26:36-38

[36] *Then Jesus came with them to a place called Gethsemane, and said to His disciples, "Sit here while I go over there and pray."* [37] *And He took with Him Peter and the two sons of Zebedee, and began to be grieved and distressed.* [38] *Then He said to them, "My soul is deeply grieved, to the point of death; remain here and keep watch with Me."*

Gethsemane was familiar ground on the west side of the Mount of Olives, having a full view of the temple mount in Jerusalem across the Kidron Valley. Jesus came here for a time of humble, earnest, heart-rending prayer. The entire band was with Him there (except for Judas), but Jesus separated out three of His disciples. We often call them the inner circle: Peter, James, and John. For reasons not given, the Lord included these three in occasional special intimacies of ministry. Peter seemed to be a leader among the Twelve, or at least the most outspoken. John referred to himself (in his gospel account) as "the disciple Jesus loved."

James was not especially noteworthy, other than that he was John's brother and one of the first of Jesus' disciples, and the first apostle martyred after Christ's resurrection (Acts 12:1-2). Although Jesus' selection of these three must remain a mystery for now, one thing we can infer is that it was not based on their sterling qualities and accomplishments. (Remember, also, that Judas was one of the Twelve!)

Jesus separated Himself from the rest of the disciples, taking these three with Him. His task was to pray. One would think that after three years of following their rabbi, they would have been accustomed to doing what He did. In fact, as recorded in Luke 22:40, Jesus instructed them, "Pray that you may not enter into temptation." But this must have puzzled them, What could possibly tempt them in the middle of the night?

The temptation was about to become obvious: temptation to sleep when they should be praying; temptation to flee when Jesus was arrested; temptation to deny Christ when accused; temptation to abandon faith when Jesus would be buried before the next day was out.

Is it any wonder that Jesus' soul was "deeply grieved, to the point of death"? But there were other things grieving Him as well.

Lord Jesus, I am sorry for causing You grief when I fall into temptation, and even when I fail to take Your warning seriously about falling into temptation.

Grief Unshared–part 2

Matthew 26:36-38

[36] Then Jesus came with them to a place called Gethsemane, and said to His disciples, "Sit here while I go over there and pray." [37] And He took with Him Peter and the two sons of Zebedee, and began to be grieved and distressed. [38] Then He said to them, "My soul is deeply grieved, to the point of death; remain here and keep watch with Me."

The grief Jesus experienced weighed heavily on Him. Matthew used three separate words to describe it. The first is *grieved* (v. 37), meaning "deeply saddened." It is the same word used in relation to the Holy Spirit, "Do not grieve the Holy Spirit of God, by whom you were sealed for the day of redemption." (Eph. 4:30). The sadness of the human predicament finally came to this: the suffering of the incarnated Son of God. It weighed heavily on Him, overwhelming Him. As the psalmist wrote, "I am poured out like water, and all my bones are out of joint; my heart is like wax; it is melted within me" (Ps. 22:14). Jesus knelt before the crushing prospect of taking on the sin of every human being.

The second word, *distressed,* carries the sense of being anguished to the point of being incapacitated. The idea here is like a scene from an old movie that depicted a police detective who wanted a scar for an undercover assignment. He had two men hold him down and a third took a red-hot poker and touched it to the inside of his upper arm. The only way he could do it was to voluntarily make himself incapacitated. That is the idea here. In bracing Himself for the onslaught of God's wrath, Jesus experienced the incapacity of the emotion of the moment. Judas was already dispatched to his mission. The die had been cast. There was no turning back. He was constrained to move forward.

The third word, rendered *grieved,* is a more intensified word in the original Greek. It conveys intense sadness. Luke used it to describe the rich young ruler who walked away from Jesus' challenge to discipleship (Luke 18:23). We normally associate this kind of grief with the deepest losses. The more we love someone or something, the greater the sense of loss and the experience of grief. For some, the loss of a dream, a job, a position, respect, or possessions, can bring on grief. Jesus was not concerned about losing any of these things. What weighed heavily on Him was the imminent (though temporary) loss of fellowship with His Father that He would experience when God, in His holiness and justice, would judge Him for the sin of the world. Shortly His grief would be poured out in the words, "My God, My God, why have You forsaken Me?"

Lord, I am overwhelmed by what You went through for me, for us. Thank you that You were constrained to do it out of love for Your Father and for me.

An Impossible Temptation

Matthew 26:39-41

[39] *And He went a little beyond them, and fell on His face and prayed, saying, "My Father, if it is possible, let this cup pass from Me; yet not as I will, but as You will."* [40] *And He came to the disciples and found them sleeping, and said to Peter, "So, you men could not keep watch with Me for one hour?* [41] *Keep watching and praying that you may not enter into temptation; the spirit is willing, but the flesh is weak."*

Intense emotion gushes out at us from this passage. We've previously seen the Lord praying and teaching His disciples how to pray. We've seen the disciples praying (that is, crying out) to the Lord in their desperate situations (think, boat on the stormy Sea of Galilee). At some point after leaving the upper room (John 14:31) Jesus voiced His high-priestly prayer (John 17). But prior to that we do not see Him praying with such emotion.

Jesus collapsed with the crushing weight of what lay before Him. The third chronicler of our Lord's life put it this way, "And being in agony He was praying very fervently; and His sweat became like drops of blood, falling down upon the ground" (Luke 22:44). This was real, not just a show for the casual reader. God invites us to sit front row center to view this intimate, emotive outpouring in prayer. We tread such ground carefully.

How could Jesus, who was the Christ, the Son of the living God, utter such a petition as, "Let this cup pass from Me"? True, in the end, He submitted to the Father's will, but He *was* tempted. What does that mean? Does that mean Jesus could have actually resisted His Father's will? If that were the case, then the perfect union of the Father and Son was in danger of a breach—a division in God Himself and an utter failure of the mission. A failure in God Himself! Yet that was impossible, for it would contradict everything we know about Christ being God, and therefore the very existence of God Himself. The Scripture says, "He cannot deny Himself" (2 Tim. 2:13).

The temptation was very real; Jesus was also human and was "tempted in all things as we are" (Heb. 4:15b). Praise God, however, that "He did not sin" (Heb. 4:15c). How can both things be true: the reality of the temptation and the impossibility of sinning? Our own experience of temptation renders us suspicious, for we often succumb to temptation. But the fact that we mere mortals do occasionally succeed in resisting it reveals that temptation does not *require* failure in order to be real. Therefore, the reality of the temptation of the Lord does not require that He be *able* to sin. He was perfect man, and therefore resisted the very real temptations that are "common to men" (1 Cor. 10:13).

Lord Jesus, please come to my aid when I am being tempted (Heb. 2:18).

When Jesus Winced

Matthew 26:42-46

[42] He went away again a second time and prayed, saying, "My Father, if this cannot pass away unless I drink it, Your will be done." [43] Again He came and found them sleeping, for their eyes were heavy. [44] And He left them again, and went away and prayed a third time, saying the same thing once more. [45] Then He came to the disciples and said to them, "Are you still sleeping and resting? Behold, the hour is at hand and the Son of Man is being betrayed into the hands of sinners. [46] Get up, let us be going; behold, the one who betrays Me is at hand!"

Three times He prayed; three times they slept. Three times He asked the Father to let the cup pass; three times they continued to sleep. Three times He wanted them to pray (see Mark 14:40); three times they could not. Human frailty becomes most evident when the need is the greatest. Jesus' request for the disciples to pray was not for His own benefit, for how could any human intercede on behalf of the Great High Priest? His need was greater than that.

Jesus was entering the conflict that would strain eternity, for the stress of the temptation would penetrate to the very core of God Himself. How is this? We find a clue in what He prayed to the Father: "If it is possible, let this cup pass from Me" (26:39). What was the cup He wished to avoid? Was He shrinking back from doing battle with Satan? Hardly, for He had previously dismissed Satan with a single command: "Go, Satan…" (4:10) and cast out demons effortlessly. Was it the prospect of physical pain? Again, we say hardly would this cause the One who healed the sick to hesitate to identify with this all-too-common human experience. Was it death that scared Him? He who had already raised the dead and spoke of it as "sleep" (see John 11) knew that death was not the last word, nor the final enemy. Many think the temptation was the thought of the absolutely Holy One bearing the load of mankind's sin, which caused this three-peat of agonizing prayer. However, something far more weighty loomed.

Repeatedly in the OT, God's anger in its most extreme description is seen as a "cup" that all under His judgment must drink. "For thus the Lord, the God of Israel, says to me, 'Take this cup of the wine of wrath from My hand and cause all the nations to whom I send you to drink it'" (Jer. 25:15; see also Job 21:20; Psalms 75:8; Isaiah 51:17, 22; Jeremiah 51:7). Could it be that Jesus, as God, knowing the extreme nature of divine anger, was about to enter something never experienced before—God experiencing His own wrath? What else could possibly cause Jesus—the portal between creation and eternity, divine and human—to wince?

Lord, when I see how You reacted to the wrath that should be against me, I am so thankful that You took the full blow in my place.

Weekend Reading

Saturday – Job 29
Sunday – Job 30

Personal Reflections

Treachery Defined

Matthew 26:47-50

[47] While He was still speaking, behold, Judas, one of the twelve, came up accompanied by a large crowd with swords and clubs, who came from the chief priests and elders of the people. [48] Now he who was betraying Him gave them a sign, saying, "Whomever I kiss, He is the one; seize Him." [49] Immediately Judas went to Jesus and said, "Hail, Rabbi!" and kissed Him. [50] And Jesus said to him, "Friend, do what you have come for." Then they came and laid hands on Jesus and seized Him.

What treachery! The antagonist is described as "one of the twelve"; ironically, Jesus called him "friend"! Judas's mouth dripped with disingenuous respect—"Hail, Rabbi." And with a thin veil of affection, Judas "kissed Him." Not in all of literature can one find such pathetic betrayal of friendship—one who had so much, giving away a relationship so great! Judas had a straightforward plan—to subtly catch Jesus and the other disciples off guard. But the Lord knew they were coming and had just told the disciples about the coming betrayal. A large commotion began with weapons ready and wielded. The religious leaders had incited a large crowd to accompany Judas. Knowing that past efforts to apprehend Christ had not been productive, the leaders vowed not to fail this time.

The time had finally come for His sacrifice, so Jesus yielded to His oppressors. Isaiah, many years earlier, prophesied about this moment, "He was oppressed and He was afflicted, yet He did not open His mouth; like a lamb that is led to slaughter, and like a sheep that is silent before its shearers, so He did not open His mouth" (Isa. 53:7). Jesus did not resist. In fact He prompted His betrayer, as He had done before, "What you do, do quickly" (John 13:27).

In contrast to all that had been recorded concerning the tension between the religious leaders and Jesus, Matthew describes this final abduction with few words. The leaders, using their pawn for a cheap price, took control—like a grand master of chess beginning the final sequence of moves calculated to bring the opposing player into checkmate. The finale is set in motion. It is time for the Jewish leaders to regain control of the conflict for the sake of their religion and their nation. Things had gone too far and had to stop. Fear had given way to madness, and they drove themselves to an elaborately concocted scheme which was about to unfold and ultimately lead to Jesus' death.

Little did they know that God was about to use their sinister plans to bring about the greatest possible outcome. I can imagine God later saying to Judas, "You meant it for evil, but God meant it for good" (see Genesis 50:20).

Lord Jesus, thank you for being my Lamb who was slaughtered for my transgressions.

Week 47
Day 2

The Arrest

Matthew 26:51-56

51 And behold, one of those who were with Jesus reached and drew out his sword, and struck the slave of the high priest and cut off his ear. 52 Then Jesus said to him, "Put your sword back into its place; for all those who take up the sword shall perish by the sword. 53 Or do you think that I cannot appeal to My Father, and He will at once put at My disposal more than twelve legions of angels? 54 How then will the Scriptures be fulfilled, which say that it must happen this way?" 55 At that time Jesus said to the crowds, "Have you come out with swords and clubs to arrest Me as you would against a robber? Every day I used to sit in the temple teaching and you did not seize Me. 56 But all this has taken place to fulfill the Scriptures of the prophets."

Jesus gave the disciples clear and concise instructions, rebuking them for their well-intended but misguided actions. We know from Luke 11:38 that they had brought two swords. From John 18:10 we learn Peter wielded one of them, and he was, in fact, the one who sliced off the ear of the high priest's slave. Impetuous? Yes, but in doind so he was demonstrating his loyalty to Christ. After all, Peter had just insisted that he was willing to die for Him (26:35), as did the other disciples.

This was not the time, however, for defending Jesus or protecting Him from being arrested. They thought all depended upon *them,* but the Lord pointed out that He did not need any human help to accomplish His goals; He had at His disposal the supernatural forces of God. The issue was not whether the events could be stopped. Scripture had to be fulfilled. God was keeping His word, His promise. Prophecy needed to unfold as planned.

How often do we wrestle with our circumstances, desperately trying to change them, when in fact God may have something different in mind. As Peter Kerr so aptly put it, "Our dear Lord … does not always have an easy, pleasant path for us, but He does always have a good path for us—even if that path involves suffering. His goal is NOT our earthly 'happiness.' His goal is our eternal holiness in Christ!"

Jesus questioned the crowd about their covert approach to arresting Him. Why hadn't they apprehended Him in the temple if the problem were His teaching as charged? He was no ordinary foe. Others they could dismiss with blistering diatribes, with the crowds cowering in fear. But with Jesus, public debates always ended in their embarrassment. The Lord's questions implied the obvious: their agenda betrayed hatred born of insecure, sinful hearts. Though Jesus did not resist, He spotlighted the prophetic irony of what they were doing.

Lord, help me not to run ahead of You or behind You, but to keep in step with Your plan and purpose for my life.

The Worst Time to Fail

Matthew 26:56

56b Then all the disciples left Him and fled.

What a sad response after the disciples had laid it all on the line for their Master! He had called some of them to leave their fishing business, and they had done that. Matthew had abandoned his tax career. They all left family and homes to follow Him. He had asked a lot of them and challenged them to "lose" their lives for His sake. And they followed Him even though "the Son of Man has nowhere to lay His head" (8:20). And just hours before this, He taught them that "greater love has no one than this, that one lay down his life for his friends" (John 15:13).

They dared to believe He was the Christ, the Son of the living God. They trusted that He, the Messiah, the Son of Man, had the words of eternal life. He was the Great Shepherd who loved His sheep. They believed He was the Way, the Truth, and the Life. He was the door to salvation. They understood Him to be the river of life, the fountain of living water, and the true manna from heaven that would nourish all who came to Him.

His inner circle of three had seen Him visibly transformed, talking with Moses and Elijah. They had all witnessed Him walking on the water, hushing the raging storms, giving sight to the blind, healing the sick, dismissing demons, and raising the dead. They had stood in awe as He cleared the temple, driving out the merchandisers and tossing over tables. They had watched in awe as He shut down the hypocritical religious leaders who tried to trip Him up. How many times had Jesus taught the disciples about faith? How often had He told them to "fear not"? Had they not learned that things were not always as they appeared? Had Jesus not, many times, surprised them with His solution to their many dilemmas?

Yet here in this garden, at this fateful moment in their lives, theirs was not the faith that Peter later wrote about, that "though tested by fire… [would] be found to result in praise and glory and honor at the revelation of Jesus Christ" (1 Pet. 1:7).

Having proved themselves unable to pray with Jesus for one hour, they fled! They abandoned their Master to save their own lives, just when He was about to save theirs!

Thank you, gracious Lord, that You are not deterred by the weaknesses of Your followers. Though we are often faithless, You remain faithful (2 Tim. 2:13).

Week 47
Day 4

Siding with Jesus

Matthew 26:57-58

[57] *Those who had seized Jesus led Him away to Caiaphas, the high priest, where the scribes and the elders were gathered together.* [58] *But Peter was following Him at a distance as far as the courtyard of the high priest, and entered in, and sat down with the officers to see the outcome.*

Waiting on delivery of their "package," the religious leaders had gathered back in Jerusalem at the house of the high priest. The plan that began in Matthew 26:6 was unfolding on schedule. Caiaphas, a high priest, presided over the Sanhedrin, the ruling council of Israel. He was the most powerful man in Judea next to the Roman governor. In Roman times the Roman governor filled this office by political appointment. Caiaphas was appointed eleven years before John the Baptist appeared on the scene, and he continued in the post until after Christ was raised from the dead.

This ruler was the one who had earlier calmed the Pharisees by saying, "You [do not] take into account that it is expedient for you that one man die for the people, and that the whole nation not perish" (John 11:50). Later, after Jesus' ascension and Pentecost, Caiaphas presided at the inquisition of Peter and John, following the first apostolic healing. Their response to the most powerful man in Israel was that their power to heal came from Jesus "whom [they] crucified," and in His name alone lay the power to be saved (Acts 4:6-12).

The scribes mentioned in this passage were experts concerning the law of Moses, the defining constitution of Israel. And of course there were the older, respected men, whose judgment was held in high regard. All petty disagreements were set aside (no delineating of Pharisees or Sadducees in the ruling council). The old saying, "A common foe makes strange bedfellows" was certainly true in this case. They all had the same goal—to silence Jesus, seen as a threat to them all.

Peter, loyal as he thought himself to be, followed Jesus at a distance. His mind may have been racing to devise a plan of his own to spring the Master. He even dared to enter the courtyard of Caiaphas's house. The officers there were probably not involved in the unlawful arrest of Jesus, for there is no mention of them being part of the incoming crowd. But surely some of the mob milling around would have been with those who had arrested Jesus. The servant of Caiaphas, whose ear Peter had sliced off, may have been among them. It was, after all, Caiaphas's courtyard. Despite Peter's impetuousness and the risk, he wanted to be with his Master!

Lord, help me to be faithful to You even when others oppose You and, by association, oppose me. I want to be with You when the difficult times of life hit.

He Reviled Not

Matthew 26:59-63

[59] Now the chief priests and the whole Council kept trying to obtain false testimony against Jesus, so that they might put Him to death. [60] They did not find any, even though many false witnesses came forward. But later on two came forward, [61] and said, "This man stated, 'I am able to destroy the temple of God and to rebuild it in three days.' " [62] The high priest stood up and said to Him, "Do You not answer? What is it that these men are testifying against You?" [63] But Jesus kept silent. And the high priest said to Him, "I adjure You by the living God, that You tell us whether You are the Christ, the Son of God."

Like prosecutors in a modern criminal trial, the religious leaders were determined to find some shred of damning evidence even if they had to stretch it to the point of incredulity. They had to draw upon all their skills at manipulating the law, the people, and the circumstances. The whole council was complicit in the guilt of the false witnesses. They knew they lacked any evidence worthy of executing Jesus. The only way to accomplish their objective was to find two people willing to distort the truth. Yet the leaders could justify their own actions *legally* because they could claim they *themselves* did not lie. The blame could be shifted to the false witnesses; they themselves were simply ruling on the "evidence." This is the beginning of what was prophesied in Psalm 22:16: "For dogs have surrounded me; a band of evildoers has encompassed me."

So after considering many approaches, all of which distorted the facts, they found two supposed witnesses willing to give identical testimony. Their testimony was a distortion of a statement Jesus had made much earlier in His public ministry when He had said, "Destroy this temple, and in three days I will raise it up" (John 2:19). John comments that "He was speaking of the temple of His body" (John 2:21). Jesus had predicted that even though they would "destroy" this "temple," He would raise it up. Obviously these witnesses missed the whole point of what He was saying and distorted it to sound as if He were saying He would destroy the Jewish temple building.

Caiaphas exploded at Jesus' refusal to answer the accusation, but Jesus was fulfilling Scripture: "He was oppressed and He was afflicted, yet He did not open His mouth" (Isa. 53:7). So Caiaphas pulled out his trump card. Based on the law of Moses, a person was required to testify when the high priest put him under an oath (Lev. 5:1). And the question Caiaphas demanded Jesus answer went to the heart of the matter: Was Jesus claiming to be God's Messiah?

Lord, while being reviled, You did not revile in return; while suffering, You uttered no threats but kept entrusting Yourself to Your Father (1 Pet. 2:23). May this also be my response when suffering for righteousness.

Weekend Reading

Saturday – Job 31
Sunday – Job 32

Personal Reflections

Despised and Rejected

Matthew 26:64-68

[64] *Jesus said to him, "You have said it yourself; nevertheless I tell you, hereafter you will see* THE SON OF MAN SITTING AT THE RIGHT HAND OF POWER, *and* COMING ON THE CLOUDS OF HEAVEN." [65] *Then the high priest tore his robes and said, "He has blasphemed! What further need do we have of witnesses? Behold, you have now heard the blasphemy;* [66] *what do you think?" They answered, "He deserves death!"* [67] *Then they spat in His face and beat Him with their fists; and others slapped Him,* [68] *and said, "Prophesy to us, You Christ; who is the one who hit You?"*

Some time previously, the Jews had charged Jesus, "You being a man, make Yourself out to be God." Then they tried unsuccessfully to stone Him (John 10:33). Now Caiaphas, like an amateur chess player thinking he has his opponent in check, puts Christ under an oath requiring Him to answer clearly, "Are you the Christ, the Son of God?" (v. 63). Jesus affirmed the answer: "You have said it yourself."

The Lord emphatically accepted the title *Son of God*, but He also continued to refer to Himself as the "Son of Man, sitting at the right hand of Power." He was referring to Psalm 110:1, which is quoted four times in the NT and alluded to many other times as well (e.g., Heb. 1:3). The Jews understood He was making an unequivocal claim to be greater than David—in fact, equal with God. The phrase "Son of Man ... coming on the clouds of heaven" makes it clear Jesus was claiming to be the Messiah of Daniel 7:13.

Jesus' present audience knew exactly what He was saying, and it sounded blasphemous in their ears. The high priest went berserk, tearing his robes (the prescribed response to blasphemy, according to ancient rabbinic literature). They no longer needed trumped-up charges. They had all the evidence they needed, and it was good evidence. They heard it for themselves. Thus the whole council became eyewitnesses.

Blasphemy was the charge, judgment was declared, and the sentence was pronounced: death. With the trial over, everything else was mere formality.

The council—not just the mob or the soldiers but the dignified, respectable high priests and scribes and elders—spat on Christ, physically abused Him, and taunted Him. What a pathetic degradation—not only of their Messiah but of themselves.

Lord Jesus, I grieve when I think of how Your own people treated You and rejected You, their Messiah. I reaffirm my trust in You as the Christ, the Son of the living God.

Week 48
Day 2

Bitter Failure

Matthew 26:69-71

[69] Now Peter was sitting outside in the courtyard, and a servant-girl came to him and said, "You too were with Jesus the Galilean." [70] But he denied it before them all, saying, "I do not know what you are talking about." [71] When he had gone out to the gateway, another servant-girl saw him and said to those who were there, "This man was with Jesus of Nazareth." [72] And again he denied it with an oath, "I do not know the man." [73] A little later the bystanders came up and said to Peter, "Surely you too are one of them; for even the way you talk gives you away." [74] Then he began to curse and swear, "I do not know the man!" And immediately a rooster crowed. [75] And Peter remembered the word which Jesus had said, "Before a rooster crows, you will deny Me three times." And he went out and wept bitterly.

If we did not know the outcome of these things, we would despair for Peter. Here was a man, like Judas, who had so much and more. He was one of the first handpicked followers of Christ. He had been personally discipled by the Master and had shown the greatest loyalty on a number of occasions. Often he served as the spokesman for the Twelve and had the privilege of vocalizing what they had all come to believe—that their rabbi was the Christ, the Son of the living God.

All four gospel accounts record the incident of Peter's denial. John supplies facts relating to his own presence there. The three accusations came from two servant girls and bystanders. With each, the emotional tempo increased, beginning with a simple denial, then an oath, and finally cursing and swearing. At its core, each was a refusal to acknowledge any connection with Jesus. Peter, like his Master, was tempted three times but with different outcomes. While Jesus submitted to the Father's will three times, Peter disowned the Son three times.

In one of the saddest, most heart-rending sections of all Scripture, Peter realizes his abject failure toward his Lord, the One he had so adamantly *defended* on so many occasions. His memory of what Jesus had predicted can only be described as bitter. It wasn't just that he had failed Jesus but that Jesus knew all along it would happen. Maybe Peter thought he was the one Jesus talked about in the upper room when He said, "Woe to that man by whom the Son of Man is betrayed! It would have been good for that man if he had not been born" (26:24).

From our perspective as readers, we ponder the question: which is worse, to betray the Lord, as Judas did, or to disown Him, as Peter did? At this point in the story, the jury is still out.

Lord, I can feel the utter grief of Peter. Help me not to be afraid of my association with You. In fact, help me boldly declare Your Name to all.

Ulterior Benefits Gone Awry

Matthew 27:1-4

[1] Now when morning came, all the chief priests and the elders of the people conferred together against Jesus to put Him to death; [2] and they bound Him, and led Him away and delivered Him to Pilate the governor. [3] Then when Judas, who had betrayed Him, saw that He had been condemned, he felt remorse and returned the thirty pieces of silver to the chief priests and elders, [4] saying, "I have sinned by betraying innocent blood." But they said, "What is that to us? See to that yourself!"

The religious trial concluded with a guilty verdict and a sentence of capital punishment. Since the Jews were subject to Roman rule, the council had no power to carry out a death sentence, so they sent Jesus off to Pilate, the current governor, for a civil trial. They had an uneasy relationship with Pilate because they detested Roman dominance. But their hatred of the Romans was eclipsed by their greater hatred of Jesus, who had just "confessed" He was the Christ.

For years, some modern historians cast doubt on the veracity of the gospel accounts because there was no concrete historical evidence outside the Bible of the existence of any Roman official by the name of Pontius Pilate at Jesus' time in that area of the Roman empire. However, in 1961, in an archeological dig in Caesarea Maritima (by Sea), on the Mediterranean Coast (north of present day Tel Aviv in Israel), an ancient theater was unearthed, and a limestone plaque was discovered indicating that the theater was dedicated by a Pontius Pilate. This find has been dated to AD 26-37, supporting the historicity of Pilate!

In today's passage, Judas comes back into the story. Matthew places this account of him immediately after the account of Peter disowning Christ. Both men failed their Master. Peter responded with bitter weeping, indicating overwhelming grief but no obvious effort to right his wrong. Judas responded with remorse *and* an apparent effort to compensate for his terrible act.

What do we make of Judas' attempt to return the blood money? The fact that he had betrayed Jesus for money sets him apart as a mercenary, benefitting from Jesus' misfortune. Yet it is clear that he was instrumental in causing that misfortune. We can speculate that Judas had not expected his betrayal would result in Jesus' being condemned to death.

Some have suggested he had a firm belief that Jesus could somehow extricate Himself from the arrest, just as He had done in past situations. Yet Judas's admission, "I have sinned by betraying innocent blood," reveals his own self-indictment. And the council only sneered at his remorse.

Lord, help me never use my relationship with You or my Christian associations for ulterior means, for my personal, financial benefit.

Week 48
Day 4

Guard Your Name

Matthew 27:5-10

[5] *And he threw the pieces of silver into the temple sanctuary and departed; and he went away and hanged himself.* [6] *The chief priests took the pieces of silver and said, "It is not lawful to put them into the temple treasury, since it is the price of blood."* [7] *And they conferred together and with the money bought the Potter's Field as a burial place for strangers.* [8] *For this reason that field has been called the Field of Blood to this day.* [9] *Then that which was spoken through Jeremiah the prophet was fulfilled: "And they took the thirty pieces of silver, the price of the one whose price had been set by the sons of Israel;* [10] *and they gave them for the Potter's Field, as the Lord directed me."*

Judas, in a fit of remorse, flung the silver coins—the blood money—into the temple sanctuary. The council had refused to let him renege on his "Christ for cash" contract. They were not about to give Jesus back. Judas then demonstrated a complete disregard for God's law. Motivated only by his own self-centered grief, he went out and destroyed that which was made in the image of God—himself! All he could think of was ending his horrific self-directed remorse. *Peter's* grief at denying Christ, however, did not lead to the ultimate self-centered act of suicide.

The chief priests, in a false show of propriety and hypocritical adherence to the law, refused to allow the blood money to go back into the treasury (from where it had probably come). Instead they used it unwittingly to fulfill prophecy (Zech. 11:12-13). They bought a burial ground, originally called the Potter's Field but renamed "Field of Blood." Acts 1:18-19 tells us that this was where Judas hung himself. This failed disciple's infamy included salacious details that traveled fast (just as sensational news always does).

The actions of Judas were so despicable that his name has been forever tainted. Rare is the parent who would name a child *Judas*. Even today, when well-known Christians fall into sin, for years afterward the mention of their name invokes the memory of their sin.

A person's name is his reputation—for good or for bad. That is why Scripture says, "A good name is to be more desired than great wealth" (Prov. 21:1). A name is more than a tag; it is a symbol. In contrast, Peter's name did not suffer the same ignominy. He went on to be a great leader in the church!

Lord, lead me not into any temptation that would allow the character of Judas to clothe my life. I want to guard my name by guarding my character.

Silent Before Accusations

Matthew 27:11-14

[11] Now Jesus stood before the governor, and the governor questioned Him, saying, "Are You the King of the Jews?" And Jesus said to him, "It is as you say." [12] And while He was being accused by the chief priests and elders, He did not answer. [13] Then Pilate said to Him, "Do You not hear how many things they testify against You?" [14] And He did not answer him with regard to even a single charge, so the governor was quite amazed.

Among the most difficult things to do in all of life is to exercise self-control when being wrongly accused. Even the political official Pilate was amazed that Jesus did not defend Himself. Although the Lord respectfully answered the straightforward inquiry of the governor, He did not honor the trumped-up accusations of the religious leaders with even one response. On the one hand, religious accusations, such as the ones the Jews had brought against Him, carried no weight in a political court. On the other hand, it's human nature to defend oneself at all costs. His self-control was remarkable.

Yes, Jesus was the "King of the Jews." This was virtually the same response Jesus gave to Judas when he said, "Surely it is not I, Rabbi?" (26:25). It was a risky thing to admit because it could easily be taken as a political statement of usurpation, and by extension, a new threat against Roman imperialism. At the minimum, Jesus' claim to Jewish kingship would threaten to disturb an uneasy political truce between the insecure Pilate and the hostile Jewish leaders. So Pilate would be predisposed to see Jesus in an unfavorable light.

Jesus' calmness stands in sharp contrast to the response of those around Him. Peter later wrote this commentary: "Christ also suffered for you, leaving you an example for you to follow in His steps, who committed no sin, nor was any deceit found in His mouth; and while being reviled, He did not revile in return; while suffering, He uttered no threats, but kept entrusting Himself to Him who judges righteously" (1 Pet. 2:21-23). Isaiah, prophetically, put it this way: "He was oppressed and He was afflicted, yet He did not open His mouth; like a lamb that is led to slaughter, and like a sheep that is silent before its shearers, so He did not open His mouth" (Isa. 53:7).

Jesus, the One who spoke the universe into existence, remained silent. One day, He will answer His accusers with the manifestation of His glory and they will bow before Him and confess that He *is* Lord (Phil. 2:10-11).

Lord, let me never "accuse" You of being anything but absolute Lord over my life.

Weekend Reading

Saturday – Job 33
Sunday – Job 34

Personal Reflections

Saved As a Result of Envy

Matthew 27:15-18

[15] Now at the feast the governor was accustomed to release for the people any one prisoner whom they wanted. [16] At that time they were holding a notorious prisoner, called Barabbas. [17] So when the people gathered together, Pilate said to them, "Whom do you want me to release for you? Barabbas, or Jesus who is called Christ?" [18] For he knew that because of envy they had handed Him over.

Barabbas had a unique privilege: he was the first to experience Jesus taking his place in death. As beneficial as this was for him, it was a gross injustice against Jesus. Barabbas's background, what can be pieced together of it, is interesting. His name meant "son of a father," which some scholars suggest indicates he was of noble birth. Luke records that "he was one who had been thrown into prison for insurrection in the city, and for murder" (Luke 23:19). Most likely he was a member of a group called Zealots, bent on overthrowing Roman oppression.

Historian N.T. Wright points out that the Zealots thought by rebelling against Rome, they would demonstrate their faithfulness to God. Then God would send the Messiah to raise the Jewish people to superiority once again among the nations. Tragically the Zealots failed to recognize that the Messiah had arrived; the kingdom plan was unfolding differently from the way they thought it would. One of the Zealots, however, did recognize who Jesus was and became one of the Twelve. We know him as Simon the Zealot (10:4).

There was nothing more odious to the Romans than those who defied imperial authority. Indeed they ruled with a cold, iron fist. This accounts for Matthew's description of Barabbas as "notorious." In the eyes of the Romans, he was a well-known rebel and lawbreaker. Jesus, on the other hand, was found innocent by Pilate, the Roman governor (27:24). Could the irony of this whole prisoner exchange be what Peter had in mind when he wrote, "For Christ also died for sins once for all, the just for the unjust …" (1 Pet. 3:18)?

During the Passover season, the governor customarily granted clemency to one of the Jewish prisoners. This was Pilate's attempt to placate the Jews, with whom he had an otherwise tenuous relationship. He could clearly see the Jewish leaders were envious of Jesus. Pilate could have ruled Jesus innocent and risked a riot, but he took a cowardly way out. He gave *them* the choice between the two: Jesus or Barabbas. Maybe he thought they would choose to execute the obvious criminal, Barabbas. But the Jews chose to let the murderer go free and to execute the One who spoke of love, forgiveness, and righteousness. They chose to kill their Messiah.

Lord, show me where envy has a grip in my life, and I will confess it as sin.

Contradiction of the Fickle

Matthew 27:19-20

19 While he was sitting on the judgment seat, his wife sent him a message, saying, "Have nothing to do with that righteous Man; for last night I suffered greatly in a dream because of Him." 20 But the chief priests and the elders persuaded the crowds to ask for Barabbas and to put Jesus to death.

A Roman ruler sitting in judgment of the Son of God? There is something pathetically humorous here. The psalmist saw it coming: "The kings of the earth take their stand and the rulers take counsel together against the LORD and against His Anointed" (Ps. 2:2). God's response? "He who sits in the heavens laughs, the LORD scoffs at them" (Ps. 2:4).

Little did Pilate know that standing before him was "the One who has been appointed by God as Judge of the living and the dead" (Acts 10:42). Imagine his horror when he eventually found himself standing before that One! "There is no creature hidden from His sight, but all things are open and laid bare to the eyes of Him with whom we have to do" (Heb. 4:13).

Pilate's wife, as a result of a dream, believed Jesus to be legally innocent of any wrongdoing. She warned her husband to divest himself of responsibility for Jesus. How much this played into Pilate's action to let the Jews choose whom to release, we do not know.

On the other hand, the religious authorities began lobbying the crowd to demand that Barabbas be freed and Jesus be put to death. How easily the people are persuaded! Whether this crowd involved some of the same people who celebrated Jesus' triumphal entry or not, we can't be sure. One thing we do know is that Jesus' closest disciples betrayed Him, denied Him, and otherwise abandoned Him. Would it be any surprise, then, if the crowds easily moved from celebrating Him to asking for His execution?

History definitely repeats itself among God's people. Think of Israel—Moses freed them from Egyptian bondage, but they turned against him when desert living brought hardship. They wanted to go back to Egypt! So too, in our passage, we can easily picture the crowd turning against the very One who healed their sick, gave sight to their blind, made their lame to walk, cast out their demons, and gave them hope. "For consider Him who has endured such hostility by sinners against Himself" (Heb. 12:3). The KJV translates the word *hostility* as *contradiction.* Indeed, what a contradiction that hostility was!

Lord, help me never to contradict Your work in my life. Help me to "not grow weary and lose heart" (Heb. 12:4), but to follow Jesus' example, and endure.

"What Evil Has He Done?"

Matthew 27:21-23

[21] The governor answered and said to them, "Which of the two do you want me to release to you?" They said, "Barabbas!" [22] Pilate said to them, "What then shall I do with Jesus who is called Christ?" They all said to him, "Let Him be crucified!" [23] Then the governor said, "Why, what evil has He done?" But they cried out all the more, saying, "Let Him be crucified!"

The question begged an answer. Roman authorities could be quite cold and uncaring most of the time. But this case has Pilate concerned. Was it because he wasn't completely bereft of a moral compass? Or was it because Rome, despite its ruthlessness in conquering nations, did have a sense of justice? We see their concern for justice throughout the NT, particularly when Paul used his Roman citizenship to his advantage.

Pilate's investigation had uncovered nothing that would justify a death penalty for Jesus. Apparently he had hoped he wouldn't have to deal with this messy Jewish internal conflict. That's why he offered the people a choice between a known criminal and the preacher of peace and love and religious reform. But to Pilate's chagrin and surprise, the people chose to release Barabbas. The worst Jesus had done, in legal terms, was to accept the title *King of the Jews*—but that was no crime. What was Pilate to do?

As indecisive as Pilate was, highly influenced by his wife and fearful of a riot, he abdicated his governing responsibility by putting the decision to the people. Let someone else make the decision. "If you take Barabbas, what am I to do with Jesus?" And as if to rub it in, he calls Jesus, "the Christ." He was fully aware of Jewish customs and teachings and knew this would aggravate them. Where the cries of "Hosanna!" had previously hailed Him, now shouts of denunciation thundered, "Let Him be crucified." Whether these were the same people as those at the triumphal entry, we do not know.

Pilate couldn't believe their response—though he might have expected it, given their attitude. So he asked, "Why, what evil has He done?" There was no answer to that, legally, morally, or religiously. The pagan governor could see that. The religious authorities knew it, for their efforts to find legitimate charges against Him in their earlier religious tribunal failed. Concerning the Jews, Peter gave this blistering assessment of their performance here: "The God of Abraham… glorified His Servant Jesus, whom you delivered up and denied in the presence of Pilate, when he was determined to let Him go" (Acts 3:13).

Lord, help me not to be indecisive in my loyalty to You.

Week 49
Day 4

Rebels with a Cause

Matthew 27:24-26

[24] When Pilate saw that he could not prevail at all, but rather that a tumult was rising, he took water and washed his hands before the multitude, saying, "I am innocent of the blood of this just Person. You see to it." [25] And all the people answered and said, "His blood be on us and on our children." [26] Then he released Barabbas to them; and when he had scourged Jesus, he delivered Him to be crucified.

First, Judas betrayed Jesus into the hands of His enemies. Then Peter denied knowing Him. And now virtually all the Jews were rejecting one of their own, the One who preached the good news of the kingdom of God to them. They worked themselves into a frenzy and called out, "His blood be on us and on our children!" They were now on record as accepting full responsibility for the condemnation of Jesus. Pilate had given up trying to defend Jesus. He had symbolically washed his hands of the deal, but not without one last comment about Jesus' innocence within the Roman justice system.

His decision was complicated by many factors, but at the core he feared a riot. If word got back to Rome of his inability to control the unruly Jews, his tenuous relationship with Caesar would be jeopardized. Political expedience prevented the hand of justice but not the hand of God.

However shallow Pilate's concern for Jesus may have been, the response of the people surprised him. To be sure, the religious leaders had, over time, hardened their hearts against Jesus. But how was the crowd so easily ignited against the One who had done so many good things for the people? Their rage against Christ was so inflamed that death not only seemed justified, it was demanded.

Pilate gave the Jews full latitude to take the law into their own hands (capital punishment was usually only allowed by Roman decree). As events unfolded, we discover that Roman soldiers were provided for the actual execution. So Pilate evidently turned a blind eye to the Jews' manipulation in order to take out their vengeance on Jesus.

Jesus Christ had come in fulfillment of messianic prophecy, and (early on, at least) even the leaders acknowledged Him to be a teacher from God (John 3:1-2). Yet, in their act of crucifying Him, they exhibited their rebellious hearts. Crucifixion, the punishment reserved for the worst rebels against imperial Rome, was wielded in the hands of rebels against the Lord's Anointed!

Lord, let not my heart be rebellious because of any expedience of life.
I want Christ to be my all in all. Please keep me close to You.

Irony of the Ages

Matthew 27:25

[25] And all the people said, "His blood shall be on us and on our children!"

This statement by the crowd at Jesus' trial represents the greatest irony of all time—on one hand, tragic; on the other hand, wonderful. Little did they realize the magnitude of either side of the irony! They were declaring full responsibility, conscious and deliberate, for the death of an innocent man. In their blindness, their cocky self-assuredness was nothing short of absolute foolishness. They inadvertently provided damning evidence for their own condemnation.

The religious leaders later tried to backpedal with the apostles, saying, "We gave you strict orders not to continue teaching in this name, and yet, you have filled Jerusalem with your teaching and intend to bring this man's blood upon us" (Acts 5:28). Not letting them off the hook, however, Peter and the apostles answered, "We must obey God rather than men. The God of our fathers raised up Jesus, whom you had put to death by hanging Him on a cross. He is the one whom God exalted to His right hand as a Prince and a Savior, to grant repentance to Israel, and forgiveness of sins. And we are witnesses of these things; and so is the Holy Spirit, whom God has given to those who obey Him" (Acts 5:29-32). They were guilty, and there were eyewitnesses to prove it!

Further, tragically, they fully and consciously passed on their guilt to their children. To be sure, they were using a colloquial expression to assert the forcefulness of their statement, but the truth is that subsequent generations of the Jewish people have continued to reject Christ, calling Him a spiritual imposter.

On the other hand, their statement, "His blood shall be on us ..." reflected a wonderful truth to which they were completely blind. The shedding of Jesus' blood gave them their only hope of eternal salvation from sin. The writer of Hebrews put it this way: "According to the law ... without shedding of blood there is no forgiveness" (Heb. 9:22), and, "It is impossible for the blood of bulls and goats to take away sins" (Heb. 10:3-4).

But Jesus' death provided the perfect sacrifice for sin, the only sure hope of salvation. Peter wrote, "You were not redeemed with perishable things like silver or gold from your futile way of life inherited from your forefathers, but with precious blood, as of a lamb unblemished and spotless, the blood of Christ" (1 Pet. 1:18-19).

Lord Jesus, thank you for the wonderful way in which You procured our salvation!

Weekend Reading

Saturday – Job 35
Sunday – Job 36

Personal Reflections

Bearing Shame and Scoffing Rude

Matthew 27:27-31

[27] *Then the soldiers of the governor took Jesus into the Praetorium and gathered the whole Roman cohort around Him.* [28] *They stripped Him and put a scarlet robe on Him.* [29] *And after twisting together a crown of thorns, they put it on His head, and a reed in His right hand; and they knelt down before Him and mocked Him, saying, "Hail, King of the Jews!"* [30] *They spat on Him, and took the reed and began to beat Him on the head.* [31] *After they had mocked Him, they took the scarlet robe off Him and put His own garments back on Him, and led Him away to crucify Him.*

What happened next was unthinkable. William MacDonald observes, "The Creator and Sustainer of the universe suffered unspeakable indignities from cruel, vulgar soldiers—His unworthy, sinful creatures." They stripped Him, which, by itself, was bad enough. But then they mocked Him as a clown king, placing a crude crown on His head, clothing Him with a scarlet robe imitating royal attire, giving im a reed as a scepter, kneeling before Him, and giving im sarcastic praise as "King of the Jews." One can almost see and hear the exaggerated mimicry. The abuse turned physical as they began to spit on Him and beat Him about the head. That pain would have been exacerbated by the ring of thorny branches comprising the "crown." Finally, when the soldiers tired of their "fun," they put His own clothes back on Him and brought Him to the execution site.

It is a curious thing why the soldiers treated Him this way in light of Pilate's declaration that He was innocent of any charges. The condemnation had been declared and the execution ordered, so what did it matter that the soldiers abused their prisoner? In Roman times, a condemned individual had no rights; there was no Geneva Convention, no political action committee to guarantee "proper" and humane treatment of criminals. Jesus was at the mercy of His guards. In such situations the base nature of humanity usually comes to the fore. The guards abused Him because they *could!*

In reality, the soldiers acted out the attitude of the Jews' toward their Messiah. Mocking and rejection are simply two sides of one coin. The insolence of creatures toward their Creator is as ancient as the serpent in the garden, when he said, "Has God really said …?" Satan's mocking question can be read like this, "Give me a break. You don't mean to tell me God has actually forbidden you to eat from that tree. That's ridiculous. He's trying to pull a fast one on you."

Yet, despite the opposition of sin and sinners against God, the Messiah remained on His mission—to die as a perfect sacrifice for sins.

Lord, all I can say is "thank you" for suffering such humiliation and shame for my shameful sins.

Week 50
Day 2

The Surprising Substitute

Matthew 27:32

[32] *As they were coming out, they found a man of Cyrene named Simon, whom they pressed into service to bear His cross.*

Simon of Cyrene performed a unique service for the Lord. Substituting for the One who would offer Himself as a substitute for the whole world, Simon bore the cross for the One who would bear the cross for us!

Obviously, the act of carrying the cross of Jesus was not efficacious in the sense that Christ's atoning act on the cross was. But the fact that it is even mentioned in the gospel account (and in Mark and Luke's as well) speaks to its significance. On the surface, this one line seems like extraneous detail. However it tells us a number of things. First, by this time, Christ was extremely exhausted from His ordeal. He had already gone through tremendous suffering even before being crucified. Second, Simon was not initially a willing volunteer. He was "pressed" into service. By contrast, Jesus voluntarily went to the cross (cf. Phil. 2:8). Third, while Simon's efforts had minimal impact on what happened, the results of Jesus' efforts have lasted about 2000 years so far.

Scripture tells us of other individuals who offered themselves for others. Think of Moses leading the obstinate, idolatrous people to the Promised Land. He asked God, "Now, if You will, forgive their sin—and if not, please blot me out from Your book which You have written!" (Ex. 32:32). In essence, he was offering himself in place of the people. Paul expresses similar sentiment: "I could wish that I myself were accursed, separated from Christ for the sake of my brethren, my kinsmen according to the flesh" (Rom. 9:3). The truth remains, though, that only one substitute will do, and that is the man Jesus Christ. "For Christ also died for sins once for all, the just for the unjust, so that He might bring us to God, having been put to death in the flesh, but made alive in the spirit" (1 Pet. 3:18).

On an historical note, this Simon (from the Cyrene area of North Africa, who happened to be in Jerusalem for the Passover) apparently became well known in the early Christian community—at least, his sons did. Mark records that he was the father of Alexander and Rufus (Mark 15:21), which suggests that his two sons were known to his readers. This could be the same Rufus mentioned in Romans 16:13, who clearly was a Christian. As Warren Wiersbe suggests, "Simon came to Jerusalem to sacrifice his Passover lamb, and he met the Lamb of God who was sacrificed for him."

Lord, thank you for being my sacrificial lamb. You took my place because I could not atone for my own sins.

Sovereign Truth

Matthew 27:33-37

[33] And when they came to a place called Golgotha, which means Place of a Skull, [34] they gave Him wine to drink mixed with gall; and after tasting it, He was unwilling to drink. [35] And when they had crucified Him, they divided up His garments among themselves by casting lots. [36] And sitting down, they began to keep watch over Him there. [37] And above His head they put up the charge against Him which read, "THIS IS JESUS THE KING OF THE JEWS."

In present-day Israel the Place of the Skull overlooks a busy commercial area of Jerusalem that has a bus depot at its base. People mill around with little thought of the momentous event that took place there nearly 2000 years ago. Holy Land tourists flinch at the thought that such a hallowed place could be so desecrated as a common, dirty place for the humdrum of life. Yet that is what it was like back in the day when Jesus was marched up there. It was a commonly traveled thoroughfare. Rome always chose the most public venues for crucifying its condemned. The executions of Jesus and the other two men that day were treated no differently. All the populace could see, as they carried on the normal business of life, the fate of those who dared to violate Roman law and loyalties.

Jesus was offered the customary opiate, wine mixed with gall, to dull the pain. Crucifixion was intended to be a painful and long-lasting form of death. Jesus refused the elixir, choosing to experience the full impact of the suffering.

Matthew records no details, saying only, "And when they had crucified Him..." Faithful study and reflection will never exhaust the depths of that simple phrase. God was, and is, magnified in this one stroke—the revelation of His true character in Christ, as the One who is just and the justifier of all who have faith in Jesus (Rom. 3:26). What men meant for evil, God meant for the supreme good of all mankind.

The soldiers who crucified Him, being of earthly mind, decided to play a game of chance to divide up Jesus' clothing. Little did they know that they could gain the clothing of Christ's righteousness, not through chance, but by expressing their faith in Him.

According to custom, the charge for which Jesus was condemned was tacked above His head so that all would be warned not to commit the same crime. In His case, though, the charge simply read, "This is Jesus the King of the Jews." To the Romans, this was the charge of treason. To the Jewish leaders, mockery. To the Sovereign of the Universe, it was *truth!*

Lord Jesus, You are the King of my life. You deserve my unswerving loyalty and reverence.

In Mockery, Truth

Matthew 27:38-43a

38 At that time two robbers were crucified with Him, one on the right and one on
the left. 39 And those passing by were hurling abuse at Him, wagging their heads
40 and saying, "You who are going to destroy the temple and rebuild it in three
days, save Yourself! If You are the Son of God, come down from the cross." 41 In the
same way the chief priests also, along with the scribes and elders, were mocking
Him and saying, 42 "He saved others; He cannot save Himself. He is the King of
Israel; let Him now come down from the cross, and we will believe in Him. 43 He
trusts in God; let God rescue Him now, if He delights in Him..."

The verbal abuse accelerated to a fever pitch. People walking by continued the harangue that began when they cried out, "Crucify Him, crucify Him." The extent of humankind's depravity was revealed as they threw the very grace of God back into the Savior's face. The religious leaders had purposely distorted His teachings, and the rest of the people ran with their lies despite the fact that the charge was ridiculous. Those described here as the chief priests, scribes, and elders joined in the degenerate merriment.

Throughout the passion narrative, irony overlays the words and actions of Jesus' antagonists. The ridicule that captures this irony most is this: "He saved others; He cannot save Himself." Their mockery of Christ was a mockery of themselves and their rejection of Him. For in reality, the statement is absolutely true. Jesus does save people from their sins. And because He was committed to that goal, He would not "save" Himself from God's prescribed judgment for sin: death. He could not do both, for by plan and purpose, He came to give His life in order to accomplish salvation for sinners.

With sneering words, they voiced the truth, "He is the King of Israel." They were taunting Him to come down. One wonders what they would have done if Jesus had actually done that. Would they have believed in Him if a miracle on that scale took place? Jesus had already answered that question: "If they do not listen to Moses and the Prophets, they will not be persuaded even if someone rises from the dead" (Luke 16:31). The people had witnessed enough miracles to validate who Christ was. The issue was rather one of darkened hearts.

They quoted Psalm 22:8, which shows the extent of their mocking—they were mocking God Himself! Those who knew the Scripture best—the religious leaders and experts in the law of Moses—actually used messianic prophecies as tools in rejecting the Messiah! The very hope, the promise of Israel, was being thrown away.

Lord, You are my hope. I believe Your promise that You will never forsake me.

The Correct Accusation

Matthew 27:43b

[43b] "*... for He said, 'I am the Son of God.'*"

The Jewish leaders understood clearly the thrust of Jesus' message. He never actually said the words, "I am the Son of God." His favorite self-identification was "Son of Man," as we have noted previously. But, after hearing Jesus' teaching over the span of three years, the Jews concluded that Jesus had, in fact, taught that He was the Son of God. That was precisely His goal—that people should see that in His teachings. Some modern scholars assert that Jesus was just a man—extraordinary though He was—and that His followers distorted this fact by propagating the "lie" that He claimed to be God. However, Jesus' contemporary adversaries saw it differently, and their testimony is unimpeachable. According to them, Jesus did teach that He was God. Today's adversaries of Jesus would do well to follow the model of Jesus' enemies in His day. At least they were honest in assessing Jesus on His own terms.

Satan tested Him on this very truth, "If [Since] You are the Son of God..." (4:3, 6). The demons feared Him because of this truth, "What business do we have with each other, Son of God? Have You come here to torment us before the time?" (8:29). The high priest tried to force the words into Jesus' mouth: "I adjure You by the living God, that You tell us whether You are the Christ, the Son of God" (26:63). His responses fueled the accusation.

The apostle Paul was convinced of this. Inspired by the Spirit, he wrote, "It was the Father's good pleasure for all the fullness to dwell in Him" (Col. 1:9), and "In Him all the fullness of Deity dwells in bodily form" (Col. 2:9). The apostle John wrote, "In the beginning was the Word, and the Word was with God, and the Word was God .... And the Word became flesh, and dwelt among us, and we saw His glory" (John 1:1, 14). The Bible teaches there is one—and only one—God (Deut. 6:4). "Before Me there was no God formed, and there will be none after Me. I, even I, am the LORD, and there is no savior besides Me" (Isa. 43:10-11). Therefore, since there is only one God, then Jesus is that God, the Creator God of the universe.

No wonder the Jews explained their animosity against Him this way: "For a good work we do not stone You, but for blasphemy; and because You, being a man, make Yourself out to be God" (John 10:33).

Lord Jesus, I worship You as God, the Sovereign of the universe. I submit to Your lordship today over my decisions, my actions, and my relationships.

Weekend Reading

Saturday – Job 37
Sunday – Job 38

Personal Reflections

The United Disconnect–part 1

Matthew 27:44-49

[44] *The robbers who had been crucified with Him were also insulting Him with the*
same words. [45] *Now from the sixth hour darkness fell upon all the land until the*
ninth hour. [46] *About the ninth hour Jesus cried out with a loud voice, saying, "ELI,*
ELI, LAMA SABACHTHANI?" that is, "MY GOD, MY GOD, WHY HAVE YOU FORSAKEN ME?"
[47] *And some of those who were standing there, when they heard it, began saying,*
"This man is calling for Elijah." [48] *Immediately one of them ran, and taking a*
sponge, he filled it with sour wine and put it on a reed, and gave Him a drink.
[49] *But the rest of them said, "Let us see whether Elijah will come to save Him."*

In the midst of verbal and physical abuse, Jesus did not lack the ability to do what they taunted Him to do. Even the men being crucified with Him mocked Him—although one had a change of heart (see Luke 23:39-43). He was determined to fulfill the Father's will, certainly not theirs.

Mark 15:25 notes that Jesus was crucified at around 9:00 a.m. (the third hour). In our passage here, darkness suddenly fell from about noon (the sixth hour) until three o'clock (the ninth hour). Jesus had been on the cross for six hours when He finally broke out with a mournful, eerie cry. There was darkness not only in the world, but also, as William MacDonald puts it, in His own soul.

The gospel writer recorded the Hebrew words Jesus used here (transliterated in our English Bibles) and also the Greek translation (translated into English in our Bibles). Matthew wanted to make it absolutely clear to his readers that Jesus was quoting from Psalm 22, which begins with that very phrase. In accordance with standard rabbinical practice, Jesus quoted the first line of a passage as a way of directing his hearers to the entire passage.

The unspoken reason is found in Psalm 22:3: "You are holy, O You who are enthroned upon the praises of Israel." But Jesus had become unholy. The Father forsook the Son because, being holy, "He made Him who knew no sin to be sin on our behalf, so that we might become the righteousness of God in Him" (2 Cor. 5:21). In that darkness, Jesus bore the sin of the world, and the Father could not, therefore, look upon His Son, as it were.

A breech in the eternal fellowship of the Father and Son had taken place. This is incomprehensible to our finite minds. Yet on another level, there was an eternal fellowship of purpose in dealing with sin because both the Father and the Son were working in concert, perfectly united in purpose (2 Cor. 5:19). It was a planned disconnect, agreed upon from eternity past. Bystanders completely misunderstood the point. They mistook what he said as a call to Elijah!

Father, while I cannot possibly understand fully what took place in the darkness on the cross, I thank You for the end result—the payment for sin.

The United Disconnect–part 2

Matthew 27:44-49

The crucifixion brought about the most incomprehensible (to our human minds) of all God's activities in His creation. How could there possibly be a breach within the Godhead? Traditionally, theologians have embraced what is called "the unity of God"—that is, He is indivisible. There are no parts to Him, for He is a complete whole. Jesus had earlier proclaimed, "I and My Father are one." And also, "If you have seen Me you have seen the Father." Yet He also said, "Not My will but Yours be done," implying some hint of a distinction, a separation. How can we understand, then, this separation, the forsaking, that took place at the cross?

The answer to this can be fully understood *only* in the inner council of the infinite mind of God. This should not surprise us. It makes sense that at the point of incarnation, certain anomalies or tensions should take place—things that make no sense in our lower dimension. For the mystery of the incarnation, the intersecting of the infinite with the finite, the Creator becoming a participant in His own creation—it is all beyond human comprehension. The anomalies are exacerbated at the point of greatest tension—the crucifixion. The purpose of God was to reconcile sinful humans to the One whose image they were patterned after. In the crucifixion He who was the perfect "image of the invisible God" (Col. 1:15) and who is "the radiance of His glory and the exact representation of His nature" (Heb. 1:3) became separated from the Father. How can mere human intellect ever understand that consequence of the infinite God invading the finite world?

Within the mystery of the crucifixion, there are some things we can know, however. Jesus was not primarily expressing ignorance (though this why question could be included with the discussion of the Son not knowing what the Father knows [24:36]). He was drawing attention to Psalm 22, the first part of which describes well His sufferings. Yet, the conclusion of the matter is found in the middle of verse 21: "Save me from the lion's mouth; From the horns of the wild oxen *You answer me*" (italics added). The verse begins with a plea for salvation and ends with a statement of fact. The answer, as it turns out, is the resurrection. Jesus was separated from the Father so that He could be "the resurrection and the life." As such, He could unite forever (in holiness) sinful man and holy God.

Yet, at another level, our Lord's cry reflected the anguish of bearing not just the physical pain of suffering, but also the weight of the sin of the world! His suffering was agony at the deepest level.

Father, I believe that Your Son truly did suffer in my place, the just for the unjust, to restore me to the One in whose image I was created. Thank you.

No More Separation

Matthew 27:50-53

50 And Jesus cried out again with a loud voice, and yielded up His spirit. 51 And behold, the veil of the temple was torn in two from top to bottom; and the earth shook and the rocks were split. 52 The tombs were opened, and many bodies of the saints who had fallen asleep were raised; 53 and coming out of the tombs after His resurrection they entered the holy city and appeared to many.

The Lord Jesus died with one last cry. Actually, He uttered seven statements while on the cross (not necessarily in this order):

1. To Mary, "Woman, behold, your son … [to John] behold, your mother" (John 19:26-27)
2. "Father, forgive them; for they do not know what they are doing" (Luke 23:34)
3. To the repentant thief, "Truly I say to you, today you shall be with Me in Paradise" (Luke 23:43)
4. "I am thirsty" (John 19:28)
5. "My God, My God, why have You forsaken Me?" (Matt. 27:46)
6. "Father, into Your hands I commit My spirit" (Luke 23:46)
7. "It is finished" (John 19:30)

Matthew does not record Jesus' final cry, but it was probably one of the last two listed above.

Upon the death of Israel's Messiah, supernatural things took place. First, the temple veil ripped in two. The direction of the ripping, from top to bottom, may, as many commentators note, symbolize that God, not man, initiated a new way into the Most Holy Place. Although the ark of the covenant (the symbol of God's most holy presence among His people) no longer resided there, that part of the temple, called the Most Holy Place, was still separated from the people by a thick veil. Now that the perfect Lamb of God had been sacrificed, however, believers in Him had open access into God's presence through the blood of Christ, apart from any physical building. There was therefore no more need of a veil to symbolize the separation.

At Christ's death, seismic activity also occurred as all nature groaned (Rom. 8:19-21). This, of course, was supernaturally induced. Then Matthew slips in the fact that after the resurrection of Christ, some believing Jews were raised from the dead, as well, and were seen in public. Whether these died again or went to heaven, the Bible doesn't say. But certainly this event further validated the message of the gospel.

Lord, I thank You for allowing me access into Your holy presence.

Faithful Witnesses

Matthew 27:54-56

[54] Now the centurion, and those who were with him keeping guard over Jesus, when they saw the earthquake and the things that were happening, became very frightened and said, "Truly this was the Son of God!" [55] Many women were there looking on from a distance, who had followed Jesus from Galilee while ministering to Him. [56] Among them was Mary Magdalene, and Mary the mother of James and Joseph, and the mother of the sons of Zebedee.

Fear struck the soldiers guarding Jesus as He died. What should have been a routine execution for these hardened military men turned into a nightmare. The commanding officer responded, "Truly this was the Son of God!" Scholars debate whether this outburst was a confession of faith in Christ or simply an acknowledgment that Jesus was somehow an unusual individual, a "son of God"—godlike, in the same way James and John were called "sons of thunder" (thunderous in their behavior or personalities, see Mark 3:17). We have noted earlier the favorable light in which centurions are presented in the gospels (see Matthew 8:8; Acts 10:1ff, for example). Certainly, this soldier connected the natural upheaval with the death of Jesus, and verbalized his observation that this particular man was no ordinary man.

At this point, Matthew chronicles the witness of "many women," three of whom are mentioned by name. They had been with Jesus since the early days of His ministry in Galilee and "ministered" to Him. They looked after His domestic needs (see Martha's example of preparing a meal for Him in Luke 10:40). Mary Magdalene, of course, held a prominent role as the first witness of the risen Christ (see Matthew 28:1 and John 20:1). While Mary, the mother of Jesus, and her sister stood closer to the cross (John 19:26), the three named women and the other women watched from a distance. Matthew's inclusion of them as witnesses reflects their tender affection for their Master and their loyalty to the end. And what a contrast with the male disciples who fled for their lives!

What did these women think or feel as they saw the One they had followed and served now being so cruelly tortured and put to death on the cross? The Bible doesn't say, but this isn't the last we hear of them in the story. In a world that minimized the testimony of women, the inclusion of this vignette concerning the woman is significant. Christ Himself treated women with much higher regard than did the culture around Him. In fact, wherever Christianity has gone, the treatment and honor of woman has been raised. The faithfulness of the women at the cross is clearly seen and acknowledged not just by Matthew, the human author of this book, but by the divine Author Himself, the Holy Spirit.

Lord, thank you for the faithful example of these women.
I want to faithfully follow You, as they did.

Secret Disciples

Matthew 27:57-61

[57] When it was evening, there came a rich man from Arimathea, named Joseph, who himself had also become a disciple of Jesus. [58] This man went to Pilate and asked for the body of Jesus. Then Pilate ordered it to be given to him. [59] And Joseph took the body and wrapped it in a clean linen cloth, [60] and laid it in his own new tomb, which he had hewn out in the rock; and he rolled a large stone against the entrance of the tomb and went away. [61] And Mary Magdalene was there, and the other Mary, sitting opposite the grave.

With the twelve disciples out of commission for various reasons, a man by the name of Joseph came to bury the body of Jesus properly. Left to the Romans, His body would have been simply discarded in a mass grave or burned. Joseph is only mentioned in the gospel in connection with the burial. He was "a disciple of Jesus, but a secret one for fear of the Jews" (John 19:38). Although Matthew doesn't mention it, someone else helped Joseph in caring for Jesus' body. Nicodemus, of John chapter 3 fame (see also John 19:39), accompanied Joseph, demonstrating that he, although a Pharisee, was also a secret disciple of Jesus.

Following correct protocol, Joseph obtained Jesus' body and gave it a proper, customary burial. He donated his own tomb, cut out of a rock, placed the body there, and closed it up with a large boulder. When the task was completed, Joseph simply walked away. His deed was done.

Although Joseph fades from the biblical record, we would be remiss if we simply walked away from the significance of what he did. His action was prophesied hundreds of years earlier by the prophet Isaiah: "His grave was assigned with wicked men, yet He was with a rich man in His death" (Isa. 53:9). Joseph gave Jesus a rich man's burial, though He died a cursed man's death. And Joseph's demonstrated devotion fulfilled the predetermined plans and foreknowledge of God (cf. Acts 2:23).

The other gospel accounts give more details about this burial. Matthew's record of it is brief. However, he notes the presence of Mary Magdalene and "the other Mary" (the mother of James the Lesser and Joseph). Again, while this information does not seem to advance the storyline in an obvious way, it does give prominence to the faithful women in Jesus' life, and now His death. In a few days, the stage is being set for the events about to happen. The stone grave, the linen wrappings, the burial, the large stone, and the women—all these play prominently in the resurrection of Jesus, the Christ.

Lord, I want to serve You in ways that honor You—not as a secret disciple but as one who is not ashamed of the good news about You.

Weekend Reading

Saturday – Job 39
Sunday – Job 40

Personal Reflections

The Mission Sealed

Matthew 27:62-66

[62] Now on the next day, the day after the preparation, the chief priests and the Pharisees gathered together with Pilate, [63] and said, "Sir, we remember that when He was still alive that deceiver said, 'After three days I am to rise again.' [64] Therefore, give orders for the grave to be made secure until the third day, otherwise His disciples may come and steal Him away and say to the people, 'He has risen from the dead,' and the last deception will be worse than the first." [65] Pilate said to them, "You have a guard; go, make it as secure as you know how." [66] And they went and made the grave secure, and along with the guard they set a seal on the stone.

Second thoughts plagued the Jewish religious leaders overnight, so on the Sabbath Day (Saturday), the day after crucifying Jesus, they took careful measures to prevent a faux resurrection. They anticipated the disciples might raid the tomb and claim fulfillment of Jesus' teaching that He would rise again on the third day.

This reveals a number of things. First, if the religious leaders were not aware of who buried Jesus, they were at least aware of where He was buried. Second, they understood the implications of His teachings. The Pharisees now understood that the charge which had finally been brought against Him—that He would raise the temple in three days after it had been destroyed—was actually a prediction of His resurrection. While they did not believe in that prophecy, they reasoned that Jesus' disciples *did* believe it! Ironically, the disciples did *not* believe it. They thought Jesus' whole mission had come to a disastrous end—that it had failed comprehensively.

The Pharisees concluded that Jesus had cleverly deceived His followers; therefore they wanted to contain any further deception from the disciples. Then sought provision of an armed guard from Governor Pilate and then went and sealed the grave with the seal of Rome (apparently). Tampering with such was punishable by death. Ironically, their action of sealing the grave has helped future generations of Christians: it substantiated that Christ had indeed died and was buried, and that all possible human means were taken to ensure the body remained in the grave. An empty grave on the third day could not be credibly explained away as a lack of necessary security. It could only mean one thing—He had risen from the dead!

For now, though, the Messiah of Israel was dead and buried, and all precautionary measures had been taken to ensure that this movement of His was completely extinguished. Little did the Pharisees realize as they smugly slept that Saturday night, that the greatest moment in history was about to take place.

Lord, You came to save us from the real deception, the blindness caused by sin, so that we would be set free. Thank you.

Week 52
Day 2

Central Christian Truth

Matthew 28:1-8

1 Now after the Sabbath, as it began to dawn toward the first day of the week, Mary
Magdalene and the other Mary came to look at the grave. 2 And behold, a severe
earthquake had occurred, for an angel of the Lord descended from heaven and
came and rolled away the stone and sat upon it. 3 And his appearance was like
lightning, and his clothing as white as snow. 4 The guards shook for fear of him and
became like dead men. 5 The angel said to the women, "Do not be afraid; for I know
that you are looking for Jesus who has been crucified. 6 He is not here, for He has
risen, just as He said. Come, see the place where He was lying. 7 Go quickly and
tell His disciples that He has risen from the dead; and behold, He is going ahead
of you into Galilee, there you will see Him; behold, I have told you." 8 And they
left the tomb quickly with fear and great joy and ran to report it to His disciples.

Resurrection! The report has been heralded by faithful followers of Jesus Christ for nearly 2000 years. It is absolutely central to Christianity. We are not just talking "religious speak"; this testimony is rooted in historical fact. The Sunday morning details are rehearsed every year in churches around the world: the two women as first witnesses, the earth tremors, an angel descending and rolling away the stone, seasoned military guards completely overwhelmed with fear. No wonder the angel said to the women, "Do not be afraid"!

It has been said that if you remove the resurrection from Christianity, whole swaths of the NT would have to be deleted. Essentially, Christian "life" is based on it:. "If Christ has not been raised, your faith is worthless; you are still in your sins … we are of all men most to be pitied" (1 Cor. 15:17, 19). Indeed, the very identity of Jesus rests on the factuality of the resurrection. Romans 1:4 clearly teaches that Jesus "was declared the Son of God with power by the resurrection from the dead, according to the Spirit of holiness, Jesus Christ our Lord." The resurrection pervades all the teachings of the NT.

Christians through the centuries have given their lives in the belief of this. Great minds have come to grips with the historical veracity of the gospel accounts. There is no satisfactory explanation for the rise and persuasive spread of Christianity apart from the belief of Jesus' immediate followers that He had indeed risen from the dead. They had seen Him with their own eyes!

Just as an angel heralded the arrival of Jesus into the life cycle of human experience, so also angels announced the completion of that cycle and the conquest of fallen human nature as well. Death did not have the last say! This was the message which had to be told. That was the women's mandate, and it becomes the mandate of all who claim to be followers of Jesus.

Praise the Lord for rising again to give us new life!

Unimpeachable Evidence

Matthew 28:9-15

[9] And behold, Jesus met them and greeted them. And they came up and took hold of His feet and worshiped Him. [10] Then Jesus said to them, "Do not be afraid; go and take word to My brethren to leave for Galilee, and there they will see Me." [11] Now while they were on their way, some of the guard came into the city and reported to the chief priests all that had happened. [12] And when they had assembled with the elders and consulted together, they gave a large sum of money to the soldiers, [13] and said, "You are to say, 'His disciples came by night and stole Him away while we were asleep.' [14] And if this should come to the governor's ears, we will win him over and keep you out of trouble." [15] And they took the money and did as they had been instructed; and this story was widely spread among the Jews, and is to this day.

On their way to tell the disciples the great news of the empty tomb, the women encountered Jesus in person. Immediately, they began to worship Him. The heart of a true believer responds instinctively to His presence. Jesus ratified the angel's instruction to tell the disciples to prepare to meet Him.

Meanwhile, the soldiers and religious leaders had a huge problem on their hands. Matthew, the author, in line with his purpose to show that Jesus was God's Messiah, includes some details that otherwise might seem extraneous. But the record shows that the religious leaders received a full report of the earthquake and the angel's appearance on the rolled-back stone. It was obvious that they couldn't suppress the truth of the empty grave or the supernatural events. In light of the guards' testimony of what happened, the religious leaders (led by the chief priests) concocted a story about the soldiers falling asleep and the disciples stealing the body of Christ.

The story was as unconvincing then as it is today. First, it requires that all the soldiers would have fallen asleep—which is hardly likely. Second, falling asleep on guard duty was grounds for immediate execution. Third, if the soldiers were asleep, how would they have known that the body was *stolen* and that Christ's disciples had done it? Fourth, why was there not an immediate search for the body? Fifth, the disciples would hardly have been willing to risk their lives proclaiming Christ had risen from the dead if they themselves had made up a lie about the resurrection. Sixth, if the body theft story were true, Christianity, the greatest moral system based on the greatest moral teacher of all time, would be founded on an intentional lie, a violation of all morality. That would make it the most enormous, cruel hoax of all time. It is more reasonable to believe that Jesus Christ *did* rise out from among the dead—just as the historical record shows!

Father, thank you for revealing to me the truth of the resurrection.
Because Jesus lives, I can live also.

Week 52

Day 4

Plan for Propagation

Matthew 28:16-20

[16] But the eleven disciples proceeded to Galilee, to the mountain which Jesus had designated. [17] When they saw Him, they worshiped Him; but some were doubtful. [18] And Jesus came up and spoke to them, saying, "All authority has been given to Me in heaven and on earth. [19] Go therefore and make disciples of all the nations, baptizing them in the name of the Father and the Son and the Holy Spirit, [20] teaching them to observe all that I commanded you; and lo, I am with you always, even to the end of the age."

When the rest of the disciples met with the risen Jesus, face to face for the first time, they responded the same way the women did. They worshiped Him. The women also showed fear, but the record here shows that some of the disciples doubted. Matthew doesn't explain what he meant by that, but Mark's gospel (in 16:11) records that "some refused to believe" the testimony of the women. Thomas, in particular, refused to believe anyone's testimony. He would only be satisfied if he saw Jesus for himself in person (John 20:25). Matthew bypasses the details and goes immediately to what has been called the Great Commission.

Jesus laid out the plans for continuing the mission He had begun and now validated with His resurrection. The disciples' commission from then on was to make other disciples. The Greek grammar explicitly demonstrates that the imperative is to "make disciples." The *go* is a participle form that would better be translated, "As you go ... " Then comes the command: "Make disciples ..."

How then does one make disciples? Jesus explained that it involves two steps: baptizing and teaching. Baptizing means bringing people to the place of publically identifying themselves as followers of Christ. Christians through the ages have taken this literally despite controversy over the mode or method of baptism.

Making disciples also involves teaching baptized followers of Christ to follow His teachings—all of them. Praise God for the four men who penned the narratives that now make up the first four books of the NT so we have a clear record of what Jesus taught.

Some implications here include these: (1) Jesus never intended two tiers of Christians, "believers" and "disciples." *All* are disciples. (2) The message that is for every human being on the planet needs to go out. Praise God for the missionaries who have taken this message to the ends of the earth. (3) Jesus expects every disciple to be involved in making disciples because the sum of His teachings includes this command!

Father, I recommit to learning what You have recorded in Your written Word and following closely everything that Jesus taught. Please show me when I am selective in my obedience.

Conclusion

Matthew 28:20b

"... and lo, I am with you always, even to the end of the age."

The presence of Jesus Christ with us forever—what a promise! It was the same promise Moses received as God inaugurated, at that time, a new dispensation of Law. It began with the exodus from Egypt, as the Lord said to Moses, "Certainly, I will be with you ... " (Ex. 3:12). Likewise, the angel pronounced, prior to the Messiah's birth, "they shall call His name Immanuel, which translated means, 'God with us'" (1:23). So also God promises His presence to all followers of the Lord Jesus Christ! We have nothing to fear. All authority in heaven and earth has been given to Him and is therefore at our disposal.

The message of the book of Matthew is that the Messiah has come and is now present. Jesus presented His message first to the Jews. But now, because they rejected Him, He brings His message directly to Gentiles.

Yet God has not given up on His chosen people. We see this on the day of Pentecost, through Peter's message, where God was speaking to the "men of Judah and all who live in Jerusalem" (Acts 2:14), and to the people of Israel (Acts 2:22). The message was this: "Therefore let all the house of Israel know for certain that God has made Him both Lord and Christ—this Jesus whom you crucified" (Acts 2:36). Peter continued, "Repent, and each of you be baptized in the name of Jesus Christ for the forgiveness of your sins; and you will receive the gift of the Holy Spirit. For the promise is for you and your children and for all who are far off, as many as the Lord our God will call to Himself" (Acts 2:38-39).

Despite some positive response, Israel as a nation has stubbornly and tragically continued to reject their Messiah. But God has not rejected them. His ongoing love for the Jews is reflected in the love the apostle Paul expressed for them when he wrote, "For I could wish that I myself were accursed, separated from Christ for the sake of my brethren, my kinsmen according to the flesh, who are Israelites, to whom belongs the adoption as sons, and the glory and the covenants and the giving of the Law and the temple service and the promises, whose are the fathers, and from whom is the Christ according to the flesh, who is over all, God blessed forever. Amen" (Rom. 9:3-5).

The Gospel According to Matthew continues to proclaim that Jesus Christ is the Messiah, the King of Israel, and that He is risen from the dead. The message continues to go out into all the world. And, praise God, the number of disciples continues to increase!

Amen!

Weekend Reading

Saturday – Job 41
Sunday – Job 42

Personal Reflections